No Fear Allowed

What Top Executives & Entrepreneurs Are Saying About
Laura Herring & *No Fear Allowed*

"Laura Herring's breakthrough business biography transcends her own story. In it she shares her incredible journey sharing openly the many failures that finally led her to success. It is an honest book, a rare insight into the truth of what entrepreneurs face ever day. *No Fear Allowed* is an amazing gift to all entrepreneurs who seek to follow their passion and create their vision and a legacy."

—**Maxine Clark**, Founder, Build-A-Bear Workshop, Founding Member, PROSPER Women Entrepreneurs

"Laura Herring has stared down some corporate scenarios that would leave some titans of industry themselves shaking in their Louboutins! But has managed to land on her feet and demonstrates the power of perseverance. This book and her lessons learned are great to keep you motivated till you succeed."

—**Nina McLemore**, Chief Executive Officer, Nina McLemore, Inc.

"I have had the privilege of getting to know Laura and I say about her inspiring message: awesome! Her resilience, her passion for making a difference, and her success as an entrepreneur make her a role model for all entrepreneurs and those aspiring to business success. Her book *No Fear Allowed* is an amazing, heartfelt personal story of overcoming failure after failure on the road to triumph. This is a woman who refused to let anything get in the way of her purpose to "make a positive difference" in all the lives she touched. Her lessons learned at the end of each chapter are worth the price of the book alone. *No Fear Allowed* is a must read for all entrepreneurs. With Laura Herring's words as your motivation, you can have the success you have been reaching for!"

—**Sandra Yancey**, Founder and CEO, eWomenNetwork

"True tales from the corporate front line, from a woman who literally put everything on the line—financially and otherwise—while believing that "failure is impossible." Herring tells her story in *No Fear Allowed* in a way that puts you in her shoes, feeling what she felt, and always leaving you thinking—How did she do that???"

—**Roberta Sydney**, President, Sydney Associates, Inc.

"I know Laura Herring and I know what it takes to build a brand from unknown to best known. *No Fear Allowed* is an exciting journey of how Herring knocked on the doors of the world's top companies and successfully walked through them, learning fierce lessons along the way. I am proud to call her a friend and excited to introduce you to this awesome woman who has a kind heart and is a fierce competitor and an amazing, gutsy businesswoman. If you are an entrepreneur, *No Fear Allowed* is a MUST read, not just to hear her story, but to learn from her invaluable 'Lessons Learned.'"

—**Laurie Ann Goldman**, Founder of LA Ventures
and Former CEO of SPANX

"Laura Herring was on the forefront of 'leaning in' way before it even existed."
—**Kimber L. Maderazzo**, Senior Vice President of
Global Product Marketing, Guthy Renker LLC

"For me, one of the most interesting facets of *No Fear Allowed* was that it is the story of a family-run organization. The stories that Laura, her husband Mike, and daughter Lauren (now CEO of IMPACT Group) tell are funny, poignant, and have lessons that anyone in business can learn from. Having a family-run business myself, I love their story."

—**Donna Van Eekeren**, Executive Chairman, Land O' Frost, Inc.

"If I had a daughter about to graduate from college and enter the world of business—in any capacity—I would absolutely give her this book as a gift… and then make sure that she read it. Laura Herring's *No Fear Allowed* is a story of entrepreneurial guts, savvy, and success and is a breath of fresh air to corporate America!"

—**Hannah Kain**, President and CEO, ALOM Technologies Corporation

"We're delighted that Laura's deep relationship with Worldwide ERC® and its members was foundational to her success as she helped raise both the bar, and the focus, on spouse and family issues. What an accomplishment to memorialize her journey in conceptualizing, developing and growing her vision so that others can learn from her rich experiences."

—**Peggy Smith**, CRP, GMS-T , President and CEO Worldwide ERC®

"It is extremely clear from page one that everything Laura Herring says, thinks, does is rooted in authenticity and absolute, unleashed passion. This woman does not have an off switch! Her book *No Fear Allowed* is a great life story combined with valuable lessons for anyone looking for the secret to moving beyond fear to incredible success in business and in life. A great read!"

—**Larraine Segil**, CEO Little Farm Company, Former Chair C200 Foundation

"As a business owner, I can confidently say from experience that if every entrepreneur, CEO and manager possessed Laura Herring's passion, perseverance and drive for success, we would have far more business success stories like this. If you are looking for the secrets and strategies for moving past fear to success in business-read *No Fear Allowed*!"

—**Roz Alford**, Founder and CEO of ASAP Chairwoman of Committee of 200 Foundation

"Laura is the true definition of a successful entrepreneur: confident, smart, passionate about her company and her clients. She has proven that a disruptive idea, conceived and executed before computers and social media were available, can be powered by vision, guts and perseverance. *No Fear Allowed* will be an inspiration to today's entrepreneurs who have the right product, at the right time, and the right hutzpah to make it happen!"

—**Kathryn Swintek**, General Partner, Golden Seeds Fund

"No *Fear Allowed* is a gutsy story of surviving and eventually thriving the ups and downs of being an entrepreneur. Laura's journey is one all entrepreneurs can identify with: extreme highs and devastating lows. She shows us all how to move into action and say goodbye to fear."

—**Susan Nethero**, "The Bra Whisperer," as seen on The Oprah Winfrey Show, CEO/Founder Intimacy Emerita

"I have seen Laura Herring bring audiences to tears with her passionate plea to help relocating families and relocating military spouses. Her passion for making a difference in the relocation industry made IMPACT Group the number one Spouse and Family Transition company in the world, year after year.

Her daughter continues the passion. *No Fear Allowed* is the story of how she did it. Truly inspiring!"

—**Ed Cohen**, Editor & Publisher, GlobalBusinessNews,
http://www.GlobalBusinessNews.net

"Laura is a person whose passion of making a difference is reflected in everything she does. Her book, *No Fear Allowed*, shows her passion, her commitment to excellence, her resiliency and her ability to LEAD POSITIVE. This is a must read for anyone who is a leader, an entrepreneur or a corporate intra-preneur. She has a gift of inspiring others to be all that they can be."

—**Dr. Kathryn Cramer**, Psychologist\Author of
LEAD POSITIVE What Highly Effective Leaders See, Say, Do

"With Laura, specifically when she would talk about her business, there was just tremendous determination. She always would approach it as, "Okay, this isn't working. What is a different way I can approach it? Let's try a new angle here." She was always trying to grow the business. It's like she could never get happy with where she was. She was always stretching to do more, more, more. And the business totally was who she was. Laura as a person and Laura as a business person were one in the same because she had such determination to be successful."

—**Sharon Fiehler**, Retired CAO of Peabody Energy

"Laura was speaking for the largest chamber in our area and she was sharing marketing ideas. But, what was really engaging is she was sharing stories for real, not just the pretty ones. She also told ones that didn't go well, and a lot of speakers, particularly at that time, didn't do that. I don't think being authentic was very popular back then. But she was absolutely authentic. She shared so much, and the sincerity that held everyone in the room, is what engaged me to her.

I immediately thought, "Oh gosh, any time this woman is speaking, I want to hear her. She's brilliant on stage!"

—**Karen Hoffman**, Founder, Gateway to Dreams (a nonprofit)

"Laura always had an eye on who the next person was she needed to see. She was fearless! I would watch her just zoom across the room, because there was somebody with a certain colored badge that she needed to get in front of. It was a riot to watch her! Sure, most people in those situations are a little more reserved than that, but you know, she just was passionate about what she was doing and that's how she got noticed. It's been kind of her MO ever since."

—**Marge Fisher**, Relocation Management Consultant

No Fear
Allowed

A Story of Guts, Perseverance,
& Making an IMPACT

Laura Herring

New York

NO FEAR ALLOWED
A Story of Guts, Perseverance, & Making an IMPACT

Published in New York, New York, by Morgan James Publishing. Morgan James and The Entrepreneurial Publisher are trademarks of Morgan James, LLC.
www.MorganJamesPublishing.com

The Morgan James Speakers Group can bring authors to your live event. For more information or to book an event visit The Morgan James Speakers Group at
www.TheMorganJamesSpeakersGroup.com.

Laura Herring donates all profits from the sale of this book to breast cancer research.

A **free** eBook edition is available
with the purchase of this print book.

CLEARLY PRINT YOUR NAME ABOVE IN UPPER CASE

Instructions to claim your free eBook edition:
1. Download the BitLit app for Android or iOS
2. Write your name in **UPPER CASE** on the line
3. Use the BitLit app to submit a photo
4. Download your eBook to any device

ISBN 978-1-63047-491-1 paperback
ISBN 978-1-63047-492-8 eBook
ISBN 978-1-63047-493-5 hardcover
Library of Congress Control Number:
2014921128

Cover Photo by:
Suzy Gorman

Cover Design by:
Rachel Lopez
www.r2cdesign.com

Interior Design by:
Bonnie Bushman
bonnie@caboodlegraphics.com

In an effort to support local communities, raise awareness and funds, Morgan James Publishing donates a percentage of all book sales for the life of each book to Habitat for Humanity Peninsula and Greater Williamsburg.

Get involved today, visit
www.MorganJamesBuilds.com

Habitat
for Humanity®
Peninsula and
Greater Williamsburg
Building Partner

To Mike and Lauren
I could not have done it without your love and support.
I love and appreciate you both!

TABLE OF CONTENTS

Fear Means That You Care

By **Laurie Ann Goldman**, Former CEO of SPANX

Timing is everything.

One night back in 2002 I was going to a dinner, and I needed fishnets. I was still carrying some weight after the birth of my third child. I knew about this new company called SPANX. Somebody told me they had come out with fishnets with a control top.

Perfect!

So I made a beeline for Saks, which carried SPANX. Only I found out that they were out of my size—and the next size! Are you kidding me? How can a hosiery department that carried SPANX be out of fishnets? It's like McDonald's being out of French fries.

Always the entrepreneurially minded executive, I explained to the manager that their supply chain was clearly not working, and that they needed a vendor replenishment program. As the manager stood there thinking, "Please, make her go away," a man who happened to be Chief Operating Officer of SPANX overheard me. He looked to be about twelve.

He very much wanted to continue the supply chain conversation. (To be honest, I still very much wanted fishnets to wear to my dinner.) Nevertheless, seeing the opportunity, I gave him my cell number. And then I began giving him advice, which eventually led to a lunch with Sara Blakely, the founder of SPANX, which led to me becoming CEO.

The kind of intuition that drove me to follow my gut in this situation toward a new career opportunity might be an inherited gift. My mother is an artist who never spent a lot of time reading the business media. And as far as I know, she couldn't bend spoons with her mind.Instinct has a power to pull pieces of information together in ways we don't even realize. But she woke up one morning and told my dad they had to sell their stocks. So he did. It was in 2008—just days before the market started its collapse.

Intuition is like a muscle. The more you use it, the stronger it gets. And the stronger it gets, the more confidence you have to listen to what it's telling you. Pick any successful entrepreneur or leader and you'll find that muscle is very well defined.

So many moments in an entrepreneur's life are a combination of intuition, serendipity, and impatience with the way things currently work. The business visionary wants to improve on those things (as Sara did so brilliantly with her invention of SPANX).

When I accepted the position as CEO of SPANX, a fledgling company with a handful of people and products, I was on maternity leave from Coca-Cola, an established corporation. Ironically, it was as an executive in a large hierarchal organization that I learned about and quickly fell in love with the power of the entrepreneurial spirit. Some people feel their voice stifled, working in the ranks of a big company. My experience was the opposite. At Coca-Cola I was able to take their trademark protection program, a largely underutilized asset, and turn it into a business with retail sales close to a billion dollars by licensing the intellectual property rights. In utilizing an entrepreneurial mindset more than an employee one, I was able to build a successful business within an already successful business!

Now, in leaving Coca-Cola, very much like an entrepreneur I was taking a big leap with no safety net. But I didn't exactly see it that way. The fear was outweighed by the desire to travel a new road that would be a better fit for the life I now had with young children. Although I had a passion to make a change, the passion of my entrepreneurial spirit had not died down. A hunt for fishnet stockings gave way to an incredible new opportunity. *Part of getting what you want is letting go of what you've had before.*

Being in one place for a long time is like being on a trapeze. Eventually you lose momentum, and you just hang there. It's good to let go while you're still on the upswing, especially when there is no one there to catch you. I highly recommend taking these leaps as a way to clear your head and get your heart beating! Because when your heart starts pounding, it also starts pumping blood to your brain so you can think more clearly. This is the typical heart pounding, blood pumping, and adrenaline charged state of your typical entrepreneur. Why are we like this?

For me, at the core of people who start and build a business is the fact that they're *hungry*. Hunger for financial success is part of it. But I think there is more. It's a hunger to build something solid when all you have is an idea. It's a hunger to lead, even on days when you aren't quite sure where you're going. It's a hunger to have people depend on you; to make them believe you *do* know where you're going. It's a hunger to change things, a discontent with the way things are. To me, that discontent is simply another word for ambition.

And yes, lurking in the midst of this discontent, this ambitious hunger to make a change—is fear. It's unavoidable. For instance, whenever I speak I still get scared. I've done it a million times and in front of huge audiences, but I always feel that exhilarating rush of fear just as I'm about to take the stage. Does it stop me? Heck no, just the opposite! Fear drives me!

Fear means that you care. It tells you that you care about doing a good job and being successful. No matter what level you've achieved whether you're just starting out, earning that first big promotion or running a global company—the fear never goes away.

My friend Laura Herring, the inspiring author of the powerful pages you are about to read, understands this more than anyone I've ever met. You will see in her vividly told stories, how Laura has *lived* fear throughout her career. Beyond that she has the foundation as a professional psychologist to communicate how fear works, in such a way that's easy to understand and also motivating. She has made the psychology of fear truly accessible, and brought it to life compellingly with humor, energy, and the voice of experience. Just as she does in real life, she has a brilliant way of reaching out to you the reader, hugging you and saying, "Yes you can!"

We all have our own distinctive gifts. Nobody is a "born entrepreneur." It's our job to make ourselves the best that we can be. There are simple things we can learn and observations we can make to do this—and Laura has lived through these.

I've also long thought of Laura as a great teacher. It was only while reading this book that I learned how her very first career *was* as a schoolteacher! I wasn't surprised at all since great schoolteachers are also great storytellers. They also truly see you. Think about your favorite elementary school teacher—she cared, she hugged you, and she understood you more than you understood yourself at that point in your life. She had the experience of seeing hundreds of students every year going through the same thing—but she always had a way of seeing the individual in front of her, not hundreds of students.

That's Laura. Her unique skill is getting to the essence of what each person she encounters is struggling with internally. Business is never just business. She always starts with the person who is running the business and discovers what is stopping them psychologically. She is very intentional about helping them move beyond the block into action and as she says, "making a positive difference." It's about helping people. Laura realizes that *people* are at the heart of joy!

One of the things that Laura and I share is that we both had demanding dads. The dilemma there is that you love what he made you become but didn't always love the process. I began life with a father who set the bar so high that sometimes I couldn't touch it. He was big on hard work and high achievement and that stayed with me for my entire career. The fearless confidence he instilled in me was really all about ambition; and as I said before, when I did feel fear I knew in my gut that it meant I cared.

The electrical current of caring is very powerful throughout this book! To say that Laura Herring cares—about her purpose to make a positive difference, her passion to help others, and each life she touches along the way—is an understatement.

You will feel the fear she felt in each heart-pounding situation where the corporate rug was pulled out from under her and she was unceremoniously sent back to the drawing board to start all over. This fear is proof positive that she cared—deeply—about what she was doing and the impact it would make. And now, with her message of "No Fear Allowed!" she cares about helping YOU harness that fear in your life so you can make a positive impact!

She carefully and subtly leaves a wake of wisdom wherever she goes. Being around Laura, you just *know* that she knows what she's talking about and your ears and heart open wider when you're in her presence. I invite you now to open your ears and your heart to the incredibly heart felt, inspiring lessons of my teacher, my fellow trapeze flying entrepreneur, and my friend, Laura Herring.

Introduction

MAKING A POSITIVE DIFFERENCE

Moments in Time

Isn't it funny how things turn out? You start planning your life around one idea and then it takes you to another via a simple moment in time. A traumatic family relocation when you're thirteen years old plants a seed inside you that grows to maturity twenty-eight years later.

Then it takes another turn. You think you are just going to help companies relocate people by reducing their stress and that of their families. You hope to prevent them from having a corporate relocation negatively impact their life and the lives of their family members. *You just want to make a positive difference.*

But the dream becomes bigger than you ever imagined and you wind up employing more than three hundred people and speaking around the world about helping families make positive life transitions. Then, one day, you get asked to buy part of a $2 billion company. You don't have much money, but suddenly you own one of the finest outplacement divisions in the industry (corporations hire outplacement companies to help their laid-off employees find new jobs). You never even thought of buying an outplacement firm, but then that deal leads to an opportunity that will forever change your life. This is what happened to me.

Three years later, I got another call that changed my life and that of our family forever. It was one of our biggest clients on the line, asking us to help them lay off forty thousand people. Not just lay off, but help create a "soft landing" for those people. Because of my company's twenty-year relationship with this client, we were the only outplacement company they would call. They trusted us not only to help their people find jobs, but also help the families adjust to the changes that not working for this giant automobile manufacturer would suddenly introduce into their lives.

These brief moments in time and many others have allowed me to follow my purpose of making a difference in this world, one relationship at a time. They have allowed me to follow my passion for counseling people through difficult life transitions. And, while not always quickly, these moments in time also allowed me to make significant profits because of our reputation and the quality of our people and processes. We became nearly a $50 million company.

If anyone had told me when I graduated from Webster College (now Webster University) with my Social Sciences teaching degree that I would be invited to join the Committee of 200 (the elite by-invitation-only group of business women in the world), dine with CEOs of global corporations, travel the world, speak with passion to women in business about corporate life transitions, and help family-owned businesses balance work/life issues, I never would have believed it.

Why? The dream was not made known to me immediately, yet somewhere deep inside, I realized I wanted to change things. I wanted to help people fulfill their dreams. I wanted to be an agent of change, to lift people up. What I wasn't aware of at the time, but now as a psychologist I know for sure, is that the seeds of dreaming to make a difference are sown early on in our lifetimes. We must be patient and be aware that they come to us, one at a time, in small moments in time. We must pay attention to our story as it unfolds. We must connect the dots. We must find the threads that are deep inside that allow us to become all we were intended to be.

Early in my career, I did not have a mentor to guide me through those moments, helping me see my potential and connect the sometimes disparate dots that became IMPACT Group. What I hope to do in this book is not only inspire you to recognize those moments in your own time, but also invite you to find your moments in time that make your purpose and passion in business a thriving reality. I also want to help you move along faster by sharing lessons I have learned along the way and what I would do differently today. I want to share with you the excitement, the wretched moments of fear I fought through with sheer guts and determination (failure was never an option), and how I climbed out of those moments and kept focusing on my purpose, passion and mission: to make a positive difference in the world, one relationship at a time.

I also want to share with you my business story, and how it became a success story—not overnight, but one relationship at a time, one sale at a time, one employee at a time, one client at a time, and one failure at a time. I want this book to help ignite the spark under you and help you see how *you* can truly make a difference in this world building your dream company.

No Fear Allowed

The title of this book is meant to be slightly ironic. After all, fear is a natural part of business and life. For me, "No Fear Allowed!" is almost a mantra—a battle cry.

There will be fear, but you don't act out of that fear. You act out of drive and the notion that failure is not an option. You find a way to move forward. Fear will cross your mind because it's a physiological response, part of the "fight or flight" response that sometimes gets us into trouble and sometimes gets us out of it. But that doesn't mean you have to let it take over. I have learned that fear equals feedback. It gives you a cue that you need to do something. Stop. Listen. Evaluate. Then devise a plan that moves you into a well-thought-out direction.

You're about to read stories from the journey that began when my husband, Mike, and I were nearly broke and starting a business in our basement. Then, as the business grew, I fought against the fear and waged the battles I needed to fight to become a full-fledged corporation. Along the way, whenever obstacles showed up (as they always will), it was almost a survival mechanism when I stubbornly put this mindset in place: "Yes, I may be feeling fear but I will not let it stop me from moving forward! I will keep 'driving for the basket' (as my dad coached me in high school basketball)." Fear should not freeze you, it should free you.

If you're starting and growing a business, taking what often seem like baby steps toward big dreams, it can easily seem like fear is over every hill and around every corner. Take it from someone who has been there: It is worth it. If you are following your passion and determined to reach your goal, fear is simply a series of directional signals that will steer your path. The trick is keeping your head held high and never losing sight of your vision of success, no matter what.

I hope you enjoy reading about my journey and I pray this book helps to free you from fear and self-doubt, invites you to go for it, and lifts you up to connect you to your dream. Good luck finding your moments in time, connecting them, moving beyond fear, and following your purpose with passion.

You will see me mention entrepreneurs and business owners quite a bit and you may even assume that I'm only speaking to that audience. This couldn't be further from the truth. Yes, those roles play to *my* personal experience in corporate America. However, the stories and advice contained in this book are meant to be just as inspiring and helpful to today's "intrapreneur" (an employee with an entrepreneurial mindset who "owns" his or her job). An intrapreneur, similar to the entrepreneur, is always thinking of ideas, processes and products that can make the organization bigger, better, faster and more powerful.

Whether you own the company or work for it, big thinking like this attracts risk, challenges and, inevitably, fears. As intrapreneurs, you climb the corporate ladder and take leadership roles within your organization. As a manager, you face your own unique fears as well as the fear of failure and fear of the unknown that entrepreneurs deal with.

To all those entrepreneurs, intrapreneurs and everyone who loves reading an inspiring business autobiography: We all face fear every day and are seeking ways to boldly proclaim, "No Fear Allowed!" This book is for you.

PART ONE

No Fear Allowed

Chapter 1

BRACING FOR IMPACT

September 2007

The moment my husband, Mike, took my hand, kissed it, and said, "Laura, you know we have had a great life," is the moment I really started to panic. This was mister calm, cool, collected and rational, and if he was saying the situation was bad, then it must be. I looked out the window of the plane at the ground below. We had taken off perhaps fifteen minutes before, yet the plane still had not climbed above six hundred feet. I began to cry softly, not for Mike or myself, but for our daughter Lauren, who was sitting at the other end of the plane. She had not yet lived her dreams of marriage or children. She had not yet lived a full life.

"This isn't fair!" I thought angrily.

Then I tried to get up to run down the aisle to her. More than anything, I needed to hug my daughter, to hold her in my arms one last time. The flight attendant blocked my way and asked me what the heck I thought I was doing. I told her I was going to my daughter.

"Oh, no you're not!" she said, shoving me by my shoulders back down into my seat.

I began to softly cry again, clutching Mike's hand and again staring out the airplane window at the ground below us.

We rarely flew as a family. This was a strict rule I had for many reasons; one being that Mike, Lauren and I were the officers at IMPACT Group, a $50 million-a-year global corporate career management company I had founded nineteen years earlier. I was CEO, Mike was COO and Lauren, at thirty years old, was President. At the time of our ill-fated flight, Mike and I were actually doing the combined work of four people. If that plane went down, I thought (my mind almost always processing business), it would be the end of the company I had fought so tirelessly to build from the ground up. Looking back, I realize how irrational this was, thinking of the company as our lives were in danger, but that's just the way my mind worked back then: all business, all the time.

We were flying that Friday morning from our home in St. Louis to Chicago, to attend the wedding of Lauren's roommate from University of Notre Dame. The girls were very close, as were all of us parents. This is very typical for me, as I've always placed great value on developing close personal relationships with people I've crossed paths with in life. We were all very excited about the wedding. It was a beautiful day with white clouds sprinkled across bright blue skies. Lauren had been automatically upgraded to first class with the ton of miles she'd booked flying around the world for IMPACT Group, while Mike and I were back in row twenty-five. It was a normal takeoff but within minutes, as a frequent flyer for most of my life, I knew something was wrong.

"Mike," I said, "we're not climbing."

"Give it a minute," he said, the picture of patience.

But as it turned out, it was the calm before the storm. He continued to peer out the window, grimacing.

"We should be much higher by now. This doesn't look good," Mike finally admitted.

Then, the kiss of my hand, the statement that we've had a good life and my unsuccessful attempt to rush down the aisle to hug my daughter. There was nothing else to do at that point except wait for information, for the end—for something. We didn't know anything, and that was the worst part. After the longest ten minutes of my life, the pilot finally came over the loudspeaker.

"I'm sure you can tell by now that what we're experiencing is not normal," he said, in a staccato, flat, matter-of-fact voice. "We're going to *try* to turn this airplane around now and see if we can make it back to Lambert (Field, St. Louis)."

Try? *Try?* It was the worst announcement I'd ever heard trying to calm a group of anxious passengers. All around us, despite pleas by the flight attendant to stop, passengers whipped out their cell phones and started calling their goodbyes to loved ones.

Lauren would later tell us how she and the other passengers in the front rows were privy to how bad the situation actually was. At one point the pilots opened the door and asked another pilot sitting in first class to come help them. She overheard them talking about a fire in the left engine, and the alarm was going off inside the cockpit. Back in row twenty-five, we were wondering if the wheels could even go down. Mike was behaving in a way I'd never seen before (or since). His eyes darted around, frantically searching the ground below, and then periodically calling out things like, "There! Why aren't you landing there?" to the airplane window. He would see a field, an Air Force base, and as the pilots desperately tried to turn the plane, my husband would be shouting, "What's the matter with you? We can land right there!"

I knew at that point, without a shadow of a doubt, that we were all in real danger.

"Please ladies and gentleman, you *have* to put your cell phones away!" the flight attendants continued to plead with the panicked, emotional passengers. "We've got to keep the lines open!"

Ignoring these pleas, I called Lauren on my cell phone. Lauren, as it turns out, was holding the hand of a fifty-year-old fearful first-time flyer who was sobbing hysterically. My daughter sounded calm, perhaps holding it together for her seatmate. I was so proud of her and wanted to hug her more than anything, but at that moment in time, a phone conversation was our only option. I knew what I needed to tell her.

"Lauren I want you to pray for the pilot, for steadiness and a clear mind."

She said she would, we exchanged "I love yous," and then I hung up, closed my eyes and prayed.

"Dear Lord, please guide the hands of the pilot, allow him to think through what he needs to do to safely land this plane. In your name, amen."

We were forty-five minutes into a turn that, with a working engine and functional hydraulics, would have taken two to three minutes, tops. Mike unglued himself from the window and the conversation turned in a different direction.

"Honey," he said, "if we come out of this alive, I want us to retire. We must enjoy life. We've both been working six-and-a-half days a week for twenty years. You come home at 7:30 at night and work another two hours at home. We have more money in the bank than we ever thought we'd have in our whole lives. We rarely take any time off. I want you to promise me that we will retire."

My heart instantly said yes.

"Okay. Let's enjoy the life we have built," I told Mike.

But just as quickly, my head zipped right back into strategy mode. We wouldn't be able to just walk away; we would need an exit strategy. We would need to transition, not toss, Lauren into the role of CEO, assuming she wanted it in the first place. We also would need to hire about four people to replace Mike and me. At that time, I was the company rainmaker, among other things, traveling and selling nonstop. I decided we would need about fifteen months to make the transition. Now that we knew we were going to get out of the business, we wanted to make it easy for Lauren, staying with her as she hired and trained her new team.

Mike and I continued our matter-of-fact business discussion while, all around us, passengers continued to sob into cell phones, flight attendants gave up on getting them to stop and, in the cockpit, a group of pilots tried to save us all from what appeared to be certain doom.

It never occurred to either of us to start calling our own family members. We were engrossed in planning our daughter's future. On top of that, we didn't want to scare my ninety-year-old dad, my siblings, or Mike's family. By that point, deep into our discussion about how we would exit the company and let Lauren take over, my mentality had completely switched from fear of crashing to fear that we might miss an important detail in our company exit strategy. Or worse, what if Lauren didn't even want the company? I'd completely forgotten about the fire Lauren had said was raging in the left engine of the plane. As I'd later find out, that fire was right behind us in the walls.

I just never believed that we might actually crash. Maybe it was my and Lauren's prayers for the pilot, or maybe it was the distraction of my impromptu onboard business meeting with Mike, but I just never believed that we would hit the ground at hundreds of miles per hour, or that it was even possible. "God is too just," I thought to myself.

Mike and I finally wrapped up our discussion with a plan for how we would approach Lauren about our exit strategy. By that time, the flight had made it back over Lambert Field and the tower was making us circle around to another, longer runway. Due to what turned out to be a broken hydraulic line caused by the fire, we would need more room to land. They never told the passengers to get into crash position. There were no further announcements from the cockpit. The flight attendants (and passengers) had gone silent. As we started to descend, I looked out and saw a sea of foam and what seemed like hundreds of rescue vehicles, causing a flickering moment of sheer terror in me. What if I was wrong? What if we were going to crash? Especially after all this, after Mike and I had *finally* worked out the details of our succession from the company (I'm laughing at myself now as I remember thinking this at the time). And I still needed to hug my daughter....

Shortly after that, we landed safely and the passengers erupted in deafening cheers and applause. Much to our surprise (and frustration), they wouldn't let us off the plane. Instead, about eight to ten men in silver space suits boarded and started to undertake various fire-protection duties. Mike and I were nearly the last passengers to leave the plane. We were there long enough to see the silver space men tear the walls away right behind where we'd been sitting. The insides were black; the fire had almost burned through to the cabin. If we had been in the air for just a few minutes more, the fire would have likely burned right through and that would have been the end of us all. The most unbelievable part for me, though, was as we filed out and they told us to leave all our belongings behind.

"Hell no!" I thought stubbornly. "I certainly will not. So far these guys haven't been on target about anything!" I didn't have a good sense of trust at that point with the people supposedly responsible for our lives.

Lauren had boarded the first bus off the plane to the terminal. Still counting down the moments to my hug, we arrived at the terminal to a throng of lights, cameras, and reporters shouting at us. Our flight had made national news. I could even see the captions on the overheard televisions showing cable news: "Flight on the verge of crashing in St. Louis."

I called my sister Karen from the terminal and had her start a phone chain to the rest of the family.

"You were on that plane!" she instantly exclaimed, and then strangely added, "What are you wearing by the way?"

A lime green sweater and slacks, I told her, to which she nearly shouted through the phone, almost comically, "I love that sweater!"

She had seen me on the national news, a camera shot taken from afar of me walking down the steps of the plane.

"But I didn't see Lauren …" my sister added.

Lauren had exited the plane earlier; I still hadn't seen her. Finally, ten long minutes after we boarded the bus to the terminal, there she was. That particular moment in time stood still, as I took my daughter into my arms, hugged her tightly and rocked her in my arms. I finally got my hug, and my only thought was how Lauren had survived and could now live a wonderful, loving life. All thoughts of the succession plan were wiped out of my mind at that moment.

Fifteen minutes later, though, Mike raised the subject for me. "Honey, your mother promised me she would retire and we'll discuss if you want the company at some point; doesn't have to be now though."

Without missing a beat, Lauren locked eyes with both of us and said, "I want the company."

I told her we would discuss it later, even as she kept repeating that statement, "I want the company, Mom."

Later that evening, when we finally arrived at the rehearsal dinner, Lauren, Mike and I received a standing ovation. After our landing, I had given an interview to a television reporter, which the bride's mother had seen before the dinner.

Lauren, of course, followed through with her promise to take on the IMPACT Group and is absolutely thriving today as CEO. Mike and I did retire, and have found ways to keep following our passion to make a difference, while also remembering to take vacations and live our lives.

People always tell me I'm such a positive person. Thinking back on this ordeal we went through together as a family, I realize how right they are. I never felt like we were going to crash because we kept making plans for the future. We prayed for the pilots to figure it out. We never felt like the plane was going down, yet the aircraft never got over six hundred feet into the air. I can't help but remember my dad and his message to keep going no matter what. I may not have been able to control the plane's ability to "keep going," but I could certainly control my mindset, pray and stay positive.

Right before he died at age ninety, I flew down to spend time with my dad. Still bright, alert and somewhat active, I shared with him how much his coaching, love, and support meant to me over the years, and how, because of him, I have adopted the belief system: "No Fear Allowed!"

Chapter 2

SEEDS OF CHANGE

The first relocation my family underwent was a good one. It was 1952 and my father's job at a large pharmaceutical company took us from Rahway, New Jersey, fifteen hundred miles away to St. Louis. I remember jumping up and down on the couch, and my grandmother suddenly announcing, "Mommy and Daddy are going to St. Louis." I didn't know where that was, but as a little kid, you only pray that your parents bring you with them.

As it turned out, I had nothing at all to fear. What a great life we wound up having in St. Louis! When I think of my younger years growing up alongside my four siblings (a brother and three sisters), I think of family, fun and happiness. In the close-knit community where we lived, Webster Groves, there were school picnics, parades and holiday happenings.

At home, tall, dark and handsome dad was a real up-and-comer at work, and extremely involved in every aspect of our lives. When I was in junior high he coached my school basketball team, but gave me no special treatment. He would shout at me, "Laura go directly toward the goal, drive for the basket, don't go around, go through!" I was thirsty, exhausted and seething at how he singled me out from the rest of the team. But as I drove for that basket, fighting my way through fear of failing to the center of the court, I also felt empowered, capable and invincible. Dad only wanted me to reach my potential.

"Drive for the basket" is something you will hear me mention quite a few times throughout this book. At a young age it became the battle cry that would carry me through personal and business challenges in life. I have my dad to thank for that, as well as all the other lessons he instilled in me.

Let me also paint a picture of my mother for you: a red-headed Irish woman, quick to anger, quick of tongue, and task oriented. She could stare you down in a heartbeat, put the fear of God in you with one breath, and then praise you with the next. She taught all us kids to work hard, play fair, and love your family— traits we all still share.

We lived almost a fairytale existence in St. Louis. For instance, when our dad got home from work, he would immediately take off his suit jacket, lay it on the curb and join in the game of Kick the Can we kids almost always had in progress. He was a man in love with his life and his family, and it showed. Pure joy, a sense of play, and lightness surrounded our family in my early childhood years in St. Louis. Then, like sudden curves in a road, a series of events led us in a different direction.

It started with dad's promotion at work. Suddenly we were house shopping in Atlanta. I liked the idea of this bigger city with so much to do; it seemed things would be okay for our happy little family.

But when we got back to St. Louis from Atlanta, some awful news from work was awaiting my father. Headquarters had changed directives. Dad would no longer be director of the southeast region out of Atlanta, as planned. Instead, he would be transferred to Memphis to be assistant director, a much lesser position. Once I was old enough to understand, I learned how that one corporate decision just flattened my dad—emotionally, psychologically and every other way in which you can mentally beat down a strong, proud man. Headquarters added insult to injury by telling dad that his new boss, Ed, was sixty-two years old,

"And don't worry about it. He will retire in a year and you'll take over the whole operation." That man did not retire in a year. He stayed on for nearly eight more years and finally retired at the age of seventy. My dad lived under this man's thumb for eight frustrating years.

Dad was never the same man once that decision was handed down and we relocated to Memphis. The light within him seemed snuffed out and the joyfulness, the passion for life, was replaced by sadness and anger. Even as a young girl of thirteen, I could see it: the way he lashed out in anger over little things; the sadness, frustration, and exhaustion in his eyes; his hung head and hunched-over shoulders. He was a fundamentally changed human being. It changed the dynamic of our family forever. It infused our fun with the unknown of fear.

Meanwhile, as my father dealt with this major transition in his career, the rest of us were left to deal with our own relocation challenges. Memphis was a very different world than anywhere else we'd ever lived, and everyone we encountered seemed to notice this—perhaps before we even did.

Picture a whole city of Southern women wearing pearls and dresses in the kitchen, getting their hair done every week, and hiring people to clean their homes and help raise their children. My mom wore housecoats, did her own cleaning, scrubbed our floors on her hands and knees, and spoke with a thick New Jersey accent that none of the ladies in Memphis could understand. She later said she felt like a burlap sack in a pearls and sweater-set world.

Just after the moving van drove away on the day we moved into our new home in Whitehaven, my mom (in her housecoat with no pearls in sight and up to her eyeballs in boxes) shooed us kids out of the house and told us to go make friends.

Three girls my age walked by our house and I quickly flagged them down.

"Where are you guys going?" I asked.

Three sets of condescending eyes bore down on me, examining this creature from another planet that said very un-Memphis things like, "you guys."

"To cheerleading practice," one responded.

"Can I come?" I asked brightly.

"Oh nooooo," another one drawled, clearly appalled at the mere idea. "We picked teams in April; this is August and you are waaaaaay too late."

"Besides," smirked another of the girls, "you are a damn Yankee!"

As the three erupted into laughter I smiled, as if totally in on the joke. In truth, I had not yet studied the Civil War and had absolutely no clue what was so funny. The girls continued on their way to cheerleading practice, leaving me on the curb, scratching my head and wondering what in the heck a "damn Yankee" was.

I ran inside to ask my mom and she told me she didn't have time to explain it, but there was a book in the hall bookcase upstairs called *Gone with the Wind* that I should read before I started school in five days. So, I holed up in my room for five days, reading Margaret Mitchell's classic from cover to cover until I "got it." By the time I'd finished, I was Scarlett O'Hara proclaiming, "I'll never be hungry again!" I remember making a life decision after reading the last page: "If I can't be popular, I'll be smart." This was my version of never being hungry again, never letting fear stop me from moving forward.

I still knew that our family had changed, though, after the sudden and traumatic relocation to Memphis from our untarnished, happy times in St. Louis. Just as the frustration of our circumstances was taking its toll on Dad, Mom and my siblings, it was also having an effect on me. Dark emotions were building inside me like storm clouds. I needed a release.

A year and a half after starting school in Memphis, I poured out all my ranting and raving and angst about the trials and tribulations of being transplanted from the North to the South into a novelette. When I handed it to Sister Mary Howard at the Immaculate Conception (IC) for Girls school in Memphis, I felt a tremendous burden lifted from my shoulders. The pain of the previous eighteen months had been delivered to a nun who I was sure would ease my pain, comfort me, and reach out to this lost soul who was just looking for someone to talk to. I was finally starting to feel good.

A week later, Sister Mary Howard returned my dramatic story of relocation from North to South to me. It looked like something recovered from the Civil War itself: Blood-like stains covered the pages of my sacred literary confessional, the red slashes of a pen, correcting the grammar and spelling errors. The bloodbath culminated in one dramatic circle, where she had placed the letter grade B. Sister Mary Howard handed it to me and said, "Laura, you are a B writer and you will always be one." She turned and left without a single word about the content, the feelings, the pain and the secret thoughts I had shared so intimately on those pages.

Nevertheless, my hard work throughout high school ultimately landed me a partial theater scholarship to Webster College in St. Louis, plus a student loan and fifteen hours a week of work on campus. I found my way out of Memphis.

A partial scholarship meant that I had to pay many expenses myself. I was scheduled to the hilt fifteen hours a day, every day: five hours per day of theater training (diction, movement, dance, Shakespeare, improvisation, scene study and more), several hours of elective courses, and on top of that I worked three hours every day in the admissions or theater office to pay the bills. I didn't see anything unusual about this. I was doing what needed to be done in the only manner that I saw fit: one hundred percent effort, no excuses, drive toward the basket. One of the other ways I paid for college was babysitting three to four nights a week and some weekends. It wasn't always easy.

"In an unusually pioneering way, Laura broke ground in her career that opened doors to an amazingly diverse international community. Who would have predicted that from her undergraduate days at Webster? She is just a dynamic woman and a great example of how far our graduates can go. She's also very generous in opening doors for other women and that's what I admire about her, maybe more than anything else."

—**Dr. Beth Stroble**, President, Webster University

A Guy Named Mike

In 1967, at age nineteen and my sophomore year, a friend from high school invited me to a Christmas party. This was a college party, mind you. There was no heat, so they improvised by turning on the gas in the stove, opening the oven door, and using a fan to blow the heat into the living room, hoping it would heat up the whole house. We weren't exactly rocket scientists, but fortunately we avoided the next day's newspaper headlines. My friend, my former cheerleading moderator, had invited her boyfriend's best friend at the time, a guy named Mike.

I spotted him the moment I entered the room. It wasn't just because he was twenty-four years old in a room full of college students. It was that he *acted* and looked like the only grown up at the party. In a sea of tie-dyed T-shirts and jeans, Mike was dressed in a white turtleneck, black pants, black wingtip shoes, and a sport coat. In a moment of universal synchronicity, I turned to my girlfriend and said, "I'm going to meet that guy over there," while on the other side of the room at the same time, Mike turned to his buddy and said, "I'm going to go meet that girl."

We walked toward each other across the room, me in my coordinated Villager wool shorts and turtleneck, Mike with a beer in his hand, an absolutely terrific smile on his face and not a trace of swagger (like some of the other guys at the time). He was the most handsome, neatest guy I'd ever seen. But did I know the man of my dreams was walking toward me? My sister claims that I did, saying that when I saw her later that night I exclaimed, "I met the guy I'm going to marry!"

So there we were, handsome older guy with a beer, and the young and innocent Catholic girl who didn't drink and was the only girl in our class at Webster who went to mass and received communion every day (in between my studies and part-time jobs). Some of my best friends were actually nuns and I spent a lot of my "free" time after work, classes and mass sitting with them, talking in depth about life philosophies and ideas. Maybe it was the white turtleneck, black slacks and such, but for some reason I had this idea in my head that Mike might be in the seminary studying to be a priest or something. I proceeded with caution and put my theory to the test. Once we met in the center of the room at the party, here's how the conversation went:

Mike: "So, what do you do at Webster?"

Me: "I'm studying to be a nun."

Mike: "You're kidding."

I shrugged, tossing my long jet-black hair back over my shoulder.

Me: "I'm not a hundred percent sure, but I am leaning toward the possibility."

This wasn't entirely a fib. I absolutely loved the dynamo Sister Jaqueline Grennan, known to us as Sr. J, who was president at Webster in 1967. She led the university with gusto and chutzpah (as my Jewish friends say), two distinct personality traits I would later own myself as founder of IMPACT Group.

Well, let me tell you, Mike didn't buy my story about running off to the convent for a second! He went to work interrogating me, asking me what I thought of the current state of affairs at the Vatican, my opinions about various verses from Catholic writers and more. Due to my extensive conversations with my friends the nuns, I passed the interrogation with flying colors, keeping step with Mike topic for topic. Mike later told me he left the conversation thinking, "Oh my gosh, this beautiful woman is going to be a nun!" I left the conversation more certain than ever in my suspicion that he was studying to be a priest. Nevertheless, we got along so well that at two in the morning, after the party, he walked me to my car and didn't ask me out or even for my phone number. I got mad! I thought, "This is ridiculous! This is the neatest guy I've ever met and, seminary or no seminary, I'm going to see him again!" (There's that Herring chutzpah rearing its head again.)

It was December 22, so I invited him to our family's formal New Year's Eve birthday party for my brother. After he accepted, I gave Mike our address, but without a phone number there was no way for him to call in between or for the two of us to stay in contact with each other. By the time New Year's Eve came around, I had no idea if he even remembered my invitation and certainly I had no clue as to whether or not he'd show up. Finally, on New Year's Eve, 8:00 p.m. came and went with no sign of Mike. Then 9:00 p.m. "This guy has no manners!" my sister announced. I was heartbroken.

Then, at 9:30 p.m., he knocked on the door. When I greeted him, partially relieved and partially peeved, he started apologizing profusely, explaining how with his large family and only one car, he'd been unanimously elected to play the part of taxi driver that evening, dropping off four other family members all around Memphis at New Year's Eve parties. Without my phone number he had no way of letting me know he'd be late.

Things only got better from there. Next, I had the pleasure of introducing Mike to my dad, who immediately gave my date the once-over, but with a strangely curious look on his face. "Oh gosh," I thought, mentally burying my head in my hands, "what now?"

"Son," my dad asked, "haven't I met you somewhere before?"

Mike bowed his head like a disobedient puppy and answered, "Yes sir ... at the seminarian's dinner last evening at the bishop's house."

My father turned on his heel and sternly confronted me.

"Laura," he said, "I've worked much too hard finding good young men for God and getting them into the priesthood, only to have you invite them to parties and pluck them right out."

I was right! I should have known that not many twenty-four-year-olds in 1967 would show up at a college party in black dress slacks and wing tip shoes if they weren't in the seminary. I was right, but in the moment, I was also absolutely mortified in front of my family. It turned out Mike had been in the seminary for six and a half years already and was scheduled to be ordained as a priest at the end of May.

We had a really nice time that evening and so we stayed in touch after that, writing back and forth into springtime. I invited him to our spring formal at Webster. It was April 1968 and, as far as I knew, Mike was still in the seminary down in New Orleans and slated to become an ordained priest in mere weeks. For the second time, Mike had a surprise in store for me when he showed up and knocked on my door. I opened the apartment door and gasped in shock at the sight of him in shorts and the worst case of knee calluses I'd ever seen, at least one inch in thickness.

"What on earth are those from?" I asked him.

"From praying," he replied.

"For what?" I asked, staring at what looked like battle wounds.

"You," he answered.

Need I say more? His class's ordination came and went without him. Mike left the seminary and thus began our two-year courtship. This upset his family tremendously (especially his grandmother—she was devastated) and to this day, I have so much respect and love for my husband for following his heart.

We dated into June, at which time I was already scheduled to continue my studies in Europe for fifteen months. I was headed to Europe to study psychology among other subjects. While I did not have a lot of extra money, the admissions office at Webster made an exception and allowed me to transfer my scholarship and grant money to The Institute of European Studies in Vienna, Austria.

Before we parted ways, I told Mike I was crazy about him and was sure we could develop our relationship through letter writing (remember those things with stamps and envelopes before email and Skype?). He agreed and promised, "I'll wait for you." True to our promise, we wrote each other almost every single day, and through 1968 and 1969, did our part to keep the United States Postal Service in business.

When I finally returned to Webster (reuniting with Mike who had found a job in St. Louis), due to the stringent courses of the theater conservatory, I was unable to continue my studies in the theater department unless I retook my junior year. By this point, I'd come to the realization that as much as I loved to act, I didn't have all the "other things" (such as singing and dancing) it takes to make a career in the theater. Besides, I'd fallen in love with psychology and history in Europe, so I switched gears and pursued a social sciences degree, which enabled me to get my teaching certificate.

These early career twists and turns taught me how important it is to be true to yourself and follow your passion. Sense your skill sets and be honest with yourself about whether or not you can be successful in a certain area.

Wasting no time, by spring of my senior year we had decided to marry. I graduated May 13 and Mike and I married June 13. When Mike and I had our heart-to-heart discussions about what we really wanted to do in this world, the common ground was crystal clear: *we both wanted to make a difference*. He was already happily immersed in his teaching career, loving every moment that he got to make kids feel good about themselves.

Lots to Learn

I was a beginner in the field, twenty-two years old, and having just landed my very first teaching job. I was so excited about the interview for this job in a top-notch school district. I wore a polyester peach dress I had made especially for the occasion. It was my first interview ever and I was nervous. But I fought through my fears, expressed my passion for the job, and the interviewer offered me a job on the spot.

From day one, I knew I had a lot to learn, especially as I was still playing catchup on my college teaching requirements after switching over from the theater program. Similar to maximizing the impact of every available hour during college, I devoted every moment of free and prep time as a young teacher to learning. I singled out one particular mentor, Nolan Stivers, a social studies teacher of twenty years, and became a constant fixture in the back of his classroom, auditing his classes. Then, I stayed after school for an additional two to three hours a day with him and another new male teacher, asking questions, listening and learning the do's and don'ts of teaching from them. Nolan was a master in his field and someone who truly made a difference in helping his students develop critical-thinking skills. I was so grateful that this passionate teacher and amazing man was willing to mentor me.

Whatever your profession, and however long you've been in it, always put in the time to be the best you can possibly be. Mastery takes time and effort. Find a mentor: someone to learn from, someone who has the wisdom to help you sharpen your existing skills and learn new ones. You can't be the best by bluffing your way through life.

Continuing my devotion to mastering my craft into the evening hours, I would get home around six each night, Mike and I would fix dinner together and talk about our day, and then I'd spend another two to three hours preparing lesson plans and grading papers. Determined not to be another Sister Mary Howard, I wrote pages of feedback to my students to let them know that I heard their words loud and clear, and was there to help them.

With this initial valuable teaching experience under my homemade polyester belt, I soon set my sights on moving up to a brand new high-tech high school currently under construction. But my principal wouldn't let me leave my current post. Fiercely stubborn even as a young woman, I told him that if he didn't let me go I'd quit. Can you imagine? Twenty-three years old, making $4,000 a year and I was threatening to quit my very first teaching job. So, much to that principal's surprise, having saved half our salaries for two years, Mike and I headed to Europe for six months, studying, traveling and living.

Once we'd returned and Mike was off to study counseling at Washington University, I realized one of us needed to get a job and it wasn't going to be him. So I got a job selling educational courses door to door in the evenings from five to nine, when people were most likely to be at home. Since I always thought of teaching rather like sales (where I had to "sell" kids on learning about topics they normally had no interest in), this job felt natural to me even though, as with teaching, at first I had no clue as to what I was doing. But as usual, I put my head down, learned as much as possible about the job, and worked every day to do my best. My supervisor on this job later told me how surprised he was by my high close rate—not because I was new to sales, but because he had intentionally given me the worst leads. He said the fact that I closed almost every lead showed that I had the makings of a great salesperson. At the time, at this young age with so much going on, this idea of sales being a potential new skill didn't resonate beyond receiving kudos from a boss on a job well done. Once again, I had my eyes set on returning to teaching.

Meanwhile, Mike came home from Washington University every night fired up by what he was learning. He would hand me his books and say, "This counseling program is *so* you!"

Like Mike, I saw counseling as a way to make a greater difference, to take my passion for teaching to the next level. But first I would need to forge a pathway there from teaching. I was still selling door to door when the school where I'd previously hoped to get a job got wind that I was back. They promptly called and offered me a job teaching history and social studies at the very best senior high school in their district. I was euphoric. No more door-to-door sales!

At age twenty-five, I still looked much like a hippie in my blue jean skirts, long hair and colorful bandanas. I didn't exactly blend in with the rest of the staff, who were more of the sweater vest, plaid corduroy blazer and pleated skirt contingent. Apparently, as a young schoolteacher in the early '70s, this naturally meant that I was the obvious choice to talk down euphoric students flying high on hallucinogenic drugs. This began my transition from teacher to counselor. The counselors, all in their fifties and sixties, naturally assumed that because of my age and the way I dressed, I was clearly a druggie and spoke their language. If only they knew how I once considered becoming a nun and married a man originally studying to be a priest. When called upon by the counseling office, my "job" was to coax the acid-dropped student out from under the desk, patiently pull off the imaginary spiders, and then hold them while awaiting the ambulance. I was only twenty-five and I'd never done drugs, yet the experience taught me how important it is for people to feel listened to. If that young person truly believed that spiders were crawling all over their skin, then I would play along with that reality until I could coax them over to join my reality.

Waiting with those kids, talking them down, listening and soothing their anxieties, absolutely cemented the notion in my mind that I needed to become a counselor. This was not just a new career path for me; it was a calling. I decided then and there to go back to school and become a psychologist.

I wasn't aware at the time of how powerful those experiences would be, contributing to my future success as a leader of a global company. Leading people to see things as I saw them demanded that I walk in their shoes for quite a while before I could successfully influence a change in their perception. This is one of the most important lessons in business: understanding the views of others and being willing to walk alongside them in their world before trying to change them.

There were other lessons learned during those early career years that would later serve me in business—like the power of politics in the workplace. A female vice principal of one of the high schools I worked with came up to me one day when I was wearing a suit and heels (counselors in the 1970s wore corduroys and turtlenecks). She said, "Laura, you are awfully dressed up today. Let me remind you, I am the vice principal, and you are a counselor." I simply smiled and said, "Oh, I know that, but I was always taught to dress for the next job I want, not the one I have." She walked away in a slightly befuddled huff. Rather than getting upset about the vice principal, I was immediately reminded of my Aunt Marge's shoes.

Aunt Marge's Shoes

Around 1958, when I was ten and our family still lived in St. Louis, I was sent to visit my Aunt Marge in Rahway, New Jersey, for two weeks. She was the first woman VP at McCrory's. Visiting her home was my very first experience seeing how "successful women" lived. They had a swimming pool, ate fancy jam on their toast, enjoyed an exotic dish called "lobster," drank wine and drove Cadillacs.

One day, I got to go to work with Aunt Marge. I sat on her bed that morning, watching in awe as she got dressed. She had the most beautiful clothes I'd ever seen: matching black lace bras and panties folded neatly in separate drawers, fine black and navy dresses from end to end in her closet, and over forty pairs of matching black and blue shoes. It was a magical moment for me. My mother generally lived in housecoats. She never worried about herself. She always put our needs first.

Aunt Marge also wore makeup, which my mom only did for church or rare dinners out with my dad. From my vantage point at age ten, what I saw in Aunt Marge was a woman driving into New York City every day in her Cadillac, wearing beautiful lace underwear and perfect shoes. I felt like she was a movie star.

After work that evening, following our impromptu "take your niece to work day," Aunt Marge accidentally locked herself out of her office. Well, earlier in the day she had already taken off her nice high heels and slipped into comfortable flats and we were headed out to dinner in the city. Unruffled, Aunt Marge said, "Don't worry, I'll just go downstairs and buy a new pair of heels so we're not late." I was gaga! Who goes and buys another pair of shoes when all they have to do is track down the building superintendent and ask him to open the office door? Aunt Marge, that's who.

We went downstairs to a department store and she bought an identical pair of navy blue heels, the same ones she had in her office. She slipped on the new shoes and we went to dinner—no scene, no drama, no panic, just calmly moving on through the problem. That taught me how a woman can earn her way in the world by taking control of each situation. But the big lesson I learned from my brief visit into Aunt Marge's world was to dress the part you want to be known for, not the role you currently have. I started imitating Aunt Marge after that:

her hairstyle, wearing sweaters and pearls for our family portraits, etc. I tried to look like her in hopes of becoming her someday. To this day, I am a woman in love with shoes.

Standing Out—Too Much

In addition to dressing "as if I'm successful," attacking my work with gusto, and going above and beyond all expectations of the job, my teaching and counseling style had a dramatic flair—one designed to engage the student.

It wasn't long before this notion of dramatic flair was also reflected in my annual reviews. I was standing out—*loudly!*—from the pack, and the pack (the older counselors) didn't take kindly to it. I look back and can't help but laugh about some of the more ridiculous comments on those early teacher reviews, such as, "Writes too loudly on the chalkboard." The reviews also addressed my constant, lifelong work habit of going above and beyond. When the powers that be in the school heard how I was showing up at six in the morning to meet with working parents about a problem student, or learned about my morning peer counseling group, or found out how I offered to take over another teacher's class and teach a values clarification course, the head of my department interpreted these actions as, "Was trying to do too much; should stick to tallying up students' earned credit hours." They literally just wanted me to add up kids' credit hours, a task I'd delegated to one of my math students. The department head was aghast at finding this out, exclaiming, "Laura, that's your job!" to which I responded firmly, "No, my job is helping these kids and their parents." Finally, the real truth came out when he told me, "You're putting more pressure on the other counselors by setting the bar too high." This often happens in life, (and unfortunately in the workplace, as I've seen over the years) when "overachievers" unintentionally cast a revealing spotlight on those performing at or below expectations.

I saw the truth of my situation and realized that my talents and passion for my work would never be valued in that job. I possessed more drive to help those kids than the school's vice principal and my future department head could handle. I wasn't a rebel; I just always saw all the possibilities.

Sure enough, confirming my suspicions that my passion and hard work would never be rewarded there, when it came time to pick the new department head, I was passed over for the guy who played politics with the vice principal far better than I could (or was willing to). In that moment, I decided that I wanted my own private counseling practice.

As I handed in my resignation, walking away from the public education system for the private sector, the principal put forth one last effort to keep me.

"Laura," he said, "you are walking away from a steady fifteen-thousand-a-year job (and I would have received a raise with a master's degree). Why not start your private practice at night and keep your job in the schools in case you don't succeed?"

I sweetly told him, "Failure is not a possibility. It has never crossed my mind."

To which he replied, "I really admire you Laura. I have been trying to leave education for fifteen years!"

Well, I'm not sure if my act of passion and bravery had anything to do with it, but just two years later, that man finally quit his job and opened a bed and breakfast. When you make a decision to fight back your fear of failure and follow your passion, you never really know how many people are watching and may be inspired in return. Just as my dad taught me, and just as I taught the kids I coached: Always drive toward the basket, never around it.

—∽— Lessons Learned —∽—

1. Don't let other people define who you are.

Those three girls I mentioned, the cheerleaders I encountered on that first fateful day in Memphis outside our home, are all lovely women today, all married, and we occasionally still keep in touch after going to school together all through high school. My decision to be smart, not popular, simply led to approaching life in a dramatically different way. If those girls had smiled, embraced me, and not called me a damn Yankee, who knows how that would have changed the course of my life? Instead, I learned a valuable lesson about rejection that would later serve me extremely well in business, especially sales.

We're all born one way, and then we're changed along the way by events and things that happen to us. It's up to us to pick and choose how to relate to things and the decisions we make in light of our circumstances. When I got to high school and finally tried out for cheerleading, I practiced and practiced (the same way I studied and studied), and tried out in front of the teachers every year—and got picked for the squad every year. I set a goal and did what it took to achieve it. If I had let those girls initially define who I was (a damn Yankee, non-cheerleader, outcast) none of this might have happened.

2. Don't let your fearful inner child define the outcomes of your life.
Choosing success can be lonely. During our first year in Memphis I learned that working hard, focusing on succeeding, and striving to be the best at everything can keep you focused, but definitely will not win you friends. "If I can't be popular, I'll be smart." As I said earlier, I could have easily let a brief conversation with three teenage girls set off a chain reaction of beliefs that would then guide my everyday actions. Ask yourself: Would you give a six-year-old your checkbook to balance? Probably not. Why, then, would you hand over the emotional balance sheet of your life to your younger self—a self who didn't know all the rules of life, exceptions to the rules, and all the fine print in between?

It is never a good idea to turn your life decisions over to a child. Yet that is really what so many of us do when we continue making decisions in life based on a mistaken belief formulated by a childhood happenstance: a word, a phrase, a look that was interpreted for some other purpose than for which it was intended. It's time to take the checkbook back and determine how much value we have today by our own updated calculations. Life decisions are choices we make every step of every day. Decide for yourself who you are and who you want to be before you pick your purpose. Don't get stuck on a curb, believing an inadvertent label about you, slapped on casually by others, that just isn't true.

3. Embrace Who You Are.
I knew in my heart and gut that my time as a teacher had come and gone and it was time to move on. The lesson is to know when to walk away from one journey and start the next. Listen to your heart. Surround yourself with people who see your value and your worth. Seek like minds and share the journey with people who see the same possibilities for your life that you do. Looking back, I am certain that it wasn't just a thirteen-year-old's awkwardness that

kept me from being a part of the crowd. I think that deep down I was already a budding entrepreneur. I believe that most entrepreneurs never really fit in because of who they are and who they are not. Clinging to isolation was my way of taking hold of my aspirations to fly away and become a "somebody" somewhere, somehow. I am convinced that not "fitting in" preps you for becoming a successful entrepreneur, filled with vim and vigor, destined to prove that you are a "somebody." It is a deeply rooted yearning to stand up and take control of making something happen, using whatever resources you have because you are not certain that you can count on anyone else to make it happen. Not fitting in can breed determination and a strength that comes deep from within.

Looking back now, I think of how often we hear that entrepreneurs have a certain type of personality, a unique blend of unbridled ambition, daring, and unrequited passion for crossing the finish line—whatever the finish line may be at any given moment. I see myself back then, this teenage girl thrust into a strange land with only her brains and personal mission to win in life. I see the seeds of an entrepreneur. Back then, of course, I only saw the next obstacle to be conquered, the next academic goal to achieve. I have no doubt that the character I was building during the adversity of those years created the foundation of my business success later in life. It's true: That which doesn't kill you makes you stronger.

4. Your kids are watching.

When happy, playful dad from St. Louis became angry, brooding dad in Memphis, our entire family dynamic downshifted. Seeing how quick to anger dad was and how we never knew what would set him off, I made the decision early on to protect my siblings from getting in trouble. At the age of thirteen, I began coaching them, saying things like, "Don't do that, daddy will get really upset." I was trying to protect the family dynamic by running interference. The lesson here, also cemented by my psychology studies later on, is that kids notice the psychological state of their parents—whether the parents realize it or not. Put on your own oxygen mask first; check your frame of mind so you know what your children are receiving from you.

5. Take control of your life.

Walking away from a $15,000-per-year teaching job (a lot of money at the time) was a risk, but I had to follow my heart. I decided at that point that I couldn't allow a company to determine my future. I had to take control of my own life. Remembering the lesson I'd learned from watching my dad's circumstances, I left my teaching career to open my own counseling practice. The principal suggested I keep teaching and make a more gradual transition. "No," I told him, "I've got to be happy and true to myself."

6. Truly dress for success.

When you want to be seen as a successful businessperson, dress as if you are going to meet someone who will want to do business with you. Dress the part you want to be known for, not the role you currently have.

Even with today's casual business dress, there are ways to dress consistently in a style that makes you stand out. I still buy quality shoes, and wear dramatic hats, pins and jewelry. Distinctive people usually comment on one or all three. Pay attention to your personal style details, and people will pay attention to you.

7. Rid yourself of negative people.

As a result of your courage to do this, it will become easier and easier to see your truest and most loyal cheerleaders—those who will link arms with you and join you on your journey to success (and invite you on theirs). When this synchronicity occurs, it is magic. This is when you begin building your army of supporters, one by one. Awareness of and willingness to take action in these situations are important leadership traits for everyone in business or in life.

Throughout this book you will hear this theme over and over again: Your beliefs about yourself and the world in general will determine who you are and who you become. They will spill over from your moments in time, to others' moments in time, unwittingly shaping their lives as well. If we all embrace a model that we truly can make a difference in the lives we touch, then we realize how powerful we are as human beings. Why not find a way to move beyond fear and make a positive impact? Why not make it a mantra in business and in daily life to make a positive difference in the lives we touch? This is the foundation of our purpose.

Chapter 3

TAKING CONTROL, CHOOSING SUCCESS

One lesson I came away with from my brief yet impactful teaching career was crystal clear: I was at my absolute happiest when helping kids and their families work through family problems. This, however, was the only thing I had certainty about. I had just walked away from a very stable teaching and counseling job, as the principal reminded me multiple times while I sat in his office delivering my resignation. He thought I was out of my mind to start a private family therapy practice at twenty-six years old and, to his credit, in many similar situations that would have been the truth. I think about all the people who take these leaps of faith, sometimes torching bridges along the way to break free from a toxic environment, in favor of starting fresh in a new career or starting their own business. There are so many who get lost in the twists and turns every day, especially after making their dramatic career/life leap. I could have been one of them, and I feel blessed that I wasn't. Surviving such a leap really does take a combination of courage, ambition, and the willingness to do whatever it takes to succeed.

Starting out with my very own private counseling practice, I learned quickly that when you take risks you never really know what you're getting yourself into. But, like so many other eager entrepreneurs, I dove into the deep end of self-employment for the first time of my life with gusto. I proudly hung my shingle outside our converted garage, separated nicely from the rest of the house.

Then I focused on getting the word out about my practice. I knew that plain old business cards with only verbiage would not be enough to draw in clients. They would need to see whom they were entrusting with their stories, innermost thoughts and feelings. They needed to meet the human being who would help them and, in many cases, change their lives. What people needed in a counselor was trust; they needed to see me interacting with people I'd helped. I called a friend to take photos of me with the kids I counseled and their parents, and another friend to design a brochure using those photos. I knew that pictures— photos of real people—evoked feelings.

With brochures in hand, I then cold called and visited churches, schools and community centers, offering to speak about any appropriate topic they chose. If a community organization in the greater St. Louis area needed a free speaker well-versed in parenting, helping kids with homework, bullying, shyness, divorce—*anything*—I was determined to be the first person they called. This is an important thing for fledgling entrepreneurs to realize: Getting your name out there and establishing credibility and a good reputation is often more important than chasing your first dollar. Once enough people know who you are and what problems you can solve for them, word will spread and the clients will start knocking on your door. And when they come knocking, you'd better be there to hear them, as I was about to learn the hard way.

One morning in my office at the back of the house, I got a call from my 10 a.m. client, who wanted to cancel his appointment. Mind you, at this point in my career in 1976, I was twenty-six and only had three clients per week, each at $25 an hour for a grand total of $75 in weekly revenue. That phone call had just cost me one third of my whole week's pay. I was absolutely devastated! When clients cancel they don't usually explain why. They don't say, "I don't like you,"

"I don't want you," or "You're not good enough." They just tell you, "I have to cancel today." So, of course, my sensitive new self-employed imagination went berserk with possibilities. Then, I did what any other professional would do: I lay on my office floor and bawled my eyes out, wailing, "Oh my God, what have I done?" The cumulative effect of my tantrum was that I fell into a deep sleep from emotional exhaustion, right there in the middle of my office floor. So, when my 11 a.m. client came knocking on the back door of my garage office, I didn't hear them. I was out like a light, wallowing in self-pity as I slept. As a result, I lost my second out of only three clients for the whole week!

The words of wisdom here are: Never take anything in business personally. Whether you are an entrepreneur, employee or even the boss, remember it's usually not about you; it's always about them. If you wallow in your disappointment, you are almost guaranteed to miss out on other opportunities while you're curled up crying on your office floor.

Because I was down to only one client, just $25 in income for the week, I had no choice but to get up off the floor, dust myself off and find new clients and new opportunities. I may not have seen it this way then as I knocked on doors, frantically cold calling any prospects I could think of, volunteering as a way of expanding my reputation, and working here and there on several projects. In retrospect, though, I see that this was just the shocker I needed to stretch beyond my comfort zone, and what I would have done with just those same three clients. It was my wakeup call: "No Fear Allowed!"

Clients come and go, change their minds, and cancel appointments and contracts—if it can start, it can just as easily come to an end. This is a reality that exists at the intersection of human nature, life and business. It's something that as an entrepreneur you must accept and prepare for. Therefore, you can never afford to rest on your laurels, not if you want to continue turning a profit. You have to keep creating more and more business; it's a continuous cycle with no ending point. Once I understood that I could no longer count on those three clients, for the next week, the week after and beyond, I knew I had no choice but to go get more.

I have always been motivated to be the best that I could be; to that end, shortly after starting my private practice, I traveled around the country for years, from St. Louis to San Francisco to San Diego to Boston and all points in between. I studied with some of the best therapists, often for six weeks straight. I was never afraid to ask industry leaders to teach me something. I would boldly march up to them at conferences and announce, "I want to learn from you," and then ask about their next seminar. If they didn't have one (which was rare) I would ask if I could fly out and observe their practice for a week. I would read a therapy book, call up the author and ask if they did training. I was relentless in my pursuit of knowledge. During this travel learning odyssey, I really learned to listen while also rediscovering my passion for teaching.

My confidence grew as I studied and implemented these techniques in my work. After a while, in St. Louis I was becoming known as "the therapist's therapist." The entrepreneurial lesson here is to sharpen your skills continuously, and never stop learning. In order to become a sought-after expert in your field, you must keep growing as a professional.

Therefore, I balanced my business hustle with my desire to learn, grow and (in my mind) become the best therapist I could be. Let's pause for a moment and look at that simple statement I used to open the door to all these wonderful learning experiences: "I want to learn from you." I've seen and heard of far too many entrepreneurs who seem to think they know it all, have seen it all and are the end all in their industry. There's no such thing. The truly great success stories in business that I've seen are about individuals who refuse to quit learning and spend every spare moment seeking out mentors, training and new knowledge. I would challenge any entrepreneur or intrapreneur reading this book, no matter how experienced, to seek out someone with more knowledge and experience, track this person down and tell them, "I want to learn from you." See where this one simple, bold act takes you.

Another thing I did to expand the reach of my reputation was to work with corporate Employee Assistance Program (EAP) counselors who worked for various corporations. I found out that companies were paying for their employees to have counseling to help deal with issues in their personal lives, such as marital problems, alcohol abuse, child rearing and other emotional and family issues. Once again I started knocking on doors, this time big fancy corporate ones, with my little brochure. I zeroed in on the directors of the EAPs and let them know I was doing private counseling. I got a positive response immediately and it wasn't long before things really started to take off. Because I was trained in so many different therapies, a major EAP in St. Louis asked me to train their entire EAP referral staff—eight therapists total. Once I started training them, the therapists started to refer to me on a regular basis. They started referring their corporate employees to me (because employees were allowed only two to six visits in the employee assistance programs), and my biggest surprise (and honor) was that many of those referring counselors valued my work so much they started coming to me to deal with their own personal concerns. One thing about therapists is they're always looking for a good therapist for themselves because they absolutely believe in the impact of therapy.

Making a Difference

The next phase of my counseling career saw me expanding my private practice to train other counselors in the city. It had taken me five years to build a solid foundation for my practice. By that point, I was working forty to fifty clinical hours a week (often more) and then on Saturdays from 9 a.m. to noon.

I was passionate about making a difference in the lives of the couples and families I worked with. Thirty years later, a former client called out of the blue and validated this passion. She began with, "Laura, this is Mrs. X. Do you remember me?" I told her "Of course I do." They were a very strong family. She then proceeded to tell me, "I am calling to thank you for changing our lives. I don't know if you remember what you told me specifically, but we came in when the middle of my three sons was acting out in school and we were crazy with fear that he would be a hoodlum. You refused to see him as a client individually; you made all three of my sons and my husband and I come to see you." I remembered the situation well, as I believed in helping families change their system of interaction and not assume the one problem child was really the whole problem in the family.

She continued, "You told me after several sessions that you were not so much concerned about our middle child, but you were more concerned about our oldest child who seemed to say nothing and sit off by himself. You said, 'I am afraid he will leave the house in two years and all your focus will have been on your middle child and not your oldest.'

"At the time I was surprised by your assignment for me and my husband that we were to ignore the middle child for a month and focus on the two others. My particular assignment was to really get to know my oldest son as an adult and to befriend him, and I did—for the next thirty years. He and I became great friends and we talked weekly. I am calling you to thank you for that, as I am not sure that I would have ever done that without your urging. You see, we just buried my oldest son last week. He was killed in China crossing the street visiting our middle son, who is a vice president of sales for a major U.S. company." She said, "Do you remember what you said to us in the very last session? 'You are good parents. You only have to remember to focus your love on all three of your children.' You also told us you thought our middle son would become a great salesman one day. You were right."

I was numb at this point in the conversation.

She continued, "I am calling to thank you for allowing me to have no regrets regarding my oldest son. We were friends, we loved each other, and I have you to thank for that."

After sharing my condolences, I thanked her profusely for being so kind in her moment of grief and telling me I had made a difference in her life. My heart broke for them, but it reaffirmed I was on the right path and achieving my purpose in life.

As part of my counseling education, I scraped together just enough money to attend Ericksonian training in Indianapolis by Jeff Zeig, a master in the field whose work I'd been studying for the previous three years. I felt very strongly that the information I would receive at this training was the missing piece of a puzzle I was working on: a counseling and training program for corporations. In short, Jeff helped guide me toward the answers I was looking for and I had sudden clarity on how to combine my mission to make a difference with my experience as a counselor.

When I got back from the training in Indianapolis, I eventually set to work on my new mission to create "Take Control, Choose Success" seminars for corporations. With Mike's supportive blessing, I borrowed $7,000 from our savings account and his retirement fund and told him, "This program will be my entry into corporate training." And so it was.

But first, there was the matter of fine-tuning my new corporate program and making absolutely certain that it would deliver the value that I envisioned. So, in what would end up being an integral, lifelong business practice for me, I put together a focus group. I'm always looking for feedback and I wasn't about to do this seminar without really testing it through my professional and personal friends. I wanted them to poke holes in all my ideas, and really challenge me so I could get it right.

I invited about a dozen friends, fellow therapists and others I trusted, over to the house for cocktails, cheese and wine, sharing that I wanted them to honestly—and even brutally—critique my ideas, my flow, my transition slides and my training exercises. I wanted their honest feedback: Would they be willing to pay $99 for this one-day seminar?

As they enjoyed cheese and wine, I had my friends review a brochure I had written for the seminar and offer up comments, critiques and recommendations. I asked them specifically for feedback on my marketing plan. We decided that I should sell seats for $99 each and limit the seminar to seventy people (which would give me back my $7,000), and their greatest contribution that night was the suggestion to invite corporate training directors for free. I went to work creating and distributing brochures based on the focus group feedback. In an earlier lesson about the value of bartering, I approached a friend of a friend for help marketing the program. I told her I couldn't pay her then, but vowed to pay her at some point. In the meantime, I gave her some free counseling in return for her hard work. The lesson here is to never be afraid to ask for help, even if you don't have big bucks to pay for it. I was determined to do whatever it took to make my vision of "Take Control, Choose Success" a reality—always driving toward the basket, just like my dad taught me.

Nevertheless, I was astounded when the seminar happened exactly as I'd envisioned with my friends the night of the focus group. Seventy people showed up, along with the training directors for McDonnell Douglas Corporation, Southwestern Bell (now AT&T), Anheuser Busch (now AB INBEV), Ralston

Purina (now Nestle Purina), Monsanto, and a handful of others who had accepted my free invitation.

By the following quarter, I had "Take Control, Choose Success" training programs lined up with Ralston Purina, Monsanto, and McDonnell Douglas. Focus groups and feedback were more important than ever in devising the right program for each of these clients (and every client to come, as my company grew over the years). I would sit with the training directors, relocation directors and employees at each corporation and, putting my counseling skills to good use, listen as they told me what kind of issues they were dealing with, reflect back what I heard, and then create a seminar tailored to each company's needs. This one exercise would help singlehandedly launch the corporate consulting piece of IMPACT Group.

This single business decision to do corporate seminars would flourish into a $50 million company specializing in transition services to corporations worldwide.

In retrospect, I am amazed by the mere thought of it. But I must tell you, if I had set my goal there to begin with, I would have felt defeated from the start. Fifty million is just too big a number to set as a starting goal. I had written on a cocktail napkin with a friend: "I want to grow IMPACT Group into a $1 million company!" We both enjoyed the moment and I remember to this day thinking, "If I could do one million, I would feel successful." That number I truly believed I could achieve.

I Won't Teach Cocktail Chatter

An intuitive person once told me that when I walked into the room, she felt a giant wind blowing and waves rolling. The woman said she saw three boats with three packages being unloaded by two others and me from a small ship. She said larger ships wanted to take over our small ship, but I waved them off, weathering the storm and keeping on course. She added that I was going to be known around the world for my work!

The chronology of events in my eventual company, IMPACT Group, would corroborate everything she said that day. Three Herrings would run the company, delivering four major "packages" in the forms of Employee Development

Solutions, Global Mobility, Outplacement, and Talent Development. We rode it out, waving off larger ships as we weathered the storm, steering our ship beyond swells of fear, and becoming extremely successful. What's your vision for future success? How will you translate your purpose and passion for what you do now into future profits? At the time, I had no idea what our future held. What I did know was that I was passionate, as was my husband, about making a positive difference in the lives we touched.

I was always a forward-moving ship, enduring the entrepreneurial storms from day one. This also meant doing my best to shore up my little ship before boldly casting off into the sea.

By 1987, my foot was firmly in the door of some of America's biggest corporations. I was teaching my stress-management model, initially in the form of my "Take Control, Choose Success" seminar. But, seeing an opportunity to do more with it, I picked up the phone and called seminar clients like Ralston Purina and Monsanto and (based on the results of my impromptu focus groups at each company) made suggestions as to how they could use the program across their entire organization. I was then invited to teach entire corporate divisions about stress management, which is how I got my foot in the door at McDonnell Douglas. As the aircraft manufacturer was getting to know me through my stress-management courses, I was getting to know what some of the greatest stressors and roadblocks were within their organization.

McDonnell Douglas moved their people around the country like they were players on a Monopoly board. At any given time, hundreds of them were simultaneously passing *Go* and collecting their next $200, which was good for the employee, but not always so great for the family. Being plucked from yet another home, another neighborhood, another school, another church, and another community left many employees begging for a *Get out of Jail Free* card.

I desperately wanted to help these families, but first I figured I would have to sell one Mr. John McDonnell, CEO at the time, on the idea. And before that, I'd have to make it through the front gate. John and I were both on the St. Louis Regional Commerce & Growth Association Board, now called the St. Louis Regional Chamber (stlregionalchamber.com), so it gave me a head start.

Then one day, opportunity struck, or so I thought: "Ms. Herring, we'd like you to conduct a class, but we have a different topic in mind than stress management," John McDonnell's secretary, Carol, said to me.

"Really?" I asked. "What are you looking for?"

"Something along the lines of 'How to be a Corporate Spouse.' Maybe you could use the day to cover 'Corporate Cocktail Chatter.' We'd like to build up the spouses' confidence so that when they interact in a corporate setting, they have some tips to fall back on."

The words came flying out of my (historically uncensored) mouth, before I even realized it, "No, no, no! Absolutely not. This won't work!"

"But Laura, we want to build up their confidence," the secretary implored.

I stood my ground, completely certain that this was a terrible idea.

Realizing how harsh I might have sounded to her, I then tried to soften my response by explaining that fifty percent of these spouses had their own careers and, I was sure, were quite confident in carrying on at corporate functions. And then I quickly added, "I think this would be insulting to men and women and any of the spouses who will be there. I won't teach them cocktail chatter," and turned the job down.

"Fine," Carol told me, "we'll find someone else then."

I told her I was sorry, but if any other opportunities came along then yes, I would truly welcome the chance to present to the company's spouses.

So they found someone else.

It didn't take very long to receive the validation I needed in my gut that I'd made the right decision. Word came back to me that they did indeed find someone to teach the 'cocktail chatter' course. The spouses who attended were so unbelievably furious and insulted, that they didn't come back after lunch.

Shortly afterward, I received a phone call from Carol.

"Well, they didn't like that," she admitted.

It wasn't exactly a "you were right and we were wrong," but honestly I didn't need that. It wasn't about "winning" or putting the other guy down for me, it never has been in business. I just really wanted to help these spouses.

"So what do you think? What do you want to teach them?" she asked.

"Carol, you know it doesn't really matter what *I* want to teach them. Why don't we find out what *they* want to know?" I said. We put together a focus group of five to ten spouses from throughout the company.

In the end, I adapted my "Take Control, Choose Success" seminar for McDonnell Douglas spouses. I taught that program quarterly for several years. That's when the seed for my corporate company really came into full bloom. I'd been counseling relocating couples for several years, and I knew I could help them. I just needed a client who was willing to pay for the solution.

However, there was still one other person I wanted to involve in the process.

I called up Carol and said, "Would it be possible for you to arrange for John to stop by my seminar to welcome everyone this time?"

"Laura, you know his schedule is very busy," Carol responded.

"But I only need him for five minutes, I promise."

I think I surprised her a little when I backed down, calmly responding with, "I understand."

The morning of the spouse seminar, the employees and their spouses mingled together in the larger management conference room. I noticed, with some amusement, that none of them seemed to be having any trouble making "morning cocktail chatter." After a few minutes of mixing, they were segregated into their own rooms: the spouses with me and the executives across the hall with John.

I put my plan into action.

"If you ladies and gentlemen don't mind having another cup of coffee and chatting amongst yourselves," I said, "I will be right back."

I slipped outside and literally stood outside the door across the hall so I could catch John McDonnell as he was leaving the management seminar.

"John," I smiled at him, "do you have five minutes, just *five minutes?* I want the spouses to meet you personally and I think you'd like to hear this opening exercise."

Well, what could he say? I had him cornered. We walked back into the room together.

"Welcome everyone, to 'Take Control, Choose Success!'" I greeted the group. "I've asked John McDonnell to join us so he can get to know everybody. Could you please go around the room and say your name and what you do for a living?"

I wanted him to realize that many of them were working spouses as well. I really wanted John to connect with these people and one of the best ways to do that is to learn their names and realize that most of them were part of a dual-career couple. They all went around the table and introduced themselves.

"Now," I continued, "Mary would you mind starting? Could you tell John, as honestly as you can, what's the hardest part of being a corporate spouse?"

"Without a doubt, it's relocation," she answered.

"Okay, relocation," I said. "What about the rest of you?"

"Relocation."

"Relocation."

"Relocation."

Every answer was the same; all fifteen participants said that relocation was the most difficult part of being a corporate spouse.

It was as if my soul was instantly transported back in time to Memphis and the struggles our family went through during my dad's traumatic relocation. My new life's purpose was coming into focus: Combining teaching, counseling, and my stress-management seminars, I would give these corporate families all the knowledge and resources they needed to dissolve the trauma of relocation.

"John," I said, "this is a major issue for spouses. Not only for McDonnell Douglas spouses, but all corporate spouses. I hear the same thing in my private counseling practice."

Then John McDonnell looked at me and said, "So, fix it."

"Okay," I said, "I have some ideas. Where should I go with those?"

I didn't want to put him on the spot in front of all these people, but at the same time I knew enough to seize an opportunity and follow it through, right when it's presented.

"Go see my Senior Executive Vice President."

"When?" I prodded.

"Monday," John answered.

I think at this point John started turning toward the door, I'm sure hoping for an early exit from my impromptu meeting, but I wasn't done yet.

"Would you tell him I'm going to be calling?" I asked John.

"Yes," John agreed, still inching toward the door.

But he was still in my force field and I think at this point a few of the spouses must have been amused at our little scene, my exercise in seizing the opportunity and getting what you want.

"Because I have a whole box of ideas I have been saving for four or five years, John. This is a problem I can solve," I said.

With a bemused look, he repeated, "So fix it," before finally escaping from the conference room.

The lesson here is to trust your gut, hear a need, know that you can develop a solution, and have a vehicle to implement it. Then, do whatever you need to drive toward the basket.

I will admit that sometimes this level of chutzpah comes with consequences. Carol, for instance, was absolutely furious with me! But, being the good Catholic girl that I am, I was able to seek forgiveness, smooth things over, and continue driving forward to help these spouses.

The following Monday I met with my contact, John McDonnell's right-hand person at McDonnell Douglas. He closed the door and opened our meeting like this: "Laura, I want to tell you that relocation almost ruined my marriage. And so," he said, "I believe in this. Now, what are you thinking of doing?"

Immensely overjoyed to finally have someone who "spoke my language," I dove right in, explaining how for years I'd been gathering information and research on coping with change and what people feel during relocation. I also shared with him my own personal story on the subject. My plan, I told him, would entail detailed job search materials for the dual-career spouse who would want to recreate their job in a new location. The materials included audiotapes on résumé writing, interviewing techniques, planning workbooks for the spouse and family, and audiotapes (remember, there were no computers, no iPhones, no Google in 1988) the whole family could listen to for positivity. I also wanted to have it so either myself or someone else could personally get in touch with the employee and their spouse after they relocated, to find out how they were doing and if they needed anything.

"That sounds wonderful," he said. "How much do you think it will cost?"

"Oh," I said, caught off guard. In all my enthusiasm to get someone on board with my idea, it hadn't even occurred to me to price it. The wheels spun round and round in my head, crunching numbers.

"Remember," he said, "that we do a thousand relocations a year, so it's got to be affordable."

"One hundred and fifty dollars a person," I said firmly.

"That sounds great!" he responded immediately, to my delight.

One thousand times 150 is $150,000. I sat on the edge of my seat, eager to do whatever else was needed to close the deal. At this point I still had my therapy practice generating income, with fifty-plus clinical hours per week. I was well aware that this brand new $150,000 venture and all the work it would entail was a whole new ballgame. Bottom line, though, is that this was what I wanted and I would move mountains to make it happen.

"Why don't you do five thousand relocation kits?" he asked.

I did more mental math, thinking of both the overhead it would require putting the kits together (workbooks, audiotapes, etc.) as well as the revenue five thousand kits would generate—almost $1 million. I agreed, we sealed the deal with a handshake, and it was off to the races.

Making it Happen

Unwilling and financially unable to close my therapy practice that early in the game, I simply juggled both commitments for the time being. For the next six months, I got up every morning at 4:00 a.m. and started writing and brainstorming this program I was creating. The goal was to teach people how to maintain both their personal and professional momentum during relocation, and the workbooks included exercises that could help them achieve that goal. This required a complete core dump of all my ideas, experiences and knowledge I'd gained through years of reading and counseling, and pulling it all together into one cohesive, clear program. I covered everything from how the stages of grief in relationships paralleled leaving one location for a new one, to a section on managing stress throughout the move, and all with a heavy emphasis on positivity and how to infuse it throughout the transition. Despite literally being surrounded by positivity that I was writing into the program materials, negativity managed to sneak in every once in a while as I worked. I would sometimes look over and find that little devil Sister Mary Howard perched on my shoulder, dripping her toxic thoughts into my ear: *You still can't write, Laura. You'll never be a writer.*

Occasional bouts of negativity aside, I was very pleased with the materials I was developing in the wee hours of the morning, but at the same time I knew I could probably use some help. In a leap of financial faith, I hired a woman who helped me organize, write some of the materials and edit my work. I also brought on a manager/bookkeeper, an additional writer, a researcher and a counselor to provide that crucial follow-up phone support to the relocating families. This was all being paid for by my private practice, leaving very little money for Mike and me to live on.

In the midst of my long hours and financial headaches, I kept in touch with my contact at McDonnell Douglas and cheerfully kept him apprised of our progress.

"We're doing great, and it looks like we can deliver the kits in about three months," I told him. "We're beyond the writing stage and are now manufacturing the tapes and workbooks."

"Three months sounds good," he said. "Let me know as soon as it's ready."

Meanwhile, as our bookkeeper continued crunching numbers, I looked for other ways of earning money. Mike was making $20,000 a year at the time as a high school counselor and I had cut back on my clinical hours to devote myself to completing the materials for the five thousand kits.

There is one thing I did that I regret to this day. Hopefully sharing this story can help other entrepreneurs in this same position. At this time, I had between nine and eleven therapists working for me part-time in my practice, increasingly taking on more of my clients as I dedicated more and more time to the relocation program. I was training and supervising the graduate school PhD candidate therapists, and signing off on insurance until they got licensed. At that point I was allowing them to keep the clients they were working when they'd been certified. So, rather than keeping those clients and arranging a buyout of the contract (i.e. a percentage of the fee for a year or two) and using them to increase the value of my practice, which I could have eventually sold to fund my relocating-spouse business, I was basically handing my therapists their own $30,000 private practices, while closing down my own. This is how I learned to always realize your own value, know what you are worth, and make decisions that reflect that.

Also on the financial front, to fund the production of the materials needed to make the kits, we took out a second mortgage on our house. We bought it originally for $126,000 and the second mortgage—along with equity we signed over on our cars, and our savings—totaled $350,000 in borrowed money that was riding on this pilot relocation program for McDonnell Douglas. I was a bit nervous but confident. I still had money coming in from my practice, but the big picture showed this gigantic number $350,000 looming over our heads. Our home, our cars, our savings, our lives—*everything*—was riding on the sale of these five thousand kits.

Finally, the day arrived. Driving to McDonnell Douglas with the five thousand kits, ready for shipment in my basement, I felt a three hundred and fifty thousand-pound weight lifted from my shoulders. I strode cheerfully and proudly into the Senior Executive Vice President's office, theatrically placed one of the kits on his desk with a flourish and announced, "It's done! We are excited! What now?"

"Great, I will invite Bob in."

The sound of brakes screeching permeated every fiber in my being and, without knowing why, my heart sunk into the pit of my stomach. "Who in the heck is Bob?" I asked.

"He's the Director of Relocation."

I quickly gathered myself together, tapped into my second wind of enthusiasm and showed the kit to Bob.

He looked it over, and then said, "We don't need this."

I started repeating what I'd heard from all those spouses. I told him that John McDonnell knew all about this and had agreed. I kept talking until Bob stopped me.

"I've worked in this area, in relocation, for fifteen years," he said, "and I have never heard one complaint."

I was beyond terrified. The number $350,000 popped into my head, and then I thought of our home and Mike's face. I thought I was going to be sick, right there on the spot.

I looked at Jim, who was still standing next to me.

"Jim, you even told me how difficult relocation was for you and your family."

"Laura," he said, "I can't make him use it."

I felt the bile rise in my throat and, for the first time since the "damn Yankee" cheerleader incident in Memphis, I was speechless.

"We shook on the deal. I have four thousand nine hundred and ninety-nine more of these kits in my basement!"

"I still can't make him use it," Jim said helplessly.

"Yes, but you can still buy what you ordered," I insisted, going from sick to just pissed at the entire situation, but mostly at my own naiveté that led me into this mess.

"Laura, I'm sorry," Jim repeated, "but I can't make him use it."

The bottom line was, we shook hands—but I never had them sign a contract.

This was the most powerless moment of my entire career. I sobbed half the drive home thinking, *How am I going to tell Mike?* I kept churning and churning, trying to find the right words to tell my trusting husband that we were going to lose our house. But the words never came.

So I didn't tell him.

—⁓— LESSONS LEARNED —⁓—

1. Always get a signed contract.

There was a point in the history of business when deals were sealed with a smile and a handshake. As I learned the hard way, with McDonnell Douglas, this is unfortunately no longer the case. It is so important to protect yourself—your time, assets and money—by building a strong foundation to every deal and transaction you enter into, with a solid contract. A contract is by no means an indicator of lack of trust by either party—not at all! It simply puts all the pertinent details and agreements in writing from day one. Then, all parties can move forward with clarity and peace of mind, to develop a stronger business connection and create great things together!

2. Trust your instincts to follow your passion.
As a teacher, I sold my students on the fact that they would learn something from me. Then as a counselor, I pitched the idea that I could change lives. Opening my own practice catapulted me into a whole new life of self-employment and owning a business; the money I earned would be up to my ability to sell. Then, I expanded my private practice to reach even more people and help them while also expanding my opportunities to create revenue with my new corporate programs. Are serial entrepreneurs born or made? Probably a combination of both. When did you first see the telltale signs in yourself? When did you realize that you had a desire to do your own thing—and get paid for it—more than anyone else around you? What did you do about it? We all have a purpose, just waiting to be escalated into a passion. It's there somewhere; it's just up to each of us to recognize it and then to take action.

3. Use your friends for feedback.
I see focus groups as an extremely valuable vehicle for harnessing the years of business, personal and intuitive experiences that other people can bring to the table and using that information to help power new ideas. Jack Welch did this on the golf course. He floated trial balloons time after time, soliciting honest feedback from those he would eventually sell to or collaborate with.

4. Be willing to have some skin in the game.
When it came time to launch my first "big idea," my "Take Control, Choose Success" workshop, I put down $7,000 of our own money to create the brochures, rent a room and hire a secretary to get the mailings out to corporations. I made my desire to sell training to corporations a reality rather than a pipe dream. I had something at risk, something to lose. I put my name and neck on the line. You can do it, too.

5. Drive toward the basket.

This is what my dad taught me when he coached me in basketball, along with my mom's advice that, "If you put your mind to it you can do anything." My parents' advice was so crucial in giving me confidence, especially during this later period of my life. Even when I was kicked in the gut, as you just read, and had the $350,000 rug pulled out from under me, the seeds of my purpose were still there, bruised but not broken. I also stepped back and noticed that I had gotten a *yes* from two business leaders before a third one had put the kibosh on the deal. Keeping perspective is so important in such situations; it could be considered failure but it is actually feedback.

Finally, I reminded myself constantly of all of the spouses in the conference room that day who, one after another, repeated the source of their biggest stress: relocation, relocation, relocation. This kept me going. I knew that my solution was needed by so many! I always believed there was a path forward; I just had to find it. So I kept going, driving toward the basket, even when there were obstacles along the way.

6. Act as if.

Call it my theater background if you want, but I think every entrepreneur or intrapreneur could benefit from the lesson of "acting as if." So many people have a belief system based in fear that they can't do something, all that negative self-talk shouting to them from inside, "No, no no. You can't do it!" What if you "acted as if" you could do it—do anything—and pushed through it? What if you made the choice to "do it afraid"? What might happen? I'll share a little secret with you: My husband, Mike, has told me on many occasions that I "take up so much space." No ladies, this isn't an insult! What he's saying is that when I walk into a room, there's a confident swagger in my walk; I lead with my arms, and act from a place of strength and confidence. My secret is that I've always tried to emulate Katherine Hepburn in these moments. I was always profoundly affected by her elegance, charm, strength and even sportsmanship, so I began emulating her in professional situations that require me to be at my most confident. In my mind, pearls + pants = chutzpah!

7. Elbow to elbow.

Remember that I already knew Mr. John McDonnell prior to these events. We served side by side on a major civic board in St. Louis at the time, and we were both members of a St. Louis dinner club. I wasn't new to him, so when I told him about my relocation program idea, he respected me enough to listen. It was my community involvement that led to my invite into this invitation-only dinner club where the majority of other women were widows of successful businessmen, rather than businesswomen standing on their own. My goal from the get-go, in all my community involvement, was to increase participation and membership by women. For twenty-six years now I have been trying to pull women up and get them to the boardroom table. Finally, in recent years, I'm seeing progress toward this goal!

8. Lesson of *no*.

Always stay true to your passion and purpose! Don't feel like you need to say *yes* to every opportunity that comes your way. By turning down the "cocktail chatter" class, I gained credibility and, more importantly, it allowed me to feel good about myself, and that what I had to offer was truly of value … so they begged for more. The lesson of *no* is an especially important one for eager entrepreneurs.

9. Bypass the gatekeeper.

Driving toward the basket means being willing to go around obstacles in your path. This is not a popular decision (I later apologized to Carol for putting her in that position), but a necessary one in business. Create a route to the decision maker.

10. Find out what you don't know.

People often ask me, "Why, in the face of rejection (by Bob), didn't you just march across the hall to John and tell him his people screwed you?"

Corporate America was a brand new game to me, that's why. I had no idea how these deals worked. If I did, I would have made McDonnell Douglas sign a contract on day one and avoided the whole mess. Every entrepreneur must learn the rules of the game so they can play it successfully. Know your industry, know how details are done, and know how much you're going to charge before you start selling.

With the Internet, so much of this information is now available. As far as I knew, we were the first provider of this thing called "spouse assistance" for the relocating spouse. So there was no one to ask. But I quickly learned there was an Employee Relocation Council (ERC). Start with what's out there. Research, research, research!

Chapter 4

FAILURE IS IMPOSSIBLE

T alk about fear! Three hundred and fifty thousand dollars, our home, and life as we knew it—our entire secure world was on the verge of collapse and my husband had no idea. After having the rug pulled out from under me that day, I spent half the drive home from my meeting at McDonnell Douglas sobbing. All I could think of was, "How am I going to tell Mike that the deal fell through?" That the client was just having a casual conversation versus actually entering into a deal for a real product? How could I look him in the face and say, "Did you like that one-bedroom walk-up apartment we had when we first got married?" My next thought was, "I need to go buy some actual paper contracts!" What was I was thinking? Of course they operate off contracts!

Then, I wiped my face dry to hide my heartbreak from Mike, and went into brainstorming mode. Every entrepreneur should adopt this version of Pareto's Principle, a formula for expending energy toward success: 20% pity party to

80% problem solving, 20% fear and 80% resolve to fight through it and keep driving for the basket.

Now, what to do with the five thousand kits my team and I had been working months on that currently sat in our doubly mortgaged basement? I racked my brain, thinking, "Dear God, who else in this town relocates lots of people?" The answer hit me: a moving company. They move thousands of people every year. I went to my office, not making eye contact with anyone to avoid distraction from my new mission, shut the door behind me, and made the call.

"I originally developed this program for McDonnell Douglas," I told the man at the national van lines, omitting the part that they'd reneged on their agreement to purchase it.

I described it in detail, sharing my story, going for the man's heart and trying to get him to react emotionally. Just one teardrop, I thought, and I can close him.

"And I thought this would be a premium you could give to every one of your customers," I concluded.

"That sounds wonderful," the VP of marketing said. "Can you come in tomorrow for a meeting?"

Of course I could. Armed with one of my completed relocation kits, I made my presentation. Jim, VP of Marketing, was completely blown away.

He kept saying things like, "Wow, this is incredible; this is perfect; our offices all over the U.S. would love to have this as a premium to give all their corporate transferees."

He stopped then, looked at me with a huge smile and said, "Would it be okay if we put our company name on the cover, rather than *Momentum*?" (the name I had given our spouse program).

Of course it would. *I would print any legal thing you want on that*, I thought to myself. Heck, I would put a picture of his pet dog on the cover if it would make the deal.

"How much does it cost?" he asked.

"How many kits do you want?" I countered.

I was learning to play defense here.

"We'll probably start with one thousand," he responded.

"Well, that will be two hundred and fifty dollars apiece then," I said.

"That sounds reasonable. We can sell a kit to each of our private van owners," he said, and then added, "Would you mind leaving the kit overnight?"

The bitter taste of business betrayal was still fresh in my mind.

"I'm uncomfortable with that Jim. I'll leave it, but only if I can come back here at 9:00 a.m. tomorrow morning with a contract," I said.

"Fair deal," Jim said, and we shook on it.

I made three stops on the way home: first, to the office supply store to purchase a blank contract and carbon paper; second, to buy a bottle of champagne to celebrate; third, by the office to share the good news with my staff that we had the deal. Mike was not there. He still had his day job as a high school counselor.

Once I got home, I finally broke both sets of news to my husband.

"Honey, I have bad news and good news," I started.

He looked at me, waiting nervously.

First I shared the bad news about McDonnell Douglas but then, as sugar for the bad medicine, I quickly added the good news that a van line had agreed to buy the kits for even *more* money, and that the first order was for one thousand kits. I was jumping up and down as I told him the last part, excited for morning to come.

The next morning I got up at 6:00 a.m. and went to my office to draw up the contract with carbon paper in my typewriter (truly, I was still using an electric typewriter). The phone rang in my office at exactly 8:15 a.m. It was Jim.

"Laura, I hate to tell you this…" My heart dropped to my stomach.

"But I showed your kits to our in-house marketing person Betty …" *Oh no, I've pitched to the wrong person again.* My heart dropped to my knees.

"And she said we already do stuff like this, so we're not going to be able to use it," he finished. My heart fell to my feet.

My first thought, even as a nearly-nun, was *Why would God do this to me, especially so quickly after the initial defeat?* But then I had another thought: God let me have a window of success, albeit briefly, to give me the confidence to confess to Mike about my McDonnell Douglas failure. Also, I was able to celebrate a success with my team, at my brand new company. Both of those moments, although short, helped me to keep from feeling like a failure. This was enough to propel me onward, past the pity party, and toward more solutions.

"The Visor"

So, when my head cleared and I picked up my *Momentum* program from the van line, I sat in my office with one thought in mind: *Where did corporations go to talk about relocation?* I quickly found the answer: the Employee Relocation Council (ERC). Their annual conference was in New Orleans in the fall (1988). I told Mike I had to go, and charged the whole thing to a credit card. I knew I'd need to stay at the hotel to meet the right people, so at the same time I packed a bunch of sack lunches to take with me to cut down on meal costs. As a startup business owner, I wanted to save money wherever I could.

Mike was amazingly supportive, credit card and all. He even made a visor for me that said *Momentum* to wear at the convention. This seemed a little silly to me because a visor with a business suit wasn't exactly the fashion statement I was going for, but I was touched by the gesture nevertheless. He wanted to help and support me in any way possible.

I packed ten kits and headed to New Orleans. But as it turned out, my plan was half-cocked. When I arrived, I found out that only those who had purchased a booth were allowed to sell anything, and those who violated the rule would be expelled from conference—sack lunches, visors and all.

Now what was I going to do? I just couldn't face Mike with bad news again. I couldn't tell him that I'd racked up further debt but was prohibited from selling the product. Instead, I brought Mike into the equation and wore that darn *Momentum* visor every waking moment of the convention—with my business suits, casual attire, and even with my cocktail dresses at evening events! I was determined more than ever to be a walking brand and conversation-starter about my product.

My Catholic training taught me how to fudge the concept of selling: If someone stopped and asked me about my visor, "What is *Momentum*?" then I would be able to answer them directly with all the details. I wasn't selling. I was answering a question!

At first, however, not many people stopped to ask me, so I had to come up with a plan B. Every day, I would stop people in the hotel hallways and ask them what brought them to the conference. I was like Julie the cruise director on the television show "The Love Boat." Once I engaged them in conversation, they would ask questions, we'd sit down, I'd show them one of my kits, and ask what they thought about it. I turned my living room focus group into a traveling road show. The goal was to make myself available while creating a forum to talk about the product. But after dozens of casual conversations with convention goers, I realized it wasn't working. I was talking to individual attendees, not corporations. I needed to snag a big fish to come even close to recouping our investment and getting *Momentum* off the ground.

A Johnson & Johnson representative attended the ERC conference. This was exactly the kind of company I wrote this program for, but I was pretty sure that my hallway tactics wouldn't work with an organization of that caliber. I knew from my counseling training that an unconscious approach is much more powerful than a direct approach, and I decided to test it out on Gary Gorran, the Director of Finance, to whom the relocation department reported. Gary had been in a recent car accident and was wearing a neck brace (unfortunately for him), which made him (fortunately for me) easy to spot on the crowded convention floor. I never looked at him but was always in his peripheral vision: at meals, during the sessions, visiting vendor booths.

I was like a puppy dog, following him everywhere, hoping he would stop and ask me, "What is *Momentum*?" You see, I felt if he asked, "What is *Momentum*?" I could then describe it in detail, not having violated the rules. I didn't try to meet anyone else from that point on; no more aimless hallway conversations. This was targeted prospecting at its finest: situational hitting in baseball, driving in hoops (indirectly) toward the basket. I kept myself within Gary's peripheral sights at all times, which was easy to do with his bright white neck brace as my GPS.

Since he had not yet approached me to ask about my *Momentum* visor, I decided to talk to him face to face after the conference. I had my eye on him during the very last speech, and when the speaker began to wrap up, I raced out the door, anticipating where Gary would exit. I figured, *They can't throw me out now, it's over!*

As he came through the exit, I stuck out my hand and said, "Hello, Mr. Gorran. I'm Laura Herring and this is my first ERC."

"Who are you, and what is *Momentum*?" he asked with enthusiasm, pointing at my ever-present visor. (*Thank you Mike!* I thought gratefully.) "I've been seeing you everywhere!"

I took a deep breath and started my story. "I've written a program called *Momentum* for the relocating dual-career spouse, and if I could just have five minutes of your time, just five minutes ..."

He agreed, and I told him about the relocation kits I had developed to help relocating dual-career spouses find jobs.

"We're looking for something exactly like that," he said. "Here's my card. Please call me."

"When?" I asked, fervently hoping that this time I was selling to the right person.

"Well, I'll be back in my office in New Jersey on Monday," he said.

It was Saturday afternoon.

"Really? What time?" I asked, which drew a light laugh from him.

"I'm always there no later than 6:00 a.m.," he said.

"Sir, is it okay if I call you at 6:00 a.m.?" I asked fearlessly.

"Of course," Mr. Gorran said.

"I was watching her (at ERC), as she would stay near the doors and things of that nature as I moved through the crowd. And at the end, she came up to me and I asked, 'What is this Momentum (on her headpiece)?' She explained what the company did, for spouses and their children, in schools and activities and job search—all these different things. From my perspective, I thought it sounded very interesting and something that Johnson & Johnson could be very interested in, because we are a family-oriented company and this would fit right into our programs. Fortunately, I was in a position where I could get an answer very quickly, too, from our decision makers. They thought it sounded like a great program and would fit with our needs. From there on, it's all history."

—**Gary Gorran**, Johnson & Johnson

So, the Monday morning after I got home from New Orleans, I got up at 4:00 a.m., put on a suit and makeup so I would feel powerful, went to my office and stood as if presenting in person to all the executives at Johnson & Johnson. I made that phone call standing up at precisely 6:00 a.m. (EST). How much power do you infuse into your phone calls? Just because the person on the other end can't see you, doesn't mean you shouldn't train your conscious and unconscious mind to "act as if" you are in the room with them.

I delivered my pitch for the relocation kits with poise and confidence. It worked.

"That sounds wonderful. Can you be here next week?" he asked me.

"Sir, are you serious?" I asked in disbelief.

"I am very serious," he replied.

Johnson & Johnson was located in New Brunswick, New Jersey (in a full circle coincidence to my New Jersey roots). As with the ERC convention, I charged the plane ticket out of necessity for the sake of the business. This was my first sales venture outside of St. Louis. Fly in, rent a car and figure out directions from the airport with an actual map (again, this was all before GPS!). I was a bit nervous, but once in the meeting with Gary, I got to the point quickly and my natural passion shone through.

He asked good questions, kept nodding awkwardly (he was still wearing the brace), and had the kindest smile on his face. So, I went directly for the reason I came, heading straight for that goal!

"How many kits will you need? How many employees do you relocate?" I asked.

"We relocate about one thousand a year. So, how much are you thinking per kit?"

Now I was nervous, because this scenario had played out twice before with disastrous results. So, to protect my company and myself, I doubled the price to $500 a kit and added three additional coaching calls directly to the spouse so we could support them through the process.

"Sounds good," he said. "This is something we would like to add to our new family program that we're launching in January."

It was October.

"But first …" he said. My heart dropped to my stomach. "… I'll have to set up a meeting with the two senior VPs who I report to. One is the executive VP of HR and the other is the Senior VP. You can come back in two weeks," he said.

I just looked at him numbly. I almost grabbed him and shook him out of frustration, but managed to control myself … for the most part. I was learning a very important lesson here. There is a certain channel to selling in a corporation. I was to learn each one is different, but there is a specific channel you must follow.

I swallowed my pride and said, "It's expensive to come back," almost with tears creeping into my eyes, "but if you really think they would like this, I will come back."

"I really think they're going to like this," Gary reassured me.

At this point I knew what was coming next and I began to pray silently, repeating over and over in my head, *I won't leave one, I won't leave one … not again.*

"Can I keep one?" he asked, of course.

"No sir," I said, summoning all the courage I had left to stand my ground. "I had a bad experience in a situation like this and I would rather show the kit myself, in person, to the executives."

Then, I held my breath … waiting. He thought about it for a moment and then nodded his head slowly in agreement. Like I said, he was kind.

"You're right. I can see you're passionate about your product and you should be the one to present it," Gary said, as I exhaled deeply in relief from the very bottom of my feet.

Then I started to ponder how I would afford to come back, calculating the MasterCard balance in my head. Mike, Lauren and I were living on peanut butter and jelly sandwiches, spaghetti and ramen noodles by that point. Our savings were blown in producing the kits and securing the loan.

I returned home, cautious about what information I would share with Mike and my team. So I just reported, "They appear interested."

Planning for my return trip, I decided to research all the large companies in New Jersey. I was determined that if I was going to fly all that way, I might as well call on several of them during that uncertain journey. I set up three other appointments, my thinking being, *Surely one of them will show interest*, just in case this Johnson & Johnson appointment fizzles.

The next issue that confronted me (and I know you might laugh) was what to wear to present to two senior executive VPs. But between my mother and Aunt Marge, I knew how important it was to make a good impression no matter what. So, I went out and charged a new suit for the occasion because I knew "costume was paramount."

Next, I focused on my presentation. I put together a slideshow featuring the story of a relocating family to support my argument that relocation is a great emotional strain on families. I never told Johnson & Johnson that the slideshow told the story of my sister and her family. I had flown up to Des Moines, Iowa, and taken pictures of her family, who were moving to Tampa. They had moved eighteen times before. Her husband decided to get off the executive relocation train, so they bought a company in Tampa, and all four kids (ages four to fifteen) were moving with them. They were dealing with a very difficult relocation. I took pictures of my sister crying as she said goodbye to her best friend; of my six-year-old nephew, hands propping up to his face with a sad look as he sat on his front stoop; and of my four-year-old niece, faced pressed up against the car, sadly waving goodbye. I then told how we helped them. My sister was a nurse and we wrote her résumé and identified all the hospitals in the area to where they were moving. We had the recruiter for each hospital identified so she could send it to the right person. Basically, I just told their story. We helped the kids find ball teams, schools and music lessons, and we listened when things got tough. This is how we helped them.

"This is terrific," said Senior VP Joe Michalcewicz and Executive Vice President of Human Resources Mike Carey at the end of my presentation.

I restrained myself from jumping up and down on the spot.

"But the problem is …" the other one said. Now I was restraining myself from jumping out the window. "… it only deals with one-third of our relocating families. Do you have another kit for non-job-seeking spouses? And what about our singles? We have a lot of singles in their forties and fifties who have children and are single parents. Could you design one of these for them?" the executive continued.

"Absolutely," I said instantly, ready to do whatever it took to close the deal. "How much are they?"

"Five hundred dollars apiece, with three coaching calls," I reiterated, from my initial conversation with Gary.

"We'll take one thousand," said Joe, and then, "How would you like to be paid?"

Honest to God, this is what happened next.

Looking right at them I raised my hand, slammed it down on the desk and firmly said, "Cash—*now!*"

That's when all three of the Johnson & Johnson executives broke up howling in laughter at me. They laughed so hard they cried. It was apparent I was a newbie at corporate selling.

"Is that not possible?" I asked, red-faced, wondering once again what unspoken law of business I'd inadvertently broken. (They were kind and sympathetic, and I realized later that Johnson & Johnson was supportive of small, women-owned businesses.)

"Well, why don't we do this?" they said. "Why don't we pay you for the ones you've done already—fifty percent down?"

"I will give you a discount if you take one thousand and pay for them in cash for a total of three hundred and fifty thousand," I countered.

All I could think about was the $350,000 mortgage and other leveraged assets hanging over our heads.

"Okay, we will send you one hundred and seventy-five thousand if you will sign this," they finally agreed.

I promised them a contract, they promised to sign it, and they did!

I flew back home to share the great news with Mike and Lauren and with my incredible staff, Joyce and Maureen, who worked night and day like a bunch of crazy people to finish all the new kits. New plan books, developing special programs for children of all ages, and me rewriting the script for each specialized group that I wound up taping again at night, Lauren in tow.

It had taken us more than a year to get the first batch of kits done, but we completed these next two in less than three months. They had a January deadline to roll out a new family-friendly benefits package, and we were going to make that deadline!

We shipped them all on schedule, the first week of December. But by December 15, there still was no sign of the promised check. I needed it desperately and called Gary to find out what was going on at Johnson & Johnson.

"Laura, it just takes a couple of weeks. If you don't get it by the end of the week, call me," he reassured me (or attempted to).

When the check failed to materialize, I called again and Gary redirected me to the Senior VP.

"Joe," I implored, "this is really important because I owe the printing company and I have also signed over my house. I really need this check."

As green as I was in business, I knew I was probably being more transparent and vulnerable than was typical in corporate America, especially back then. But I didn't care. All I could think about was getting that check and saving our house. The lesson here: Do what you need to do, and if that means being vulnerable, so be it. Besides, what may be considered weak to some may be seen as a show of authenticity, passion and inner purpose to others.

"I called the accounting office and they promised me that you would have the check no later than the twentieth," Joe called to let me know.

The twentieth came and went—still no check.

When I called Joe again, I was almost crying.

"Joe this is really critical. I know you're going to be closed during the holidays … I need this check."

"Okay," he simply said.

I didn't know what to make of such a succinct response. At that point I'd almost given up. But the next day Joe called back and I heard trains and buses in the background.

"Joe where are you?" I asked him.

"Up until now I've been calling you from my home. I've been on vacation this week, Laura," Joe said, "but I came in to Johnson & Johnson today and stood there in the accounting department while they wrote your check and they handed it to me," he continued.

"I put it in a FedEx box just now and you will get it tomorrow," he finished.

All those broken promises and heartbreaks earlier, and this is how the first true chapter of our business ended. I wasn't trying to take over the world at that point. I just wanted to avoid being homeless and prove to my husband that his faith in me had paid off.

Mike and I have stayed in touch with Joe over the years, and in the summer of 2000, we heard that Joe was at his condo not too far from our home in the Sierra Nevada Mountains. I called him and his wife, Pat, and invited them over for dinner to show them the area, but more importantly to say thank you.

I was able to share with Joe that having Johnson & Johnson as our first true client gave us the credibility we needed to bring on over the years more than two hundred and fifty Fortune 500 companies. But it all started with Johnson & Johnson believing that what we created would truly make a difference for their transferees. Twenty-six years later, we are still serving them and appreciate their commitment to help their relocating families.

As we all enjoyed a lovely dinner together, I raised my glass to toast Joe in appreciation for his initial impact on our company.

"Your faith in me all those years ago has paid off, and I want to thank you from the bottom of my heart," I said.

Johnson & Johnson is truly one of the most caring companies we have ever served. It is an honor to call them a client, and to this day I call Gary and Gail Gorran dear and trusted friends.

—⁓— LESSONS LEARNED —⁓—

1. Never let fear defeat you.
Always believe there is a tomorrow. This one thought kept me going through the first year of IMPACT Group. I made it a point to get to the office early, with a smile on my face, waiting for the next opportunity to respond *yes*. My friends marvel as to why I didn't just quit back then. Well, quitting wasn't an option. It is like the enthusiastic child who asks for a pony for Christmas. On Christmas morning, that happy child finds a pile of horse manure at the foot of the tree and

exclaims, "There's gotta be a pony in here somewhere!" I still look for the ponies to show up.

2. Trust in the goodness of a few people.

Not everyone you call on will buy from you or like you. Keep going anyway. The kindness of Gary Gorran, Joe Michalcewicz and Mike Carey taught me to have faith in businesspeople. Joe did not have to leave his home to ride a train to headquarters to mail my check, but he did because he felt my pain. They later told me that Johnson & Johnson loved to support new businesses, especially women-owned businesses. It was one of the reasons they did not run when I demanded cash. They got it. Keep looking for the good people to sell to.

3. Don't be afraid to be transparent.

It is not like I planned to be so vulnerable in front of all of them; it's just who I am. I always try to be my true self, so that I don't have to pretend to be someone else (other than Katherine Hepburn!). Being genuine allows people to connect with you. Now I don't cry in front of everyone, but I couldn't help it in this case. My openness gave all three of them the chance to be genuine and gracious to me.

4. Stay connected to those people who made your success possible

I continue to stay in touch with Gary Gorran and his wonderful wife, Gail. It is fair to say we are friends. He knows how important he is to me and his kindness of referring more than twenty clients to me was just Gary being Gary. To this day he says, "Laura, I just wanted the best for our people and after looking at all the others over the years I still think you are the best!"

Mike and I visit Gary and Gail once a year in Florida, where they retired. He even visited my dad, three hours away in Tampa, when he learned my dad was ill. Despite high winds and dangerous driving conditions, Gary and Gail attempted to cross the state to my dad's funeral. Calling me he said, "Laura, I am sorry, the roads are blocked now." He is such a special person, and I make sure he knows what he means to my employees and me. We named our first employee service award after Gary. It is a coveted recognition in our company. Always honor those who honor you with their business.

5. Find your purpose!

The seeds of my purpose were planted in my childhood during my father's traumatic relocation to Memphis. I did not realize this until much later, after creating a solid foundation for my future career that included teaching, mastering psychology and opening a successful counseling practice. The only thing clear to me all along was that my purpose is to make a difference in this world. With the creation of *Momentum*, persevering through those early failures and finally, *finally* experiencing that first taste of success with the Johnson & Johnson deal, my purpose was cemented. It was to help families in the midst of relocation have a better experience than I did. My passion for succeeding in that purpose would be the fuel that kept me moving forward from day to day, sales call to sales call, heartbreak to heartbreak, and joy to joy.

Section I

CONCLUSION ON FEAR

> *"Failure seldom stops you. What stops you is the fear of failure."*
> **—Jack Lemmon**

There are things that happen every day in business that invite fear to crawl in and nestle in your brain, leaving you lying there flat on the ground, dormant, scared into inaction, and afraid to take any forward movement. You are sleeping and awaken to the thoughts: *Do I really have what it takes to be successful? Can I truly risk all I have to move forward? What if no one wants what I am selling?*

The important part here is seeing all the questions you need to answer *before* you risk the house, the savings and the energy. You address them once, do your homework, make informed decisions, and keep moving forward, taking your pulse only occasionally, and *never* in the middle of the night after working all day and night. You just have to remember fear can paralyze you. Do not allow that to happen. How? Do your homework.

When I started my private practice, I planned on it taking two to three years to make as much money as I was making as a school counselor: $15,000. But I did not wait for it to come to me. I did everything I knew how to do in order to get the word out that I was in business. I knocked on school doors offering free workshops, I made professional brochures with pictures of me meeting with the families I served, I mailed them out to pediatrician offices and gave cards to my hairdressers and neighbors so they always had my number to give out. That was 1976. There were no computers, no cell phones, and it was almost thirty years before the advent of social media as a means of promoting your business. I had to create my own "social network." I researched who in our industry referred people. I called them, took them to lunch, and shared my vision, my story.

In other words, I said "No Fear Allowed!" Take action instead. Even if that action is to revamp, rethink and refinance. Stay on your toes, think, rewrite your game plan, and interview other successful entrepreneurs. Form relationships with the media, locally and nationally, and with networking organizations. The important thing is to keep moving, create a strategy and follow it until you get feedback otherwise. I often taught my clients my belief system: F = Feedback, not Failure. This single mind shift is the difference between fear and moving forward with a shift in plans.

My dear friend Dr. Kathryn Cramer, creator of the Asset Based Thinking (ABT) process (assetbasedthinking.com) and author of *Change the Way You See Everything* (2006) and *Lead Positive: What Highly Effective Leaders See, Say and Do* (2014), outlines in her books how to "widen your perspective beyond the negative." Asset Based Thinking means looking at yourself and the world through eyes of what is working, what strengths are present, and what the potentials are. This is exactly what you should do when you get scared, in order to determine what needs to be revamped in your plan so you can keep moving forward. You must be open to feedback and realize it is always giving you a new way of looking at things.

What will you choose? Who will you choose to help support these beliefs? How you respond to fear is all a matter of choice.

"There is no courage without fear. What you need to do is shift from fear to desire, and once you get your sights set on what you truly desire, out of that desire will come strategies for achieving it. As long as you're keeping your eye on strategy, you will find the courage to move forward toward your goal."
—**Dr. Kathryn Cramer**, Bestselling Author

PART TWO

FEAR OF THE UNKNOWN

Chapter 5

TAKE OFF

I was recently at a meeting with a small but elite group of women, The Committee of 200, which includes some of the most successful women business leaders in the world. I love being a part of this group, but there are moments when I feel like the little gal amongst giants. Like when I find myself sitting across from Ellen Kuhlman, the CEO of Dupont, at a dinner in a member's home. Sure, I grew IMPACT Group to $50 million, but I still feel like a scrappy entrepreneur at times, managing from every possible angle. At this council meeting, listening to larger-than-life stories from corporate giants, the feeling of *How do I fit in here?* started to creep in. Suddenly, the president of a division from Johnson & Johnson leaned down the table with an intense look on her face to tell me something in front of the whole council.

"Laura, I just want to tell you that as a single mom, I've moved five times with my company. If your company, IMPACT Group, hadn't taken all the details of moving off my hands, I wouldn't be where I am today. Thank you," she said, grasping my hands warmly afterwards.

In one moment, that woman telling me how special our services are provided a powerful reminder of what happens when purpose fuses with passion to make a difference in people's lives.

After two false starts, with McDonnell Douglas and then the van line, the Johnson & Johnson triumph validated my purpose. Two false starts to one true validation. Don't let false starts sway you off course if you know the truth in your gut that people need your product or service. Look for the positives, the *yes*. Purpose and passion together will get you through those false starts and guide your growth. Getting to *yes* might take awhile, but the rewards are so personally fulfilling.

Growth

We officially had a business to grow, and its name was IMPACT Group (*Momentum* was the product name).

Growing a business is very different than starting a business. The startup part is exciting. You live on adrenaline (and peanut butter and jelly), putting in twelve to fourteen hours a day, burning the candle at all possible ends. You're powered by hope that you'll reach your goals, that you'll make a sale, that you'll survive to see tomorrow. But you don't care. You just want your first *yes* and your first check.

Well now, thanks largely to Joe Michalcewicz's Christmas Eve FedEx adventure, I had both and it was like the dog that finally caught the speeding car: *What on earth do I do now?*

That was my prayer: *Lord, please tell me what I do now.* The answer came when Mike, Lauren and I decided to fly home for the holidays. We were sitting comfortably in our seats with Lauren on the aisle, excited to be flying and ready for fun. The next thing I knew, the flight attendant came on the loudspeaker: "Ladies and gentlemen, we have unfortunately oversold the flight and I need three volunteers to give up their seats and we will give you a ticket to anywhere in the continental U.S." It was the holidays, for gosh sakes; people were wired and ready to take off. No volunteers.

Second announcement: "Okay we are upping the ante. Two tickets each and we will put you in a hotel for the night with food vouchers and get you out early tomorrow morning, guaranteed," the flight attendant said in her best cheerleader voice. Looking around, we saw there were still no takers.

I then said to Lauren, "If she offers three tickets each, I want you to jump out and run down and get them."

She looked at me like, *Are you kidding?* She was a somewhat shy eleven-year-old kid. *Don't make me do this,* her expression said.

I said, "Honey we need those tickets!"

She sighed, was truly uncomfortable, but unfastened her seat belt with a new expression on her face that said, *You owe me mom!*

Sure enough, the perky flight attendance upped her offer to three tickets. I helped launch Lauren out of her chair and then put my hands up in the air, shouting, "We'll do it. We'll do it! We'll take the three tickets."

Lauren was mortified, and shuffled quickly up the aisle, red-faced, head down to claim the tickets. Little did she know that nineteen years later she would be CEO of IMPACT Group, giving international speeches to Fortune 500 companies and signing her own big deals. That night, we found ourselves dining out in a nice hotel and upgraded to first class first thing the next morning.

Unintended events in life can lead to serendipitous outcomes. Those nine tickets financed our sales and marketing for the next year. Lauren told me she thought at the time that we would go on nine vacations that year. I later told her, "I am so glad I did not tell you what I was thinking when I was begging you to run down the aisle and claim those tickets!" What I didn't say, and I am serious here, was that she may never have had the chance to become CEO if she hadn't expanded her boundaries that day. And that is the truth.

Back at the office, after the champagne had worn off from celebrating the big final payment from Johnson & Johnson, I wrote checks to the vendors we owed (starting with the mortgage company for our home) and put reserves down for our growing payroll. Then I sat down with my IMPACT Group team to create a growth strategy. Joyce Edelbrock, the editor and designer of our booklets and our *Momentum* logo, and Maureen Kammerer, a really smart McDonnell Douglas spouse who I had hired to help build our materials and determine next steps, were the other two on the team. Between the three of us, we had to figure out how to reach the Fortune 500 companies that relocated 100 people or more a year. Volume was key, as I had four thousand kits still sitting in my basement. This was somewhere between door-to-door vacuum cleaner sales and email blasts. It was up to us to identify our prospects and then find a way to connect with them and make the sale.

We joined the Employee Relocation Council (ERC), identified our top prospects by volume and ZIP code, then went about literally cutting up the ERC membership book member by member to create our own user-friendly paper copy directory according to ZIP code. I then determined the cities and states that had the majority of the moves, chose the top nine and started "dialing for dollars," trying to get as many appointments as I could in each area. Finally, I set a schedule and used the nine airline tickets Lauren had run red-faced up the aisle to claim, to fly to each city.

Thank you, God, for showing me the way! I thought.

I was literally making up my sales and marketing plan based on bare instincts and somehow capitalizing on those nine tickets. Now it was a matter of sales and pure guts. I became a maniac. Dialing for dollars every day, determined to find a buyer for what I thought might be the last four thousand *Momentum* kits that IMPACT Group would ever produce. We called our program *Momentum* so as to help the spouses and families create positive personal and professional momentum throughout the move. It really never dawned on me until much later that year, that not only had I created a company, but I had also created an industry.

No one else had come up with a national spouse and family transition service. Another woman in St. Louis had just started a company, Vandover (vandover.com), doing similar work (which Lauren bought on IMPACT's twenty-fifth anniversary), but IMPACT Group quickly became the national leader in the industry. I found myself elated at how many companies realized, after I shared my stories, that they needed this service. I had given birth to a new industry: Spouse and Family Transition Services for the Relocating Family.

With the help of Gary Gorran supplying the much-valued and much-needed VIP reference, we signed clients such as Bell Labs, AT&T, Lucent

Technologies, BOC (now Lindy Corporation), and Pepsi Bottling Group—just to name a few. I presented to each prospect my self-made marketing slide show of my sister's relocating family. I knew if I could get them to feel the need for our services, perhaps make them shed a tear or two, I would strike a chord and create an opening to make a positive impression. Then I would ask for an opportunity to present to their relocation team. So many companies approached me afterwards, asking me to call them, that my travel agenda filled up fast.

Serendipity

Then something happened that absolutely blew my mind. One day back at the office, I got a call from a man at the executive offices of McDonnell Douglas: our first failure, or as I'd come to think of it, our first stepping stone to success.

"Laura, we need your help."

I sat up straight, ready to pack up those four thousand kits and ship them over.

But they continued.

"We have a very confidential deal going on. The top ten people in the company have been meeting at our president's house for the past ten days in the basement, planning a re-organization. Our plan is set. We will move our top seven people there to oversee it and we want you to come and tell the spouses that they are moving to Long Beach, California."

I was speechless. Once again, I thought I was going to have to say no to McDonnell Douglas. But then I gathered my wits about me and decided to offer an alternative.

I activated my psychology training and made my counter offer.

"Wow, congratulations! You sound really excited. I am thinking though that the spouses may not have time to feel as excited as you all do. In fact, they might be in shock (to name just one emotion that was going through my mind), so I recommend that we do this in two stages.

"For the first stage, have the employees tell their spouses tonight that they will be moving in a matter of weeks and what that means for them personally, career-wise, and for McDonnell Douglas as well. Then, for the second stage, let them know that a specialist in family relocation will be there at Bob's house to help them think through what's next." Trying to lighten the moment, I added, "The reason I am suggesting this is it would be really uncomfortable to get blood all over Bob's carpets if they weren't told beforehand. I'm afraid that some of the spouses might not be as enthusiastic as their husbands."

The man on the other end of the line laughed and said, "I think you are right. The shock might be too much. Let's give them a reason to want to come tomorrow night."

With this, I learned that John McDonnell and the executives truly valued my services and knew to call when they needed me.

That same fateful evening allowed me to start a successful relationship with a real estate agent, Judy, from the West Coast. She was at the McDonnell Douglas meeting to explain Los Angeles housing costs. I helped her put pamphlets together and we hit it off. Her team member Jenny and I were to become great friends.

Judy and Jenny had many West Coast clients, including Chevron, The Gap, Seagate, Apple, and Amgen. All were to become good clients of ours in the first four to five years of IMPACT Group. In fact, the day Judy had arranged for me to present to Chevron, I was quoted in the front section of *The Wall Street Journal* (wsj.com) taken from a presentation I made at an HR conference. That was a delicious moment, to be able to bring the paper with me to Chevron and show them the quote. It was only a quote, but it was worth a million in credibility.

Trial by Fire

Here is what I learned in the first year of business: Just because you can sell a product doesn't mean you have all the tools to deliver a product. Those first few years were a true trial by fire.

Now that we were mailing out these *Momentum* spouse programs, in order to counsel people effectively and ensure quality, I felt we needed master-level coaches in counseling to deliver the follow-up phone calls to help counsel the spouses in case they became emotional. Eventually we needed a tracking system to make sure we could provide reports to our corporate clients who wanted feedback on the viability of our services. Who knew? It had never been done before.

That reminded me of an interview I'd recently read in *Bloomberg Businessweek* (businessweek.com) about Fred Smith, who created the concept of overnight mail now known as FedEx. It was relieving to me that he said, "I think you meet circumstances the way they come, and then you adapt to them. ... FedEx would be self-limited if we couldn't constantly improve what we were doing. If people were going to use FedEx ... it *absolutely, positively* had to be there when promised."

What I realized very quickly is that, if we were to grow this company, we had to create systems and processes that would make it run smoothly and make it appear seamless to our spouses and our corporate buyer. We were inventing everything as we went. First, handbooks for training our coaches; then, a billing system process; then, a mailing of the kits procedure; then, hiring procedures and quality control surveys to both users and clients—and the list kept growing. Oh my, if I had thought of all that while pitching to my first client, I probably would never have knocked on the door! I realized quickly, once talking to my new friends in corporate America, what it would take to be successful. One of those things was that I'd need a sales force; I could not do it all. Also, how did this thing called relocation work? While I had my purpose clearly defined and my passion knew no bounds, I was still unaware of the many details of the relocation industry. I needed to understand how the industry worked, who did the home sale, who set up the mortgages, and who referred the employee to the real estate agent. Unfortunately, while you can learn details, you have to live through all the nuances. Sometimes things just fall into your lap. Referrals were the name of the game.

What I did know was that presenting at conferences was a sure-fire way to get my story out and my product in front of the right people. In fact, people within the real estate and relocation management firms (those companies that oversee corporate relocation) would see my presentations and started referring me to their major clients. We got to know each other by working with mutual clients as well. One such relationship that started early on was ignited by a large corporate headquarters group move to Omaha from St. Louis by ConAgra Corporation.

I was asked to help the families and executives relocate all their families. This was the first time I had heard of a group move. I was delighted to be a part of this dynamic company's adventure and to learn there would be times when companies (other than Johnson & Johnson) bought and paid for product in large quantities.

While I presented to the group of employees, other service providers were sitting in the same room waiting to present their services to the employee and spouse. That is the first time I had met anyone from a California company called Paragon Decision Resources (now Paragon Global Resources). Through their future referral to us, we received a very wonderful piece of business and one of my favorite stories to tell about the growth of IMPACT Group. This is the (somewhat funny) story of how Paragon hired us to help MCI move its corporate world headquarters from Washington D.C. to Richardson, Texas.

MCI

Relocation is a stressful time no matter who is relocating. When relocating a corporation's world headquarters, it is more critical than ever to make it a seamless, smooth and positive experience for all the employees, their spouses and their families. It was our job as the family transition company to ensure that all three hundred employees and their families' experiences would be positive, without exception. During this time of transition, it was also our job to recognize that the corporation had to maintain business as usual without interruption. Keeping the employees and their families happy was our number one job. From the very beginning, we strived to work in synchronicity with the corporation and its relocation manager, and the keys to success on our side were me, the sales people, the account managers, and all the consultants working closely with the families. It was our job to understand the goals of the corporation as well as the goals of each individual relocating family. All of these principles were true back then for the MCI relocation, and remain true today for each and every relocation we do. Here's how we landed MCI:

Paragon Decision Resources' CEO Joe Morabito referred me to make a presentation to the relocation manager at MCI, who wanted to learn about our services.

I did my standard formal presentation, showing the slideshow of my sister's family relocating from Iowa to Florida. I told the story in pictures of the children saying goodbye to their friends, and the mother doing the same to their neighbors, best friends and co-workers as she turned in her resignation. The emotions in those photos, as always, were palpable throughout the room. Then, in the most poignant photos in the presentation, the young relocation manager watched images of children pulling away in the car, with sad faces pressed against the window, waving goodbye to the life they loved.

I've talked about how profound this presentation is, from back when I first gave it to Gary Gorran and the executives at Johnson & Johnson. But I believe this was the most profound presentation to date because most relocation managers have never themselves relocated and are unaware of the emotional toll of relocation.

After the slideshow, I presented our expanded services: calling the spouse, family and employee before the move; and inventorying all personal needs, from finding the right school for the children (including special needs children) to finding a football coach or ballet teacher, so not a single member of the family missed a beat in continuing life as they knew it. I explained how we could also help the spouse start his or her job search even before the move. This service always piqued people's interests because close to half of the couples we worked with were dual-career couples.

Since this was a sales presentation and because we were growing, I needed cash, as opposed to just getting paid one family at a time. Therefore, moving well over three hundred people for MCI was a significant opportunity to receive a large sum of money, to pay off some of the debts we quickly were taking on as a startup business.

Immediately after the presentation, the young relocation manager said, "This is a fabulous program. We want it for MCI."

I was thrilled for two reasons. One, as mentioned, we needed the injection of cash. Two, I wanted to show Dorothy Jones (my longtime friend and new sales rep who was with me) how easy it was to sell a client when you hit their needs right on target.

Because it was a large group move, I boldly told the MCI relocation manager that I needed to get a purchase order immediately so we could begin getting things organized, and to ensure we had enough counselors to begin servicing their employees. The woman was apparently an inexperienced relocation manager, but she heard my request, went back and got a purchase order, brought it to her manager, and had it signed.

I was amazed that it took no more than twenty minutes to make it all happen. That was the first and last time in my entire career that I would make a sale during a presentation and receive the purchase order all in the same day.

That was another lesson I learned: If you don't ask for it, you won't get it. You can only imagine how excited I was to have Dorothy witness this incredible sale. We both left there flying high. It sealed her desire to work with me again and to become a member of the team.

When I returned home two weeks later, however, I learned that the executive relocation director was furious at this young woman for having her manager sign a purchase order for more than $350,000.

In fact, he called me to say, "Laura, I'm sorry to have to do this, but I have to cancel this purchase order. This is something we can't afford to do."

By this point, two weeks had gone by and I had already started hiring other coaches and consultants to manage the job. I had also ordered computers and desks. I was not about to let this sale slip through my fingers.

While I was scared, I still had an ace in my hand: I'd had the president of MCI Networks over for dinner just three weeks before, so I knew that if needed to, I could call him and expose this flaw in their relocation plan. I was not about to accept this decision to back out of the deal, so I called my new best friend Joe Morabito, the CEO of Paragon who had referred MCI and a lot of other business to us, even though he and I had personally never met.

"Joe, I have already spent money on desks, computers and recruiters hiring qualified consultants. I cannot cancel this contract. I have already committed one hundred thousand dollars in spending toward fulfilling the contract—computers, desks, added office space, materials …"

I told him about knowing the president of MCI Networks personally, having just spent an evening in my home with him, and that I was not going to let this go. I informed Joe that I was going to call said president and let him know I had already begun spending funds on the fulfillment of the contract.

Joe said, "Give me a moment and let me call Brian, the director of the relocation program who signed our contract."

He called back ten minutes later.

"Don't worry, you're not losing the contract. I shared with Brian that you knew the president of MCI Networks and that you would bring this to his attention if Brian insisted on canceling the contract. "

Joe told me his exact words were, "Brian, how much exposure do you want to have in this situation? Because Laura will take it to the president of MCI Networks. I suggest you let it go."

It was at this moment that I truly understood the value of not giving in, not giving up, and going up the pecking order as high as needed to maintain a contract. Get buy-in from the implementer of the program, and then move your way up. It also taught me the incredible lessons of being strong, not being afraid to do what is right, and standing up for what I believe is the right thing to do.

The power of networking also came out as a byproduct of this situation. I had done a really good job for Paragon when it moved ConAgra to Omaha, Nebraska. For this reason, the woman we worked with on the ConAgra account told Joe, her CEO, how wonderful we were—so wonderful that Joe later felt comfortable standing up for us to his client, MCI, stating that they needed our services and that we were worth our weight in gold to the company and its employees. Joe also felt that our services were valuable enough that Brian would certainly not want to be seen as a villain to the president of the network.

My networking in St. Louis, which always involved inviting executives who'd recently moved to the area to my house for dinner, had paid off. To this day, Lauren and I continue entertaining new corporate leaders who move to St. Louis. We establish firm relationships with leaders of corporations in our local marketplace and nationwide. After this incident with MCI, I continued to do business with Joe Morabito's relocation management company for more than twenty-five years. Our reputation has led almost every other relocation management firm to our door.

The $350,000 allowed us to make the final payment on the books, workbooks and tapes we had sitting in our basement, and all our other outstanding debt. It also facilitated another special moment in time, one where I got to give back to the people who helped me along the way. Shortly after the MCI group move, another customer called me to help with their group move and provide them with our family transition services to a new location as part of a corporate group move. They were looking at another relocation management company to provide their group-move services. I shared with them the wonderful job that Joe's company, Paragon Decision Resources, did for MCI and they immediately hired Paragon.

Entrepreneurs should always pay it forward. You never know how you might be able to help someone when either given the opportunity, or when you seek out the opportunity to help the people who help you. Since Joe Morabito had helped me so much with saving the MCI deal, and even though we had *still* never met in person, I called him to arrange a meeting at the next ERC conference.

At 11:00 one night in Reno, Nevada, Joe and I agreed to create a consortium of shared salespeople. I thought my life had just gotten easier, but when Joe's competitors heard about it at the convention, some of the ones who helped me with McDonnell Douglas said they would never do business with me again. I was dumbfounded. What I had failed to understand, and I have since corrected, is that my decision to partner in sales with Paragon was not the right long-term decision. To form a sole partnership with any one company created the impression that their competitors felt I would never refer to them.

Oh my goodness! How could I not have thought that through better? Fortunately, it happened very early in the life of my company and I was able to correct it, but it cost us significantly in potential business with the other relocation management companies throughout the years, and gave my competitors an edge with the larger relocation management companies. This is a case where "size matters." Knowing who in your industry would be the biggest referral source and courting them is a very effective sales strategy. Partnering with as many people within your industry as possible is critical for your growth and your reputation.

I am proud to say that we now partner with most of the large relocation management companies, not just because we don't have an exclusive relationship with any one company, but because we have been rated number one in customer satisfaction since the start of the surveying process sixteen years ago. Like I said before, selling isn't enough. You must have the systems and processes to keep the business and keep your client and recipients super happy. There is always a competitor waiting for you to fall.

Even though we gave up the joint partnership after about eighteen months, Joe continued to support IMPACT Group because he felt we were the best spouse-and-family transition assistance service out there. We have stayed friends for twenty-six years.

The following is what Joe shares about our first meeting

"I first met Laura around 11:00 at night at a casino/resort in Reno. We were sitting in an empty bar that was closed, and it was the very first time I had met her in person. My impression of Laura was of absolute intensity. So there we are in a closed bar in a casino at night, and Laura is giving me her sales pitch for IMPACT Group! She never stops selling. I could instantly see, in that first meeting, her passion, her focus and her discipline, which are the three elements that I believe are necessary for success in life or in business. Laura had all three of them—there was no doubt about it."

—**Joe Morabito**, CEO, Paragon Global Resources, Inc.

Spherion—Part One

In this chapter, I have one final story that stands out in my mind about the future expansion of IMPACT Group … well, the beginning of the story, anyway. Some things are just meant to be together. In our world, that perfect couple was IMPACT Group and Spherion HRC (Human Resource Consulting).

The Spherion story started in the early 1990s when I hired Kathy Flora as one of my first outplacement counselors. She was easily one of the best I ever had the pleasure of working with. During our time together, we closed a huge Contel contract for outplacement when they merged with another big company. Kathy and I spent weeks preparing materials and making what we lovingly referred to as a "Job in a Box" (audio tapes and plan books which mirrored our *Momentum* program) that would support the phone counseling our master's-degreed coaches would provide. These items were, in my mind, state-of-the-art new technology job search materials. In contrast to what we have today, they were merely cassette tapes and books. But in the 1990s, they were definitely out-of-the-box thinking for corporate job search assistance—so to speak.

Kathy and I were both very proud of them, and Kathy did a terrific job of tying up all the loose ends and creating a quality piece of work that we would be proud to market. In fact, we did such a great job of marketing that we needed more hands on deck than just Kathy and I to deliver the twenty-plus seminars that the Contel contract required.

With two small, demanding young children at home, Kathy came to me one day and said, "Laura, I would love to do all of these but I have two kids I have to drop off and pick up from school every day. You have been great letting me have flexible hours, but I can't do all the seminars."

I said, "Okay, I understand." And this was my big mistake.

Years later, I know the perfect response should have been, "Fine. Tell me which ones you would like to do."

Understanding the push of work-life balance, and wanting to respect her decision to be with her family, I moved forward and did what I needed to do to fulfill the contract: I hired another full-time coach to help deliver the services. My expectation was that Kathy would do some work and the new coach would deliver the rest while I kept marketing the product. That was my intention, anyway.

Hell hath no fury like a trainer scorned! Unbeknownst to me, Kathy felt like I had given her job away, when in reality I only gave away half of her job because I thought she said she didn't have time for it. I guess I wasn't listening between the lines. What I didn't hear was how much she wanted to do it, but felt torn that she shouldn't do it due to the demands at home. I'm still not sure how we could have resolved it at the time, but I now listen "between the lines."

It came to a head when Kathy called one day and said she couldn't do an already scheduled seminar, leaving me in a huge lurch, embarrassing me in front of the client, and leaving me scrambling for coverage. Kathy left the company with a slew of unresolved issues hanging over our once-solid relationship like storm clouds in a once-sunny sky. Then she left the area, relocating once again for her husband's job.

Continued in a later chapter...

―ᴡ― LESSONS LEARNED ―ᴡ―

1. Know the rules of your industry.

I can't emphasize this enough. When you start designing a product to sell or produce, you need to know the spoken and unspoken rules of that industry's marketing game. You need to know the process flow: who buys, who can sign for such large orders, what is the decision scheme from "I love your product" to signing a contract to getting people to actually use the product once sold.

Know who your competitors are and make sure you know what the unspoken competitive alliances are: who is aligned with whom. It's like Star Wars out there and you have to know how to team up with those who will support you without scaring off, or even worse, offending someone who could really become an ally.

If I had to do it over again, I would have interviewed and gotten to know the relocation industry better—particularly all the relocation management companies—before setting out to sell to corporate America, because it was from the recommendations of these valuable partnerships that the majority of our sales would eventually come. Know who buys, who recommends, who your competition is, and with whom they are aligned.

2. Know your buying power pyramid.

I should have known that this young MCI person reported to someone with much more authority, having presented to many a VP since I started. Always do your homework well ahead of that first sales meeting to ensure that, whenever possible, you're not selling to a non-decision maker (as I learned at McDonnell Douglas). Ask, "Who in your organization will have the authority to buy our services? Would they be available for our presentation?" If this isn't possible, try to reach the person who is no more than one rung below the decision maker. And if this isn't possible, you can still put on your strategic thinking cap, listen carefully, and find out how to get buy-in from a higher up in the company, even though you're pitching to someone lower on the ladder.

Selling to the right person is a critical component of saving time and preventing lots of disappointment and frustration. Before you dial for dollars (or in today's world, send out meaningless emails and phone calls to the wrong person), do your homework.

3. Create strong relationships on many different levels within your industry.

Each industry has myriad vendors, competitors, complimentary products and services. It is important to become acquainted with all of these divergent, but relevant potential connectors.

Make friends and acquaintances with individuals at all levels within the organization. Not you necessarily, but your team, your salespeople, account managers, and even your accounting department will come into contact with people who can spread the word of your valuable services. Ask them to do so consistently.

You will be surprised how, at each level, you will find people who can refer business to you. We now try to have relationships three levels up within a client organization to establish inroads: at-the-door, decision-maker and executive levels. You never know when someone will leave or get fired. You'll want to know their bosses and subordinates so that the relationship will continue.

4. Hire only the best or the best you can afford!

My first year taught me one of the most important lessons that I have since passed on to Lauren: hire the best account managers you can, so that you continue to service your clients every day with good customer service. I had not hired account managers until I saw how other successful firms managed their accounts.

This lesson was invaluable, teaching me that I could not single-handedly keep all our new clients happy. It took losing a few solid clients who I could not visit regularly, to make me aware how important client management is. I mistakenly thought just being the best was important. I quickly learned you must stay in front of your client in person, by phone—and now by email and social media—in order for you to be "top of mind" for them.

5. Find a mentor in your industry.

One of the most important things that you can do early on is find a mentor inside the industry whom you can call on for fresh perspectives and feedback. I had many mentors: Gary Gorran, Walter Hall, Kathy Curtis, Ruth Davis, Marge Fisher, Marita Strickland, Patti Puglia, Marion Usdan, Linda Beranek, and Joe Morabito, among others whom I will write about later—many of them clients. It is critical to seek out their feedback and advice as to how you are doing and what you could be doing better. I will talk more about this as we go into the next few chapters.

Chapter 6

WIN SOME, LOSE SOME

O ur purpose was always to make a positive impact and our passion was
to lift up others in their personal lives and professional careers. To
accomplish these things, however, I knew that I also must make a profit.

This idea was a lofty one when we first started growing, especially considering
that at the beginning I was just grateful to make payroll and cover our expenses.
One of the keys to our growth was to find the right person to help take us from
breaking even to turning a profit.

I started looking at our systems and realized we were continually adding staff
members, rather than asking the question: "What could we do to improve our
processes in order to reduce our cost of service delivery, all without sacrificing
quality and while increasing profit?"

For instance, Mike noted one day that all of a sudden we found ourselves
with a mailroom boy. We were only a $6 million company and we had a

young man whose sole responsibility was to ship out materials and sort mail. The receptionist used to perform these duties, we recalled, which led to our next musing.

"Laura, we only have five or six people visit us a week, usually our accountant, our lawyer or vendors trying to sell us something. Why do we have a receptionist?" Mike asked.

I didn't have an answer but I knew enough to keep digging. It's amazing how efficiently you can shape the bottom line of a company when your goal is to cut expenses in pursuit of turning a profit.

Our informal little efficiency audit came to a head one day, when Mike heard the receptionist announce over the loudspeakers that the mailroom boy's 1:00 p.m. appointment was waiting for him in the lobby. Mike's jaw dropped. Who on earth was the mailroom boy meeting with and why?

It turned out that the FedEx, UPS and postage meter salesmen were all calling on our $10 per hour mailroom employee to eagerly vie for his business. They were plying the (undoubtedly thrilled) young man with football and baseball tickets and sending him liquor and fruitcakes at Christmas. (Do people still romance businesses with fruitcakes?)

The lesson was loud and clear: Mike and I both recognized that we were spending too much money on unnecessary job positions.

One of the risks of rapid growth is that you get fat and start hiring people willy-nilly, without doing a proper assessment as to whether their positions are really necessary, and the effect they will have on your bottom line. As a result of our realizations, I did some research and found out that other consulting firms of our size typically earned annual profits of 15% to 30%. At the time, we were only making 2% to 6% profit, so realizing that we should not be satisfied with the current state was liberating to me as I started looking at other inefficiencies.

While we were crawling along at 2%, our general manager told us everything was great. We didn't see it that way. This certainly didn't automatically place him in the wrong, but rather it alerted me, as the company leader, of a need to align his expectations with my own. This is an important lesson for all business owners, especially during times of rapid growth when a flurry of constant activity and motion can easily cloak pertinent details of the bottom line. The good news is: If you are keeping a thumb closely on your business and you are communicating clearly and directly, you will be able to hear and anticipate most problems brewing below the surface before they escalate. But knowing accurate details of your profit and loss are critical. Many entrepreneurs I have met get excited about closing the deals and bringing in business, but do not realize they need to accurately assess the costs of delivering the goods and total expenses. Just because you can pay the bills doesn't mean you are running the company efficiently. Keep your eye on the bottom line.

In addition to staying closely connected to what's going on, another way you can ensure you are heading down the right path is to have an advisor who can help you determine what your next steps should be. So, I sought a business coach to offer some clarity, guidance and the wisdom that comes from real experience in the business trenches. I found Allen Hauge, 2011 Chairman of the Year of Vistage International, an international organization founded in 1957 made up of peer advisory groups that "help CEOs and companies improve and grow" (vistage.com).

Allen had been persistently courting me to join Vistage for ten years. I never felt I was big enough to be a member. Boy was I wrong! Joining Vistage was the best decision I made, especially for my growing company. It provided me with monthly national speakers plus the shared experiences of thirteen other CEOs who helmed like-sized privately owned businesses. Vistage quickly became my peer sounding board, my advisory board and my corporate board. Once I joined, the group constantly challenged me to trust my intuition and make quicker decisions. Once I started doing that, we grew by 800%.

My fellow Vistage members were the first ones to openly and bluntly encourage me to expect more profits from IMPACT Group. As a child of the '60s, this was initially an uncomfortable thought for me. Expect and embrace an influx of money? I was afraid of being greedy or somehow selfish. But Allen and my Vistage Group calmed my concerns and reassured me that, as a growing company with big dreams of making a big impact on our clients, I had a right to expect 12% to 20% profits. That was the norm at the time for the service industry. We were looking to grow even bigger and that meant seeking out big companies.

"Laura is a natural entrepreneur, but she wasn't a businessperson. She was a psychologist who saw a need in her clients and built a business to satisfy that need. I think maybe one of the things that helped her was that I don't think she knew in advance how difficult business could be. I mean, let's face it, most of the businesses that we see, that we talk about, are above ground; they're making money, they're doing well. We don't see all the ones that have crashed and burned. And I think her lack of business experience really kind of helped her because she didn't understand what all the obstacles were and all the things that could go wrong. But I think she identified an idea and the time was right for it. I also think she's one of the best natural salespeople I've ever met in my life. I was never in a room that she either didn't command or couldn't command if she wanted to. I always used to kid her; I used to thank her for letting me run my meetings when she was in the room."

—**Allen Hauge**, Vistage International

Big Business: IBM—Part I

Sure, we were growing big, but were we big enough to shoot for the big business stars of the time? I'll never forget the day I pulled into the parking lot of IBM in upstate New York. The sun was shining brightly and above me were what I later came to refer to as "California blue skies" (as I never feel as stress-free as when traveling to California). I sat in the car for a few minutes, savoring the moment of having truly "arrived." After all, who in business in the early '90s didn't dream of one day adding IBM to their client list? I was always grateful for the opportunity to present to any company, but IBM at the time was the holy grail of all corporate moves—doing at least five thousand moves per year. This would be huge. So there I was, sitting in front of Big Blue in all its glory. In my heart, I knew that today was the day I would make that dream come true.

I couldn't help but reflect on the rocky stepping stones to this Big Blue day. About three years prior, I sat in this parking lot, nervous but excited about my very first meeting with IBM. I had met a woman from their relocation department at a relocation conference; we clicked instantly, and I asked if I could call on her someday. When someday arrived and we met, I outlined our services for her. She said that this was exactly the type of program for relocating families that she (and I assumed she meant IBM) was looking for! It addressed the emotional needs of the entire family: employee, spouse and children.

My insides were brimming with excitement when she hit me with, "Let me get my boss. I want him to meet you and hear about your program."

Not again! I realized that I'd been talking with a non-decision-maker who had told me she was in charge of relocation in the company. This is a common pitfall for inexperienced salespeople, believing the people who tell them they have buying power. But that didn't make it sting any less. Here I was thinking I was about to make the sale and add Big Blue to our client list.

Her boss was a large man. Either that or I remember him that way because I was feeling extremely small, sitting in the office of the largest computer company in the world, having just made a rookie salesperson error.

His relocation manager quickly outlined for him why I was there and why IMPACT Group's services were just perfect for their relocating families. My mind was racing and I was more nervous than in any previous sales meeting in my career. I was actually salivating at the thought of landing them as a client, like when you smell freshly popped popcorn and can almost taste the warm, salty kernels melting on your tongue. I tasted a contract coming. It was a delicious moment until …

"How many employees do you have?" the big boss demanded, startling me out of my reverie.

Puffing out my chest proudly, I announced that we were the largest spouse-and-family assistance firm in the world with thirty-two employees.

"Call us when you are large enough to handle our business, when you have *at least* one hundred people."

With that piercing dagger jabbed through my pride, the IBM boss stood up and left.

I was speechless and my newfound supporter embarrassed. Every part of me wanted to cry out, "We *can* handle your business now. Just give us a chance! I can make this happen." Instead, I thanked the woman who loved what we did, and left. That man actually did me a favor that day. He set a new goal for me: Grow to one hundred employees and have systems in place ready to go when we *do* sign IBM. Walking down the hall, I felt like Arnold Schwarzenegger: *I'll be back!*

One thing about IBM is that their people moved in and out of positions frequently. Three years later, I invited the true boss of the relocation department to a seminar I gave in New York City, where I shared "New Trends in Relocation." I was grateful that she and many others had actually paid several hundred dollars to come hear me speak. Of course, back in the early '90s, having lunch at the top of the Met Life building was one of the things that could entice relocation directors out of their offices to get updates from their business partners and potential suppliers like me. I learned that if I invited and charged people for a day of lunch and learning, they not only showed up but they usually invited me back to their offices to make formal presentations to the right people (decision-makers). I was able to make a sale 90% of the time in those situations. That's how we finally landed IBM.

Learning Curve: Pfizer—Part I

Because we won Pfizer's business early on while building the business, and because of the extraordinary friendships I had with the senior HR women and the relocation manager, when the contract came up for bid, we "assumed" (a dangerous word in business and life) that Pfizer would stick with us. Unfortunately, I wasn't aware of what was happening behind the scenes on this particular account.

In the meantime, when the contract came up for bid, another competitor swept in and significantly undersold us, thereby winning Pfizer's business. While we knew that our technology, service delivery and overall customer service experience were better, Pfizer wanted to go to hourly billing, and in our bid we stuck firmly to our existing processes, telling them that we knew from experience the extra cost and time not only for our invoicing, but the time their own accounting team would have to put in, would not be worth what appeared to be immediate savings.

Nevertheless, they were one of our biggest clients (and one of our favorites) and we were determined to keep them. I made the call and asked what we could do to keep their business.

Their relocation manager told me, "Laura, we really like doing business with you. Our colleagues love you and your consultants. But we really need to go to hourly billing. Get me a new proposal, and I'll consider reinstating you."

Problem averted. Our salesman flew up a few weeks later with the new, lower-priced hourly proposal. As it was later told to me by the relocation manager, our salesman marched into the Pfizer relocation manager's office, flippantly flung the proposal across his desk and, with bravado, demanded:"There it is! Where do I sign?"

When this story came back to me I couldn't believe it. I was beside myself. You never, ever treat a client like that. The Pfizer manager told him to get out of his office and never come back. I would have done the same thing under those circumstances. We fired the salesman immediately upon hearing that story. He was a good salesman, but through this episode, I saw he lacked the integrity I expected in our employees.

Needless to say, as long as that same man was relocation manager in NYC, we were never going to get Pfizer back as a client. Five years later, I was at a relocation conference (no visor this time!) when I caught sight of Pfizer's new relocation manager. I walked up and planted myself in front of him, and his demeanor instantly darkened with shadows of the rocky past between our two companies.

"Mike," I said, "I know we've had a bad history over the past five years, but I understand you're going out to bid now. Will you please talk to me for just five minutes?"

"Laura, I think we're done," he said, unflinchingly.

"Mike, I'm begging you, just five minutes."

He must have sensed that I wasn't going to give up because finally he agreed to talk, motioning to a nearby door leading outside. I knew my only shot was to be completely genuine and honest, so I poured my heart out.

"Mike, I don't know if you heard the full story of what happened at IMPACT Group, but let me tell you, behind the scenes I have tried to write to you ten, maybe even twenty times," I said.

Crickets. Not a change in the impassive expression on the man's face. I decided to take another shot, this time with humor.

"For heaven's sake, I feel like a jilted girlfriend starting a love letter over and over, trying to find the right words to apologize and make things right again, but then I wind up just tearing the darn thing to pieces and throwing it in the trash can. This is how obsessed I am about earning back your respect!" I exclaimed.

That got a laugh. *Thank God*, I thought, and trudged on.

"When I heard how my sales representative treated your predecessor, we fired him immediately. The way he acted is not in line with my values as leader of the IMPACT Group, nor with our company values. However, what you don't know is that the entire situation showed me that you can't control every one of your employees' actions, but you can take definitive action when they violate your values, your mission and your vision. I also knew in my heart that we are the state-of-the-art spouse-and-family transition company. We have way too much to offer, and I don't want that errant employee's mistake to get in the way of Pfizer families and colleagues getting the very best service and solutions we have to offer. We've moved too many of your colleagues and their families over the years and they and you are just too important to us."

Mike just looked at me. Things were getting serious. Desperate times called for, well, begging. I then did something I'd never done before and have never done since. I dropped to one knee in front of Mike, looked up at him, and delivered my most desperate plea as a jilted corporate supplier for a second-chance relationship.

"Mike, I beg you, I'm not asking for the business outright. I'm simply asking for the opportunity to present and bid on your business."

"I'll think about it," he finally conceded.

"That's all I want you to do," I responded gratefully, standing up and brushing myself off. But he wasn't done. The scars of our business past clearly weren't entirely healed yet...

Big Struggle: IBM—The Conclusion

Think that one was a heart stopper? As they say in show business, "You ain't seen nothin' yet." Here's another story of what can happen when false security with a client relationship leads to false assumptions.

After finally getting my foot in the door at IBM, I became fast friends with the new relocation director, who had ultimately helped me seal the deal. She was a fun person and we truly liked each other. We received all of IBM's business for the following five years, and they continued to be one of our biggest clients. Then, our contact was transitioned out of her role. She was replaced by someone I had only met once. There had been a recent transition for the client contact and that left us vulnerable without an internal coach. I learned a valuable lesson about the dangers of what can happen when a friend within the client company transitions out of their business role—just like when we initially won IBM's business.

You-know-what hit the fan in this particular situation, while Mike and I were in Reno overseeing the building of our dream home. IBM had gone out for bid, as all big companies do now, to make sure they were getting the best price for the services provided. We were told repeatedly how they loved IMPACT Group and our services. In addition, the current relocation director served under our friend, the former director of the department. We were confident that we would get the contract renewed.

During the bid process, IBM requested we lower our bid $50 per head. I was on vacation at the time, and citing how we had already generously reduced our overall fees for the purpose of the bid, my team held strong. Big mistake. They never called me to ask, "What should we do?" I would have definitely lowered the price by fifty bucks. Volume would make up for it.

Big lesson: If a company, particularly a current client, comes back to you and asks you to reduce your fees during the bidding process, you can rest assured that your competitors came in lower and they need to justify your price.

In this situation, our humongous and ultimately fatal mistake was that our manager just said, "No" and, in return, IBM said, "No." We lost one of the largest clients we'd ever had.

Mike and I were driving up the mountain to see our house when our general manager called me, letting me know that we had lost IBM's business. I asked Mike to pull off to the side of the road where I immediately threw up. I was sick and, more than that, absolutely furious. How could we not have listened to this client? How dare my team not even call me when this came up? The former relocation director had stayed in my home when she visited. I was invited to her wedding. This was *my* account. How dare they lose it?

Afterwards, when I looked at the situation again calmly and with clarity, I realized that the team was very confident in our ability to maintain this incredible client because of our relationship. Business was coming so quickly and seemingly effortlessly. They didn't even dream IBM would desert us for another vendor, especially for a mere $50 per person, considering the fact that we had already reduced our fees. But, of course, nothing in business can be assumed, and certainly nothing is effortless. Never assume the deal is done just because it's "done." It is never done. Losing our key contact there was also a blow, since without her we didn't have the inside scoop on what was actually transpiring behind closed doors. We needed more relationships at more levels. When money is involved, never ever think that just because your client loved you yesterday that they will still love you today. Everyone has to report to somebody who holds them accountable. Just like in life, love is a fleeting thing, easily replaced by "what have you done for me lately?"

Big Bid: Pfizer—Part II

When I lost an account, I took it personally. I would never give up trying to win it back. That is why we returned and I knelt down to beg Pfizer to let us bid.

"I do need to let you know, I rode into work for five years with my predecessor so I heard the whole story about your salesman," said Mike, Pfizer's current relocation manager, as I begged him outside the ERC conference for a second chance at the company's business.

I took a calming breath, dug my heels into my purpose and passion for helping those relocating families, and said, "I appreciate your honesty, but I really want to do business with you and Pfizer. I want to serve your colleagues and their families. We have been voted number one in our industry every year. I know we do a better job at helping your spouses and families get settled. Trust me, I want the opportunity to demonstrate who we really are."

So we got the request for proposal. The bid was actually a perfect fit for us because it included all the technology requirements that IMPACT Group now possessed; we finally had the opportunity to show off all the amazing changes we'd been working on! We were one of three finalists.

In addition to meeting the tech requirements, by that time I had also learned a lot about how to make a winning presentation. I made it clear to everyone in our company that I would be making this presentation. If we didn't win the bid, I wanted the blame to fall squarely on my shoulders.

I walked into the room with my trusty flip chart, a simple tool I still use in every single presentation, no matter how big or small. I always start with the flip chart. A committee of twelve Pfizer people seated around the table, including a still-wary crossed-armed relocation manager, would decide the fate of the Pfizer/ IMPACT Group relationship. I had one hour to present a case strong enough to finally heal the wounds of the past.

On the very first sheet of my flip chart, I had written out Pfizer's company values and, alongside that, I had listed IMPACT Group values, which I had taken directly from both our websites. I talked about how the alignment of their corporate values with ours was our top priority. Then I focused on the individuals around the table.

"I want to go around the room and find out each of your criteria for selecting a spouse-and-family relocation vendor for your colleagues."

So, for the first twenty minutes of our hour together, I wrote each person's name alongside his or her goal. That way, I could instantly tailor my presentation to address each individual's specific concern, rather than giving a generic presentation. Here's how that looked.

"Mary (in accounting), I see that you are concerned about how many invoices our services will generate on a weekly basis. Let me answer that for you."

"Joe, I understand you want to find out more about our technology. Let me share some features of our latest upgrades in that area," I said, presenting the technology as a live demo.

I went around the room until each need was addressed.

Then, five minutes before my time was up, I told a couple of our most poignant Pfizer spouse/colleague relocation stories before summing up the presentation by reiterating the importance of values alignment between our two organizations. And then, I put my stamp on the whole thing with a single question posed to the entire room.

"I know our time is up, so I want to ask you: Have I met your needs today and do you believe we are the right people to serve your colleagues?"

Eleven Pfizer people jumped to their feet and gave my presentation a standing ovation, another thing that never happened before and hasn't happened since. Mike was still very tough to impress.

And then I waited; rather, we waited as a company to find out if our efforts (and begging) for a second chance with Pfizer had paid off. We got a call from their procurement people asking if we would reduce our fee by $25 a person.

"Absolutely," I said without hesitating.

Then, a week later, Mike himself called to let me know that we'd won the bid, on an eleven-to-one vote. He didn't get off the phone though, without putting us all on warning: If everything wasn't perfect this time around, there would be no more chances, and no amount of begging would change that.

Message received. I put our very best account manager on the account. She ended up forming a wonderful, strong relationship with the client. To this day, she still has lunch with her contacts at Pfizer. That's not all either. Mike and I became friends, and all of us even laugh about the "jilted girlfriend begging on one knee" story at that relocation convention. The moral of this story: As an entrepreneur, you are your reputation. You must always work hard to maintain the integrity that you personally stand for, and you must rid your organization of anyone who does not share your company values. Just as importantly: Never give up, always ask for forgiveness, be the very best at what you do, and then out-sell and out-deliver your competition. To this day, Pfizer remains one of our most-valued accounts and trusted friends. Even Mike would agree. Today, the vote would be twelve out of twelve.

The Biggest Win of All

In the midst of all these professional wins and losses, I was hit with an entirely different type of challenge—a life-altering one. It was 2001 when I learned that no matter how prepared you think you are in business and in life, you will always come up against obstacles you never anticipated. You can be the best planner in business, but you don't know God's plan. And God's plan may mean that you suddenly have to take things one day at a time.

I knew it was probably not going to be good news when, following my routine mammogram in St. Louis, the nurse from the office called and said, "You've got to come back in."

I had an idea of what the issue was because my mother had breast cancer. My gut feeling was confirmed when I went back in and the nurse came out and started treating me like a child.

"Okay, we've got these new mammograms. Now honey, I'm going to walk you into the doctor and he's going to explain to you what we're doing," she said.

She actually didn't need to say a word. Her body language told the whole story (I'm very sensitive to people's body language).

"Sit, listen, ask whatever questions you can, but just absorb the information," the nurse added as she walked me down what suddenly seemed like a tremendously long hallway to the doctor's office.

I've heard that some people go numb at that point and the mind goes blank. I actually remember to this day exactly what the doctor said.

"Yes, there is definitely a tumor there but we won't know if it is cancer until we do a biopsy." And then my mind did go blank.

So, three hours later, Mike and I left St. Louis, as scheduled, for our prearranged two-week vacation to Reno.

Once we arrived, in the interest of "getting this over with," I did one of the stupidest things I've ever done in my life. As opposed to seeking out a breast cancer specialist or cancer center, I asked the only person I knew in Reno (our homebuilder) who was the best surgeon in town to do the biopsy. Now, normally I'm a very research-oriented person, but I just wanted to know if it was cancer or not and get the poison out so I could get back to my life. I very uncharacteristically put action ahead of analysis, with a continuous soundtrack in my head of: "Get it out, keep going. Get it out, keep going." I also didn't want to be living in a state of fear for two weeks, waiting to find out. I wanted a certain answer, one way or the other, so I could plan my strategy.

From a business standpoint, there was also something else at stake in my decision to get this thing "taken care of" quickly, quietly and without letting anyone find out—or so I thought. Here's how that particular thought process worked.

Being on the St. Louis Regional Chamber, as well as several other boards, I was recognized as an active member of the community. My company was very well known by this point and on top of that our biggest competitor, Vandover, was also in St. Louis. I did not want anyone in our industry to find out that I had cancer, because you never know how competitors are going to slant the marketing/PR against you. Looking back, this may seem like a case of confused priority, especially in the face of a potentially life-threatening diagnosis.

But at the time, all I could picture were industry whispers of "Laura is the face of the company and if she's sick, then you can't always guarantee that she'll be there, and if she's tied down for a while you don't know what direction the company's going to take."

I later found out that the "enemy at the gate" (our competitor) was a lovely and wonderful person who never would have done anything like that; it's just not who she is as a person. But when you're doing business, and the slings and arrows are whizzing by in the heat of battle, you can't count on anything for sure. Fear of the unknown definitely took hold of me in this situation.

Botched

In Reno, it was soon biopsy day. Now, one thing you have to know is that my tumor wasn't huge—maybe the size of the fingernail on your pinky finger. But, as Mike said later, a surgeon's job is to cut. So cut he did, and deep. He literally removed all the tissue between my breast and the tumor. When I woke up, three quarters of my breast was gone.

That was not what I expected. Having had several small needle biopsies before, I knew the goal was to only take a sample of the tissue out. I'd mistakenly assumed that all doctors doing this procedure had the same technology and followed the same procedure. To briefly explain: a small needle biopsy is not surgery; therefore there is no need to "dig" into the tumor, removing tons of tissue for the sake of a sample. That is not necessary. The job of the biopsy surgeon is to lay markers around the exact margins of the tumor so later, when the surgeon goes in to remove the entire tumor, it gets clear margins. My biopsy surgeon got the sample, but he missed the margins and removed a sizeable portion of my breast in the process.

This is a lesson that I specifically want all women reading this to understand: All doctors are not created equal. All breast surgeons are not alike. They each approach the science from a different perspective and it is up the patient to put analysis ahead of hasty action, to make the most informed choice possible.

With this doctor, the most upsetting part of all was that he missed the margins of the tumor! So, he dug out a four-by-four-inch piece of me and still missed the mark. I now know it's because he wasn't a breast cancer doctor. He didn't know what the tissue looked like. He didn't have the roadmap of experience. He didn't have the right resources to target the location of the tumor, and the list goes on. And I chose him because I just wanted to rush and "get it taken care of" and get back to my "regular life."

Then, on August 6, 2001, I got the call confirming our fears. It was indeed cancer.

First, Mike and I held each other and cried. Then, as if saying, "Okay, got it, moving on," I moved into action. That's pretty much my style in crisis situations (recall the brief bout of tears in the car after the McDonnell Douglas deal fell through): Understand what's happening, feel it, put a plan in place and move forward.

Lauren

Meanwhile, Lauren had been in Puerto Rico doing a year of Christian social service work in economic development in the low-income communities outside of San Juan. Mike and I visited her there at one point and saw it for ourselves: dirt roads, chickens walking around and mules used for transportation. Lauren set up an incredible mentoring program there, mainly for young girls since teenage pregnancy was considered a "red badge of courage" instead of a problem. Motivated by what she saw, Lauren ended up raising $25,000 and recruiting fifteen vice presidents or higher in various corporations to become mentors. The program she developed is still alive and thriving in Puerto Rico today.

When her service commitment ended, Lauren returned from Puerto Rico to Reno. We told her about the cancer. That night, she later told me, was the first time ever in her life that she cried herself to sleep. At the time, though, she never showed me that emotion. Instead, she hugged me and said, "I'm so sorry," and went upstairs to her room. The fact that she would be so emotional honestly didn't dawn on me. My thinking was, "I'm going to be alright. It's early stage. There's no reason to worry." But a twenty-one-year-old thinks the worst, especially when it's her mom.

Lauren soon made a career-changing decision to drop what she was doing and return to St. Louis to work for IMPACT Group, as she wanted to be with me through my entire cancer process. This was the best thing that happened as a result of my cancer diagnosis, although I will admit I had mixed feelings when I received her call several weeks later asking to return to St. Louis to be with me. She was so engaged in her new mission to start her career in Dallas, and I felt bad that her plans had been interrupted. Ultimately, though, our relationship grew closer than ever before. Her joining the company has been a gift to me many times over.

Dr. Tim

Yes, the biopsy had been massively botched, but I believe everything happens for a reason. I decided to return to St. Louis to finish the job, and that's how I met Dr. Tim Eberlein, Director of Siteman Cancer Center (siteman.wustl.edu).

Up until this point, the only people at work who knew about the cancer were our general manager and our secretary. When I called my secretary and told her that I'd have to come back (to St. Louis) for another surgery because the surgeon didn't get the margins of the tumor, she told me about an article she'd just read in the *St. Louis Business Journal* that I had delivered to the office (bizjournals.com/stlouis/). There was a new doctor in town, Dr. Tim Eberlein, who had done nine hundred breast cancer surgeries in a year in Boston, so they brought him to St. Louis to run the Siteman Cancer Center. (Lesson for the ladies reading this: If you find yourself in this situation, you want a doctor who has specifically done hundreds of breast cancer surgeries.) My secretary faxed the article to me in Reno and I immediately called his office, even while realizing it was a long shot that he would see me, since he was the director of the whole center. On the other hand, when had "long shots" ever stopped me?

After introducing myself and why I was calling, here's how the conversation went between Dr. Tim's secretary Peggy Kraus and me—something I would classify as a "God moment."

"The doctor really doesn't do many surgeries, as director of the center," the secretary dutifully responded.

"Well, I'm in Reno right now. Can he at least recommend anyone?" I asked.

"Wait," she said, "you're in Reno, Nevada? Hold on just a minute."

Then she came back and said Dr. Tim would see me next week. You see, they thought I lived in Reno (solely) and one of their goals was to become a national cancer center, so I would have been one of their first out-of-town patients. They never asked if I was a resident or anything, so technically I was telling the truth.

When I saw Dr. Tim he spent an hour and a half comforting me, listening about my experience, and examining what was still a very ugly, seeping sore from the initial surgery. He would be able to operate again in six weeks once I healed. Before I left though, he placed his hand on my shoulder, looked me in the eyes and said, "I am so sorry this happened to you. I promise you, I'll get it all and I'll use the same entry point so you won't have any more scarring."

Dr. Tim followed through on his promise and got it all. And after six weeks of radiation, I was done. My last radiation treatment was on February 13, 2002. After the treatment, Mike and I got on a plane to Reno so I could rest and recover. Understand that we had somehow blocked out almost all of our emotions throughout the entire ordeal. We were in full "go, go, go" mode … until now. I sat down in my seat on that plane and started crying, and then Mike started crying. We both cried for the entire three-and-a-half-hour flight to Reno. The flight attendants periodically came by and anxiously asked, "Is there anything we can get you?" We waved them away. We didn't have as much as a cup of coffee; we just wept. Leaving St. Louis, where I'd been treated and then recovered, we felt like we were fleeing the scene of an accident.

If I had to go back and do it again, would I have shared what I was going through with more people? Yes. Looking back on it, I missed out on a whole lot of prayers that could have been said for me. I would have asked for more help. I would have called my competitor and told her the truth. I would have told my staff where I was *really* going all those afternoons—not to client meetings, but to radiation treatments. It honestly never dawned on me to go at half pace. I let my fear of the unknown spin my imagination of "what people might believe" out of control, and this kept me from getting some of the support and love and treatment I really needed. As I write this, it is 2014 and unfortunately I had a recurrence of cancer in the opposite breast in November 2013. I am proud to say that I learned from my mistakes going into this experience. I did exactly what I needed to do and got the best care, the newest mammogram and sonogram machines, and Dr. Tim was there for me again (although, heeding my own advice, I did get a second opinion). I wanted to understand the surgery in detail ahead of time. I told the doctor and his team exactly what my expectations were and it turned out to be a perfect procedure. I am now totally cancer-free.

I won yet another battle with breast cancer. I suppose some would call me a two-time breast cancer survivor. I call myself a two-time breast cancer *thriver*.

My relationship with Dr. Tim Eberlein has grown over the years as an ardent supporter of the Siteman Cancer Center. Dr. Tim has also readily accepted many of my friends as patients who believe that he is an amazing doctor and human being. I am proud to call him my friend.

The Pfizer Connection

It is very unusual when a client company's products impact your life personally. I felt very blessed to have won the Pfizer account early on in our company's history. Pfizer has always valued women-owned businesses and I was so fortunate to get to know the senior women there in procurement, who faithfully invited me to sit at their table during the Women Business Enterprise National Conference (WBENC) dinners. One year was extremely powerful for them and me.

This was several years after my breast cancer diagnosis, and I had been receiving Tamoxifen for several years. At the dinner, there was a discussion of Pfizer's new drug, Aromasin, which addressed the endocrine aspect of cancer treatment. Well, I was so impressed by the results of Aromasin they were describing that I went to my oncologist immediately and asked him to put me on Aromasin. After reading up on the drug, he prescribed Aromasin for me for the last two years of my treatment. He now treats all his early breast cancer patients with this protocol. So I feel in many ways that Pfizer was my protector, my guardian and my friend.

Fear it, or FIGHT it!

The reason I tell this story is to share a belief that has helped me look fear in the face and move on. Things happen—you win some, you lose some. But you must think things through, create a plan based on analysis, take action, grieve, and then move on—even in the face of fear.

You deal with fear not just with action, but also in the analysis stage. The who, what, where and how of the action you take makes it an educated action. That's why I am being so open and vulnerable here. I'm sharing this part of my life with you to let you know I understand what you are going through, not as psychologist, but as a fellow human being. When we are confronted with illness, financial loss, children's illnesses, divorces and business downturns, all we want to do is to get to the other side. We want it done. We want it over. That's not always the best way. You are scared and you want to just get through it, but the most important piece here is to learn from my mistake. Fear stops you and invites you to analyze all the different factors you need to understand, know, research, investigate and then talk through, so your next course of action is an educated one—not one taken out of fear.

I think mine was a fear of not wanting this cancer to interfere with the momentum I had built up in my business. I didn't want to make it the focus of my life. I didn't want pity. I didn't want the public to know. I didn't want my competitors to know. I didn't want people to use this "illness" as a reason to not use IMPACT Group. If I had analyzed it, shared it with people and gotten some advice, here is what I would have done in retrospect when calling my best clients. I would have said, "I want to share something very personal with you and I want to tell you how I'm going to handle it. I want to assure you that I've got one hundred and twenty other people doing the day-to-day work, so I wouldn't want you to think I had taken my eye off the business or that I'm not managing. Other people are in control of it. Here are the people that you can talk to at any moment in time, and I ask for your prayers and your support."

Our fear of admitting vulnerability and weakness (whether to business competitors or even loved ones); our fear of looking stupid by asking too many questions; our fear of seeming "difficult" by asking for a second opinion, and asking and asking some more until we get satisfactory answers; our fear of being a "bad patient" are fears that could cost us our life. I personally learned this about breast cancer: You can fear it or you can fight it. I say fight it!

⟿ LESSONS LEARNED ⟿

1. Hire the right people

When we hired our first general manager, he had only worked for a Fortune 500 company. Not a good fit for a $6 million company with limited resources. It would have been better to hire someone who took a $6 million entrepreneurial company and helped grow it to a $50 million company; they would have understood how to grow processes, procedures and hiring with limited resources while making a decent profit.

2. Promote solutions and skills

Rather than promoting the individual with only the solution, make it a point to advance the person with the skills and vision to manage and take your business to the next level. Yes, reward people for proactive thinking and company loyalty with a raise and recognition—but not a new position if that is not the best solution for the company.

It is critical to know when you need to upgrade the caliber of person in a specific role. One of the things you need to do is talk to recruiters who work with companies the same size as yours and are experienced in recruiting people who have led such a company to its next step up. Demand that the recruiter produce a proven, successful track record. That is the role and responsibility of a recruiter: to seek out people with the criteria that you dictate. Just make sure that you choose criteria specifically connected to taking your company to the next level and get help (from your coach, advisory board or a group like Vistage) defining what that level looks like and what is needed to arrive there.

3. It is okay—and important—to make a profit.

Every entrepreneur needs to realize the goal of going into business is not only to serve, but to make a profit to make a fair living. Therefore, it's important that you expect to make a reasonable profit. The first year or two you may not make much of a profit, if any. However, it's important that you keep in mind as you create systems and processes that the goal is to streamline the systems/processes so that your costs are reduced and there is money left over to finance future growth, which is so critical to your future success.

Knowing the profit margin in your industry for your type of service is important. It will help you establish pricing. It will help you determine realistic goals for your sales people in order to cover costs of materials, personnel and delivery services. It will also allow you to measure your growth on the same cost basis year after year.

4. Know your complete cost of doing business.

It is important that an entrepreneur accurately assess the cost of doing business. Make it a point to surround yourself with good financial advisors or financial support, so you are clear on all the details of your costs—everything from the cost of the product (whether it's manufacturing or service delivery) to understanding overhead (down to how many pencils, pads of paper and sticky notes are leaving the office each day). This is important to calculate in tracking your costs. It is only then that you will be able to determine how much profit you really are bringing in.

5. Go after clients you can handle at the time.

This means making sure you only pursue clients that you know you can deliver services to on a timely basis. In the IBM example, the relocation director did me a great favor when he said, "Come back when you have one hundred employees." It not only gave me a goal, but it gave me an insight to knowing how many people I would need in order to service five thousand transferees a year. That is an important thing to know: What type of contract will stretch you so much that it could put all your contracts and quality at risk.

That is not to say you don't stretch. You need to always have a plan that is actualized to hire more people on an ongoing basis and train more people before you get more business. Knowing your pipeline conversion allows that to happen.

6. Make sure every job has a detailed job description.

Let employees know the extent to which they can make decisions on their own, whether in dollars (i.e. you can make up to a $500 decision), or you can give them specific guidelines relevant to their job. Had I put in my general manager's job description or said verbally, "Even though I may not be in the office, I want all pricing finalized with my approval," I would have not had the heartbreak of losing IBM.

7. Understand price shopping.

If a client calls you and asks for a price reduction, it is important for you to recognize that they probably have either read something about other services being less expensive than yours and/or a competitor has called them, met with them and shown them how they could do an equally good job for less. Trust your client is not going to leave you if you take these requests seriously. Ask them, "Is there something in our quality that has come up that I need to know about? What specifically are you looking for that would satisfy this need? Do you have an idea of the price range that you are looking for now? Is there something in our current product that you would like less or more of?" It is not always about wanting more. It could be about wanting less.

8. Don't assume clients are forever.

Just because you have a client today who likes you, do not assume that they will like you even when your product costs more. There's always a competitor your client can learn to like as much as you if they can deliver the same quality product at a cheaper rate. Know that there is no guarantee in business.

9. Lessons learned from breast cancer.

A general surgeon with a knife in his hand took out almost my whole breast to get to a tumor that was closer to the back of my breast. In other words, he did not use a biopsy needle for breast cancer, which most successful breast cancer hospitals and doctors have used for the past fifteen years. This doctor just cut to the tissue, and the reason I share this is so that women don't make the same mistake I made.

Just knowing whether you have cancer is not enough; you need to know that you have the right doctor who has the right tools, the right training and the right experience. I made an assumption and I didn't do enough research, in this new area we were going to call home, to find out which doctors did breast biopsies.

The biggest mistake most women make is going to a doctor they "always" go to and they say, "Well, I like him." Liking a doctor is not a criterion of competency. You need to research by way of the Internet, and make appointments with at least two doctors (three is ideal) to interview them and learn about their backgrounds, including how many needle biopsies they and their team have done, how recently and what type of needle biopsy equipment they will be using.

Also, take a close look at the facility. Most large cancer hospitals have fabulous oncology units that have (particularly for breast cancer) diagnostic tools and resources, and materials that make needle biopsies almost painless. Ask the hospital where they get their mammograms, and how old their mammogram machine is (older than three years is not advised, according to my conversations with Dr. Tim). Go to a place that has the best technology for your diagnosis. For instance, in the case of breast cancer, old or outdated equipment can affect the surgeon's views of the margins, potentially missing them and allowing the tumor to expand, increase in stage and even become life threatening.

My cancer experiences have taught me to ask a lot more questions about what, how and why. Every doctor and hospital has a batting average. You deserve home run hitters.

Chapter 7

SERVING HEROES

Αt IMPACT Group, we are always grateful to serve any and all spouses and families who can benefit from our services. But when you have the opportunity to exercise your purpose to help the people who need you even more than most, it elevates your passion for what you do to a whole new level.

We were already serving hundreds of corporate clients at the Fortune 500 level, nationally and globally. Then, through a serendipitous series of events, I identified a new target demographic in need, a demographic I felt absolutely honored to be able to serve: military families, who move on average every two years. We wanted to provide those military spouses with mobile careers that would allow them to maintain their integrity, their dignity and their career (certifications, credentials, skillset, education, etc.) so they could support their spouses serving in the military. What was happening, as I discovered, was after four to eight years of relocating around the world and back again, the spouses were saying, "I'm not willing to move again because I've given up my whole career for you. I'm done."

Remember I shared with you the value of networking and giving of your time to your community? I had been on the board of the St. Louis RCGA for about ten years. During that time I made many friends in the major corporations and they referred me to be on other community boards. One of my favorites was the Scott Air Force Base Corporate Advisory Board, where I served for about fifteen years. The goal of this board was to integrate Scott Air Force Base leaders into the community and to help them in any way we could. There, I came face to face with a lot of military leaders and their spouses and, in doing so, really identified a need for our services. I asked spouses, when I would discuss issues of importance with the high-ranking military, what it was like being a military spouse. Their first answer was always, "It's been an honor to serve our country." Their second was, "The relocations have been difficult." That was all I needed to hear. Now, in all fairness, the military was doing its best to create solutions for this need within its own parameters, trying to set up the necessary services at each base to make relocation less difficult. This included working with family-focused centers set up on the bases to ensure there were child care, educational and resume services. Unfortunately, the base personnel were already so overwhelmed by every other family need, like traumatic care and emotional support, that there just wasn't the capacity to employ mobile career specialists. The other overriding reality was that most funds in the military need to be allocated to support the men and women who are on the ground protecting us and fighting our wars.

I served on the Scott Air Force Base Corporate Advisory Board and worked with these families through several generals' assignments, and I always took each general under my wing and hosted dinner parties to introduce them to other leaders within the St. Louis and Illinois area. One of the strongest, longest-lasting relationships I formed through my work at Scott was with Gen. John Handy, a four-star general in the United States Air Force. He and I developed a very trusting business and community relationship, and he and his wife had also become good, personal friends.

I had identified the need very early on as a result of my work at Scott Air Force Base with Gen. Handy, as well as meeting Linda Rothleder, a relocation consultant to the Department of Defense at ERC. I'd even met with officials at the Pentagon several times about how IMPACT could solve the relocation challenges faced by members of the military and their families—with no success.

This all changed when I saw a quote in *The Wall Street Journal* related to the Department of Defense that got my attention; it turned out to be a quote from a military memo by the Undersecretary of Defense for Personnel and Readiness at the time, Dr. Stephen Chu. It basically said that his greatest challenge was to get their top military people to re-up, as most were married and part of a dual-career couple. Their spouses did not want to move again. My radar shot up. I had been calling on the Pentagon for almost fifteen years. Now, from Dr. Chu's voice, I knew there was a real need. I knew I could help him solve his problem.

When I called Gen. Handy to make him aware of Dr. Chu's quote in the paper, he immediately took my call. I simply told him, "General, I can help fix this problem."

He set up an appointment with Dr. Chu at the Pentagon for me the following week for a fifteen-minute interview. There, I communicated that IMPACT Group was already delivering successfully the same relocation services I was proposing to the DOD, to more than two hundred Fortune 500 companies. We had the knowledge, skills and resources to do the same for the military. I stressed in particular how much I wanted to help the military create a mobile career for the military spouse.

I walked out of there with a $1 million pilot program we later called JEMS (Job Employment for Military Spouses) to provide dual-career assistance for military spouses at Scott Air Force Base (jemsjobs.com). We started by focusing on mobile careers with these military spouses. This could be anything from court transcriptionists to teachers, massage therapists and even lawyers; there were many highly successful women and men amongst the military spouses we worked with. Eventually we evolved into online training for career and relocation coaching, so some spouses became IMPACT Group consultants themselves.

Here's a real-life story from the pilot program that offers a firsthand glimpse of what we did to achieve our goal of getting jobs for 100% of the participants by the end of the one-year program. Our job search consultants went above and beyond to prove to the military that this is absolutely possible, with the right program and the right people in place.

We'd scheduled a job interview for a twenty-one-year-old young man, one of the male spouses at Scott Air Force Base. But he called us a couple of hours beforehand and said, "My wife took the car today and we're a one-car family."

Well, our job search consultant was absolutely determined to get this guy to his interview and said, "I will drive the forty miles to Scott Air Force Base to pick you up so be ready. When I get there, we're going right to the interview."

The young guy agreed to be ready.

Well, lo and behold, when our consultant showed up, he found the guy working in his garden in jeans and white T-shirt. When the guy saw his ride, though, he hopped right in the passenger seat and matter-of-factly said, "Okay, let's go."

Our consultant was incredulous.

"What the hell do you think you're doing? We're going to a job interview! We rehearsed this! Go inside, take a shower, get the dirt from under your fingernails, put on a clean pair of pants and a nice shirt and then we'll go."

This wasn't a stupid young man, not by any means. Like many of the other spouses, he was young and he just didn't know the rules of the game in his young life. They haven't been tutored in the ways of corporate America: how to look for a job, interview, and present themselves in that kind of setting. These were the skills at the heart of the pilot program, which we taught spouses like this young man in his gardening jeans and white T-shirt. He ended up getting almost teary that day, he was so appreciative of how our consultant helped him. And guess what? He got the job. Next, we trained him and his wife on the importance of scheduling his transportation so he could get to work every day, and all the other basics that so many of us take for granted, for navigating everyday life.

The pilot program was a huge success and we went on to win another national contract when the DOD went out to bid for more spouse assistance. I will always be grateful to Gen. Handy for his confidence in IMPACT Group and me. And to this day, I truly count him and his wife, Mickey, as dear friends.

"Laura is able to market. I mention that because a lot of it has to do with her personality and also her daughter Lauren's personality. Sometimes you just have to force people to listen and, by the force of your personality, get your point across. A lot of success that came from IMPACT Group's efforts was based on Laura's understanding of the challenges we face in the military, and then her natural marketing and sales skills to preach a solution that worked. Then it was up to us to help her blow through the bureaucracy to get to a decision maker who was willing to agree with Laura and say, 'Yes. This is the right thing to do.'"

—**Gen. John Handy**, United States Air Force (Ret.)

As with all our client relationships, I was constantly looking for ways to add value and help wherever possible. In 2001, shortly after 9/11, when I asked Gen. Handy how I could assist him, he said that it would be helpful if he could speak to leaders of major companies and share what his mission was in the Middle East. He wanted to build national support. I connected Gen. Handy with several of our clients in New York and the East Coast, including the head of the NY Stock Exchange, Dick Grasso, who agreed to host the general and his technology team for a briefing on their global technology system since Scott Air Force base was responsible for all military Transportation and Communication, better known as TRANS COM. Trips to the stock exchange were not entirely new to the general. One of the techniques he used a few times in his career, to train his subordinate general officers at Scott Air Force Base, was to take them on a tour of the NYSE. His goal was to demonstrate information technology, and more importantly, demonstrate the dynamic nature of decision making in a very high-speed, high-stress environment.

This all resulted in an extraordinary day for me with Gen. Handy and ten of his top generals. The day kicked off with the tour and presentation at the New York Stock Exchange. Then we all boarded a motorcade set up by Scott Security and rode through the streets of New York to the Met Life building, where I'd arranged a luncheon for him to speak in front of more than one hundred top executives in the Northeast. With police escorts, we went from uptown to downtown at the speed of light. It was a very special day.

—ww— Lessons Learned —ww—

1. Volunteer and go the extra mile.

When you accept a place on a board, it is your responsibility to actively pursue the goals of the board and the role that they want you to play. I took the role of being on the Scott Air Force Base Corporate Advisory Board very seriously, so I made sure I brought the leadership of the base into the community.

An unintended consequence, but a very valuable one, was that I gained access to many top corporate CEOs who opened doors for me, and forged lifelong friendships with several of the top military families, such as General John and Mickey Handy, General Norton and Suzie Schwartz, and General Barbara Faulkenbury.

The key lesson is to become involved in your community in organizations where you can show your commitment and your talent. Volunteer to lead teams and to follow through so you get a reputation for being a go-to person.

You can begin not only to develop truly valuable relationships where you can make a difference, but you can also gain credibility for your company. Your target market will dictate the type of volunteer community work you choose, but be strategic. It will pay off.

2. Take risks and be fearless!

When I called up Dick Grasso, head of the NYSE at the time, I did not know him. I networked around until I got his direct phone number. I knew what a busy man he was, so I waited to call him after his assistant would have gone home. He answered at 7:00 p.m. at his desk, and I went right into my reason for calling: to have him host corporate leaders with me for Gen. Handy to tell his story.

He was astonished. "Who are you? Are you getting paid for this?" he asked. I then told him I am a patriot just like him, I was on Scott Air Force Corporate Advisory Board, and Gen. Handy asked me to set this up. He agreed and then he and his staff communicated with the general's staff to set it up.

I then called more than two hundred top executives, clients and non-clients, and got one hundred there for the luncheon. If I had not started by asking Gen. Handy how I could help him, I would never have had the opportunity to serve him. By being fearless, I was seen as a valuable resource by Mr. Grasso, Gen. Handy and the one hundred corporate leaders whom I fearlessly called and invited to the luncheon I hosted. Do not be afraid to make those calls and ask for what you want—for yourself and others who may need your help.

3. Read newspapers, magazines and important materials associated with your business and industry and work the leads therein!

I read the *WSJ* every day with a red pen. I circled names and jotted down details of deals taking place in various industries. I followed up with phone calls and notes to people who were in the news.

If I hadn't read the *WSJ* article about Dr. Chu, I would never have gotten an audience with him, or the pilot program, or the subsequent winning bid for the DOD's Spouse and Family Assistant program. That article was worth $2 million, and it allowed us to help thousands of military families.

Stay connected by seeing where opportunities are that you may not be aware of. I read the *WSJ*, *Forbes* and *Businessweek* to keep up with which companies were growing and which ones were doing poorly. That way I knew to send our salespeople to sell them on a specific product: relocation or outplacement. Remember, even with Google and everything online today, doing your own research can really make a difference in your personal sales and relationships.

4. Connect with notes.

Send people in the news a congratulatory or "I saw this" note. I always send people a hand-written note after they have been quoted in the press; it is a way of saying, "I value you, and I am keeping up with you." Then, should I see a need that we can serve them, it is like we are already introduced. I can always reference the note.

5. Stay connected to those you meet along the way.

I feel blessed that Mike and I have gotten to stay friends with so many of the people whom we met at Scott Air Force Base. I continue to serve on several boards and feel the connections made there are truly long-lasting friendships. Nurture those relationships, not just for business, but for personal friendships. They can be lifelong treasures.

Chapter 8

LEADING WITH EXCELLENCE

One common leadership denominator shared between the military and we civilians is what it takes to attract, train and develop strong leaders and team members. And for intrapreneurs, the lessons in this chapter will hopefully guide you up the corporate ladder by strengthening your own managerial skills.

As painful (and unpopular) as it may be, you must regularly change managers who have outgrown their ability to handle the next level of management, as your company continues to grow.

Employees don't leave companies, they leave managers. Why? Because they do not like or respect their managers. Good managers need to be fair, knowledgeable and possess the ability to lead and motivate their people. As you grow, you need managers in the top spots of your company who have been there and done that before. It is just plain painful to watch as managers, who have outgrown their comfort zone, hang on desperately by their fingertips to the status quo. They try to manage to the level of their ability, not the level that is needed to adapt to new technologies, methods, processes, industry developments and procedures.

At IMPACT Group we have been blessed with many, many great managers. They get truly excited by seeing the growth and possibility of growth within the company. Our best managers lead their people and also set a tone of enthusiasm and passion for their work.

For example, when you first start your company you might need a bookkeeper. But as you grow you'll need a person with even stronger accounting skills to manage your financials, and you'll need to replace the bookkeeper with an accountant and eventually add a CFO. This can be a difficult transition sometimes, but it cannot be avoided if you want to give your company what it needs to grow successfully.

When we bought Spherion's Outplacement Division, I made sure their two top managers were part of the deal. I figured they knew the thirty-six people we bought with the company. They helped develop the programs we acquired, and they knew all the clients. These were critical considerations to address if we were going to maintain Spherion's momentum in the outplacement marketplace. Fortunately for us, both managers joined our firm and stayed with us throughout the transitions and beyond, until both felt they were ready to retire or take on different challenges. It was perfect timing for all those involved. I respect both of those managers tremendously for their commitment to excellence as well as their desire to keep their teams motivated.

As a leader you will need to develop a sixth sense as to when it is time to hire for the next level. Always start sooner rather than later, and constantly maintain a "now hiring" mindset so you can spot great talent that you may need in the future. Make it a point to take your various managers to lunch regularly and encourage them to share their thoughts.

I remember taking managers out to lunch who said things like, "Laura, I miss you walking around and asking how things are going; my new manager doesn't do that." That is how I would learn that my management philosophy was not being carried out as we grew.

Tackling the issue head on, I would take their manager out to lunch and personally coach them on all the things I wanted them to do to maintain the company culture that we'd so carefully created. For me, that meant being out there and available, meeting with their teams on a consistent basis, as well as touching base informally with individuals every week, just to let them know, "We see you, we notice you and we care about you."

This kind of preemptive Personal Touch Talk (my PTT) goes a long way in helping to lead, coach and craft a good manager. For instance, when I would walk around the office talking with people, I would ask a personal question or make a specific comment about each person's newest project. There was the time when I asked my marketing manager how she liked her new work station and she instantly started sharing a few stories about the employees who surrounded her—some favorable, some not so. I coached her on how to handle these interruptions and she was grateful. I then started to notice the behavior of one employee she'd mentioned, an individual who was not as passionate about her work and spent a lot of time doing other things. This woman's manager was informed and within a short period of personal observation, the manager let her go. Passionate people want their company to hire passionate people. The marketing manager told me how valued she felt when I took action.

If a manager chooses not to accept your offer to help, however, and continues doing their own thing, consider it feedback about them as an individual, rather than as a personal failure or slight to you as a leader. Dig deeper to understand why they're not interested in improving as a manager, or perhaps why they're unable to accept your offer. Then, you have a decision to make: Persist and help them see the value of coaching or get them some coaching to see if they can change this blind spot (and get their buy-in in the process), or terminate them. The bottom line is that the employees working under that manager want to be seen, they want to be noticed, they want to know that somebody cares. That is a role that good managers *must* perform in order to be respected (and thus effective in growing the company). Just being smart isn't good enough; good managers must be present. Nurturing their team's performance has to be their top "to do." As the owner/CEO, building relationships with all your direct reports and their direct reports throughout the company (knowing who each person in their team is and how they operate) is critical to successfully asking them to help you grow the business.

Know When to Intervene

One day, one of my favorite employees, Peggy, came to see me. I had an open-door policy so she knew she could always walk in and ask to talk. She asked if she could shut the door, and that got my attention.

She handed me her letter of resignation. After nineteen years of service, I was a bit taken aback, but I kept quiet and listened to her reasoning.

"I cannot work with my new manager. I'm sixty-two years old, a grandmother and I want to enjoy my life now. It's just not worth it to me to deal with this," she said.

Over the almost twenty years she worked with us, this woman was passionate about every job she had; she was an A performer. Remember, people leave managers, not companies, so I understood her frame of mind. But just because I understood, didn't mean I was ready to give up one of our stars without a fight.

"Yes, things are changing as we're growing; they have to. That's the nature of growth. But I value you and I need you for the next six months," I told her.

I could see that she was unconvinced so I pressed on.

"Look, do you trust me?" I asked, making eye contact with her.

"Yes," she replied.

"Good. Then trust me when I tell you that I can't explain the details right now, but we have a very large client who will be doing a ton of outplacement and I need you to help me manage that process. If you don't like the position I put you in, come back to me in three weeks again with your letter. I need your expertise now more than ever. Trust me, you will be happy."

So she stayed and helped manage one of our biggest projects ever. She was responsible for developing the processes to support over forty thousand outplacement candidates in less than six months and ended up loving the new responsibilities we gave her.

Here's what you need to know as a business manager/owner: We not only needed this A performer's experience and expertise, but we also needed her commitment to excellence at that point more than ever before. For me to try to train someone new on our systems and processes in just three weeks would have been impossible, let alone worrying if they had the passion and commitment to get the job done right.

This valued employee ultimately stayed because she trusted me. She knew who I was as a person, she respected me and we valued each other's skills and capabilities. Her manager would have easily accepted this lady's resignation because she did not have the long-term relationship and perhaps would have taken her at her word about wanting to enjoy life now. Her manager hadn't bothered to find out what was important to her team member (which was respect for her knowledge and experience). I knew that already about Peggy because we had years of history and conversation. I knew that she was the smart one in her family growing up and she relished that role. Her manager at the time was also smart, so their smarts collided.

This employee stayed on for eighteen wonderful more months. She later read touching remarks at my retirement party then took me to lunch and gave me a beautiful retirement gift. Peggy knew I had her back from day one. I shared with her over my retirement lunch the other reason I was so determined to make her stay: I wanted to do the right thing for a great employee so she would have the resources she needed (including a big bonus) to retire in the way that she deserved, because of all the hard work she had put into the company, especially after that intensive six-month outplacement job.

As you grow, one of the most important things you can do is stay ahead of the curve. You will know how your people are doing if you coach your managers to look for signs that their people are disengaged, unhappy or unable to do their jobs proficiently. Train your managers to look for warning signs, such as employees who are taking too much work home because they either can't get it done during the day or they are afraid to delegate. Are their people staying at the office working well into after hours, just to get caught up? Are they always behind?

Then, ask the same questions about your managers. Are they micromanaging others? Are they blocking progress in team meetings? What are other managers saying about them? Listen, listen and listen some more. Your managers are so often speaking to you through their own behaviors and the actions and reactions of their team. Observe, observe and then observe again. Mike always says to me when I make a statement about someone, "How do you know that?" I tell him, "Just watch and listen and you'll see too. It's intuitive because my radar is always up." This has served me well.

Expect Excellence

In addition to modeling the behaviors that we wanted our managers to adopt, Mike and I would also set the bar for the standards of excellence that we expected. We both liked the story about Henry Kissinger, and frequently recited it to anyone who would listen. The story goes like this:

An assistant hands Mr. Kissinger a behemoth proposal for review, saying "Sir, here's the report you asked for." Kissinger takes the report and then hands it back to the young man the next day asking, "Can you do any better?" The assistant responds, "Yes, I think I can." So the underling takes the paper back and works on it some more. They repeat this iteration about five times and finally Kissinger gives it back to the assistant one last time, with the same comment, "Can you do any better?" The assistant says, "No sir, that's as good as I can do." Kissinger responds, "Okay, then I'll read it now!" The lesson there, of course is to keep (gently) pushing people until they do their very best—even better than perhaps they thought they could.

A more modern-day example of this comes from Steve Jobs, who was notorious, almost controversial, for having outrageous expectations of his people. In the book, *Steve Jobs*, a story is told that after repeatedly telling one employee "this is crap, this is crap" about every idea the employee brought to him, the employee finally said, "Steve what the hell do you want?" Jobs said, "I don't know but when you bring it in here, I'll know it." And he did, and in that way, expecting more made a difference.

The difference between these stories and how Mike and I managed was in the execution. I knew darn well that if I called into the office and didn't like the way the receptionist answered the phone, and upon returning to the office, if I marched up to the front desk to confront her about it, the end result would be the equivalent of a fire alarm for that employee. The receptionist would be thinking, *Oh my goodness. I'm going to get fired now.*

This can easily be an exercise in self-restraint. As the owner, sometimes you just want to charge into a situation, guns blazing and just take care of it. The problem with this is that it breaks the chain of command and sets a precedent that whenever there's trouble or a decision to be made, call Laura or Mike and they'll take care of it. It completely undermines your managers and exhibits a lack of trust in their managerial skills.

Many owners undoubtedly struggle with this concept of giving up control, but in a small, family-run organization like ours, it can be even more of a challenge, realizing you must learn to give power to your managers (or get buried under an avalanche of details and be taken away from your real responsibilities). It's hard to do, but when Mike and I did unclench our fists and free up those reins, allowing our people to take on those responsibilities, good things usually happened as a result.

—⁓— LESSONS LEARNED —⁓—

1. Establish hiring criteria for your business culture.

I learned that, as you hire people, you are responsible to make sure they have the right knowledge, skills and experiences to truly move the business forward. And equally important is that they need to share your business culture. A business needs to have the right leadership. The entrepreneur usually has the vision, the risk tolerance and the passion to work twenty hours a day to make things happen, and this needs to be translated through the entire company. The shared passion is the key to engaging employees.

If you see that your managers are not fulfilling your expectations as it relates to the culture you want in your organization, then you must clearly communicate to them the culture in behavioral terms ("I want calm resolution of conflict; I don't want shouting or name calling in this company"), and then explain in detail the day-to-day and long-term behaviors you expect from them in order for that culture to be maintained whether you are there or not.

I have found that the most difficult thing in the world is to have a great manager who knows business and knows how to run a business, but who does not share your values or your culture.

The hardest thing to do is to let that manager go. But you must let them go if you want your culture maintained. The managers who did not succeed with me were those who wanted to micromanage and control all aspects of their staff's responsibilities, and those who did not train their people well enough in their expectations so that they could trust them to do what they were hired to do.

2. Hire slowly.

Do not hire more people to take on new business if you have not evaluated your systems and processes and the ability of the current staff to handle the duties that expanding requires. A mailroom person and a receptionist are "nice to have" but not necessarily "must-have" positions. It's important that, as you grow, you evaluate how that growth impacts personnel. Is it possible that an existing employee can add to their day-to-day duties without compromising the quality of their current work?

Sit down with them and walk them through what the new job is and tell them how you would like them to achieve it, and then let them know that you will help them set up the system or process that will not interfere with their daily duties.

It's important to evaluate the additional duties after a month or two. Is the addition of this duty impacting the performance of their other duties? After a certain period of time, it will be determined at what point a new employee will be needed to take on the additional tasks as a full-time job.

3. Know when to up-hire.

It's important to know when to hire a new manager for the next level required by your growth demands. One rule of thumb to use is to look at how efficiently the current person is working and how many questions they are asking you about what's next and what should be done. Are they capable of developing processes? Do they need additional outside resources to get their work done? So it is critical to know what the next level of job outcomes looks like. I recommend you keep printed copies of job descriptions of next levels (i.e. bookkeepers, accountants and CFOs). Review them on a regular basis so you have a clear understanding of the job demands and requirements needed at the next level of every role within your organization. These descriptions will guide you as to when you will most likely need to update your skills in that department.

Chapter 9

CELEBRATING VICTORIES

As you may recall, when we last left off in what would become the tale of Spherion (a game-changing chapter in the story of our company), one of IMPACT Group's earliest employees, outplacement counselor Kathy Flora, had first said that she didn't have enough time to deliver the load of seminars needed for the Contel contract. Then, when I hired someone else to assist with the workload, Kathy got angry, stormed out of the company, and left me in a lurch, with storm clouds formed over our once positive, productive relationship.

Fast forward to December 2006; my office phone rings and it's Kathy, calling for the first time since that fateful day. She opened the conversation in a very surprising way, apologizing for her behavior all those years before. She owned the fact that it was inappropriate and said that she'd felt badly about it since then. Then, she added that she'd followed our company since then and, in fact, had been working for one of our competitors for several years. She ran the "virtual" outplacement division of that major firm and had grown it to $19 million in just three years. I congratulated her, and then she got to the main point of her call.

Kathy's company had just moved her and her family from New Hampshire to Florida, in the middle of her chemo treatment for stage-four breast cancer. Then, they proceeded to let her go two months after the move. She explained how, as part of her recovery, she wanted to heal old hurts and hence the call to me. I was stunned. Not just that she called, but that a national firm would be so spiteful, so thoughtless and so inconsiderate to someone who was a valuable contributor—not to mention a cancer patient.

I was also touched that Kathy wanted to close our gap and bring positive energy back to our relationship (something I'd yearned to do for years). Why do we wait so long to heal hurts long overdue for healing? Having been a breast cancer thriver-survivor myself (with another recent recurrence scare and surgery as of this writing), I empathetically embraced her need for closure and assured her I had let go of any hurt a long time ago, and never held any grudge—only disappointment that two talented women couldn't find a direct way to solve a problem. I missed her friendship and her talent as we grew the company. More than one time during our company's journey, I wished that Kathy were still a part of the team. She's a woman who is truly a star wherever she goes.

We spent the better part of an hour catching up and lamenting why her company would possibly let her go when she was making them lots of money. She shared how our idea for a virtual outplacement option (something she and I first created fifteen years earlier) threatened her former employer's brick-and-mortar business. When corporate clients were offered the choice of virtual versus in-person outplacement service delivery, many of their current client companies opted for our virtual model that Kathy was managing for them. Our virtual model was supported by telephone coaching and Internet delivery. The office delivery program that most national firms sell was outrageously expensive compared to the virtual model we created and that she had introduced to our competitor. It was exciting for me to hear from Kathy that our twenty-year vision was finally beginning to pay off, although not necessarily for us yet, but for our competition.

Some Things Were Just Meant to Be

Well, unbeknownst to me, Kathy was also calling to do some due diligence, gathering competitive intelligence for SHRC, a small $12 million division of a $2 billion staffing company. They had decided to sell SHRC and stick to their core competency: corporate staffing.

Kathy called me several weeks later to say there was a company she wanted me to contact called Spherion. She could not tell me the nature of the call as she had signed a non-disclosure agreement. She gave me the number of a woman who was a Spherion manager. I was getting ready to travel for a week so I gave the number to Mike to call. When the woman said she wanted IMPACT Group to buy Spherion's HR Consulting business, Mike quietly refused. He was the back-office guy. He never told me the result of that call.

I was flying into D.C. to land another account (the Department of Defense) the following week when I called Kathy to invite her out to dinner to re-engage our relationship. I decided to make it easier for her so I said she should pick a place close to her home and I would come to her. After showing me her new apartment, we headed across the street to her favorite restaurant.

The conversation went like this:

"Laura, I am really disappointed you were not interested in Spherion. I am a bit surprised. I thought you would have jumped at the chance to buy them."

Flabbergasted, I said, "Kathy what are you talking about?"

She went on to say, "I was asked to do due diligence for them as they need to sell the $12 million HR Consulting Division of their $2 billion staffing company. After reviewing all your competitors, I knew your values and your mission statement were the best match for them."

She went on to say, "I also called several of your clients and they had rave reviews for your outplacement services, especially those who had changed from your larger competitors, Right Management and Lee Hecht Harrison. They all said your personal service, your pricing and your model met their needs to give a positive transition for their laid-off employees. I recommended you, saying that, 'Given Spherion's goal of wanting to provide the absolute best service delivery to their current out-placement clients, I believe IMPACT Group to be their best decision.'"

My mouth dropped as I thought about her initial statement that we somehow "weren't interested" in this phenomenal opportunity. Kathy must have seen that shock on my face.

"Wait a minute," she asked, "are you saying you didn't know Mike said he wasn't interested?"

After gaining my composure I simply said, "We really haven't had time to discuss it."

I then asked if making a deal was still an option, almost two weeks later.

"You might be too late, as I think their CEO is 'shopping' the company to your competitors, but a call in the morning wouldn't hurt," she said.

"I don't have the number," I replied.

She smiled and said, "I do at home. Let's go get it."

I set my alarm early the next morning so I could be the first to catch the Spherion manager, Pam, in her office. Recounting the story once more, I asked if it was too late to meet and discuss with them the acquisition.

"I am not sure. I believe our CEO was calling some of your competitors last week. Let me get back to you in five minutes," Pam said.

Five anxious minutes later she called me back and asked, "Can you get down here tomorrow?"

My heart pounding as I said, "My husband and my daughter and I will be there if you can get your CFO and CEO there."

She assured me they would be.

We walked into the meeting and before introductions were made I said two things. Why, I will never know, but they set the stage for our future:

"I just want you to know that we did not bring our checkbooks today," and "Before we begin, can you please tell us what is on and what is off the table?"

The CEO quickly responded, "The only thing off the table is we will not write you a check to take the company."

Good. Now I knew exactly what was about to happen.

The management at Spherion was convinced that we were the only company who could maintain client satisfaction while retaining their current staffing clients. We set out to see what this gift called Spherion HRC was really worth. Their financials turned out to be fantastic. They were a $12 million-a-year company and had healthy profit margins. They anticipated with the closures of the majority of their offices that they would bill $8 million in sales that year (2007). Financial documents supported their report. But they only gave us three weeks to do our due diligence. This was ridiculous, as typical due diligence takes three to nine months to thoroughly carry out. But the Board of Directors of Spherion wanted this off the books before the third quarter so we threw every resource possible at this deal.

First, we engaged Kevin Short of Capital Partners in Clayton, Missouri, to assist us. To cut costs, we had our internal controller, who had joined our firm three months before, do the numbers. He had experience buying more than fifteen companies, and any which way he crunched the numbers, it came up looking good for IMPACT Group.

Then, our accounting firm came in to give us direction, instructing us to dig a little deeper. What we found was that this company was very profitable because they, like us, were turning almost 100% of their services to virtual telephone support and their overhead was disappearing. The largest cost we discovered was the cost that Spherion headquarters was charging them for real estate, accounting, IT and marketing. We knew most of those costs would be off the books once we acquired them. Things were going at breakneck speed when we hit a wall in negotiations.

To say that their "deal guy" and chief negotiator, Bill, was a "bull in a china shop" is putting it mildly. He was pushing back and refusing to sign a no-shop agreement with us, meaning we wanted them to stop shopping their company to our competitors and make us the sole buyer in negotiations. We didn't want another competitor coming in and underbidding us at the last moment. We wanted to be the only one they were talking to.

We were scheduled to fly down to Fort Lauderdale to meet the CEO and hammer out the deal. Lauren and I would fly from Las Vegas where we were finishing up a relocation trade show and then we would be off to do our deal in Fort Lauderdale.

While at the convention, Manville Smith, the Executive Vice President of Spherion HR Consulting, and also the most gentlemanly corporate executive we have ever had the privilege to meet, attempted to reach me on my cell to confirm our Friday and Saturday negotiation meetings at Spherion. Unable to get me, he called our office in St. Louis and got my assistant, Linda Costello, who realized that I was probably in the cave of a convention center and thus unable to receive his call. She ran for Mike to deliver the message. Mike responded that because they refused to sign the no-shop agreement, Lauren and I would not be coming after all.

Linda made the call and delivered this message. Manville was dumbfounded and asked her to call back in fifteen minutes so he could go get their "deal guy," Bill, to hear this news from her directly.

Linda repeated the message to Bill, word for word. Then, she left a message for Lauren and me on our hotel phone, reporting what had just happened. When we both heard what Mike had done, we were furious. Was he trying to lose this deal a second time? What was he thinking? We were beside ourselves with anxiety that we were going to set such a negative tone in the deal that we would not be able to recoup the positive momentum and continue moving forward to a successful conclusion.

Mike, after all, was the one who originally talked to one of the Spherion employees and politely passed on the opportunity, never telling me the nature of the call. That's what I was thinking as Lauren and I sat in that hotel room in Las Vegas listening to Linda relay this conversation between Mike and the Spherion negotiator. I thought, *Oh my God, he's done it again! He may as well have sent them down the line to the next hungry competitor for this $12 million business!* My heart sank.

Well, that shows what I knew then about negotiating. I was told later that it was Mike's strategic move that forwarded the deal to the no-shop agreement, as we did not seem so desperate. It was a brilliant move because Manville was from the European gentleman's school of business and our move shocked him.

So, to have my executive assistant return his call, rather than one of the owners of the company, was interpreted as a statement of total disinterest. He saw this "maneuver" as the possible dismantling of the deal. He knew under no uncertain terms that the board wanted this division off the books within weeks. I was told long afterward that Manville told Bill (their deal maker) that by no means was he to screw up this deal. Bill immediately signed the no-shop agreement, which meant that we were the only interested party with which they would continue to negotiate. Regardless, I did demand then that they pay the $5,000 for the trip down to finalize negotiations. (Why not? Just ask!) They agreed.

Putting this deal together was one of the most fun things I have ever done. If you like excitement and living on the edge, try putting together a multimillion-dollar deal, complete with preliminary reconnaissance, in three weeks. We worked day and night.

Fortunately, we had recently brought onboard an experienced Director of Communications who brilliantly put together our communications plan. She was an angel. Christina had successfully worked on two other acquisitions in two previous jobs and we could not have successfully executed this deal without her. It was her training and discipline, particularly in regards to the timeliness of communicating the next steps to both clients and staff, that were critical to the seamlessness of our deal. Manville, who had acquired more than twenty-five companies for Spherion, said he had never seen a more comprehensive, well-executed plan. At the time, this felt like the Pope giving us his blessing.

Fast forward to the night before the deal was to be closed. We got a call from Bill, Spherion's deal maker, saying there was a problem with one of the website licenses both our companies used. They refused to reduce the cost of Spherion's fee and release the sole license to IMPACT Group because Bill had backed the CEO of the company into a corner saying, "We need this done by tomorrow night and we want the blended cost of both our licenses to be dropped by fifty thousand dollars." The CEO refused and hung up on him.

Dumbfounded, Bill called and asked, "Laura, can you call and see what you can do? I'll throw in another twenty-five thousand dollars, and we split the increase."

The important thing was to get them to agree to the terms before the 2:00 p.m. contract signing the next day. This license (or lack thereof) could break the deal because everything had to be off their books by the next day. This small detail was a potential legal deal breaker if there ever was one.

I looked around the table at my team as I shared this information. They were blown away.

I put in a call to the salesman who sold me the license; he said he knew what was happening. Fortunately, years before, I had helped him network with several companies when he first sold me the license. We had a friendly relationship.

I said, "Pete, I need your help now. Here is the deal. I need you to talk to your CEO and present to him this new deal."

I went on to negotiate. I outlined the terms, expanding the contract for another two years if they reduced the fee by $25,000. By giving him an extended contract, he was still getting the $50,000 he wanted from Bill. I explained how the deal was so important. He called back five minutes later with an agreement faxed and signed. This is yet another important example of building solid, mutually beneficial relationships.

The fun part was the next day, during what is called "the red lining of the agreement," where you get down to every incremental expenditure left to discuss and say, "Who is going to pay this?"

Bill paid way more than he would ever have prior to the licensing issue. He was so grateful for my resolving the issue, saving the deal on his end, that he threw in $25,000 here and $5,000 there just to get the deal done. And we did. It was truly an exhilarating moment.

I have to commend Spherion here, as what they wanted most of all was to ensure that their clients would be taken care of, and be given the best service possible. And we did.

After the acquisition of Spherion Human Resource Consulting, it was not unusual for me to fly to two or three cities a week to meet with our newly acquired clients to thank them for their business and to assure them that nothing would change in the quality of service they received. My personal assurances made them feel special. This single act of goodwill allowed us to retain almost 100% of the purchased clients who used virtual services—an unheard of retention rate in acquiring companies.

When first flying out to meet and greet our new office staff in Houston, Cleveland, Toledo and New York, I anticipated that they would be anxious to see what the new owners looked like and, more importantly, what we were "really" like. Many of the staff, I later found out, were already interviewing with competitors. They had already lived through four other acquisitions.

This entire, loyal staff had worked fearlessly to save their division. With a stellar client list, including Eaton, State Farm, Allstate, Grainger, Cemex and other mostly Fortune 500 companies, these dedicated employees banded together virtually (most of them having never met one another) and decided to "save the company" so they could all continue to work together and provide the same caring support to their outplacement candidates. Their passion for making a difference and for doing whatever it took to continue servicing individuals who lost their jobs, made this small leftover group of thirty-six individuals the pearl in the oyster of this entire organization.

We had the privilege of meeting only three employees before we purchased the company. However, two out of the three were star managers and were professional in every sense of the word. Meeting Carolyn Parrott and Pamela Grosiki immediately left me with the impression that we would be lucky to get these two people to stay as part of the acquisition. In fact, we made it a prerequisite to the sale. We were told, as we went through the employee roster with Pam and Carolyn, who the players were, which we should keep, who were dispensable, and who were the stars. They pointed out thirty-six stars. That is an incredible number of stars for any one organization.

The week after the signing of the contract, Mike and I set out to Houston to meet some of our new clients and to shore up the Houston office. Trying to ignore the fact that no one in Houston had ever heard of IMPACT Group was going to be impossible. I hit it straight on by first thanking them for seeing me on such short notice. I think we had all of three days to get appointments. We had a full week of meeting clients, interrupted only by Fourth of July midweek, and torrential rains the entire week.

"Bet you've never heard of IMPACT Group before, have you?" I asked each client.

No, they hadn't, and that is exactly why they wanted to meet with me.

They were playing right into my plan. I told them the truth, that we were a privately held family business servicing more than 150 Fortune 500 companies and that because we were privately owned, we chose not to spend hundreds and thousands of dollars on advertising. We chose to grow by word of mouth. Johnson & Johnson told Pfizer, Pfizer told Novartis who told Abbott who told

Amgen, and *voila!* A vertical market was formed. I then talked about how we covered spouse relocation issues at HR meetings worldwide, becoming known as experts in the field and thus growing into other industries such as finance, manufacturing, telecommunications and more.

I also outlined for our new clients in Houston how this acquisition came about in the first place. I revealed how Spherion employees approached us discreetly at first and, with direction from their CEO, they approached us to buy them. Their due diligence had determined that we were the absolute best match for their clients: quality services, outstanding staff with credentials and years of success and experience—all of which Spherion wanted in order to maintain the company's positive reputation. They wanted to keep their current clients happy since many of them used the staffing division services, thus maintaining a positive, seamless delivery that would be win-win for both companies.

"I have to say something about Laura. The woman made an enormous difference in my life, and I'm not even sure she knows it. When she hired me, I had not done very much in front of a group as a speaker or even as a facilitator of large or small groups. I was pretty young. When we got the MCI contract, she said, "Oh, we've got to go out there and do these presentations and they're going to be a day long and the spouses are all going to come together. We have to talk to them about what's going to happen and inspire them, and then give them some real practical tips of how they're going to work with us."

So, I developed it and it was pretty canned, but she came with me on the big trip to Washington D.C. We walked into the ballroom and found seventy-five MCI employees all ticked off because they had to move to Plano, Texas, from D.C. Well, to make matters worse I gave the little talk that I had put together and it bombed. It was awful. They hated everything that came out of my mouth. I felt like I was letting Laura down. But that evening she came up to my hotel room and coached me for most of the night. She didn't berate me at all. She told me, "Kathy, throw away your content and just talk to their hearts, just talk to them. I have confidence in you. You can do this. Just tell them stories." I had watched her tell stories. I had seen how she did it and I got up the next day and it was the most fabulous experience that I had had in my career, because everything she told me worked.

From that moment on, I loved giving speeches, talking to people in public, all of that. Laura unleashed something in me that I have been able to use for the rest of my career, and I will forever be grateful to her for that. She coached me in a way that freed me from that fear of public speaking and engaged me with the audience, and I have been really, really able to use that every moment since. This has been a thread for thirty years in my life, and there's not a time I don't get up in front of a group and thank her for making that be the most fun I've ever had now. That is the key thing that I love to do. I could never have done it, I could never run for office, and I could never have been in the roles I've been in if it wasn't for her helping me get over that."

—Kathy Flora

Celebration

You might have seen a little of this throughout my stories so far: bringing champagne back to the office to celebrate the Johnson & Johnson deal and (albeit prematurely) McDonnell Douglas and then, in the prior story, the Spherion acquisition. It's true: One of the most exciting things about owning a company or managing a division or a team is watching it grow. Just like a new parent records a baby's first steps, the first time their little precious rolls over, or the first time the child pedals their two-wheeler down the driveway unassisted, you feel proud and exhilarated and a bit smitten that your "baby" is growing.

I don't care how sophisticated you are in business, there is nothing more delicious than getting a new contract that you have been working on for months, or even years. Nothing beats the sense of victory that you beat out your competition in all areas to win the client. You earned the right.

Whenever we won a big contract (or a small one for that matter—a deal is a deal) the sales team and I would dance around the small office with some of the marketing staff like a bunch of lunatics. We would buy champagne for the biggest contracts and share it with the entire office. Mike, Lauren and I would then treat ourselves to a nice dinner to celebrate the big win.

In fact, very early on, when Lauren was about ten and in the classic, "Mom can I have?" and "Dad I want" age, she would ask for something specific, like a pair of Reeboks. In the nicest of ways, I would explain to her that the sneakers were expensive and we could not afford them just yet. But when we got a big contract, we would buy her a pair. For six months, every day when I got home from work, Lauren would run and greet me at the door, hug me and ask breathlessly, her eyes brimming with excitement, "Did you get a big contract today?" She kept score religiously and when we did close a deal, she joined our victory dances at home. By the way, it was the MCI deal that scored Lauren her Reeboks.

Back at the office, however, sometimes some of the staff didn't share in Lauren's excitement (despite the fact that they could afford their own Reeboks), even when we hit a big home run. IBM, MCI, Pfizer … the list goes on. I could never understand why some of them weren't jumping up and down and clinking champagne glasses with me. Mike told me later that rather than seeing the closed contracts as cause for celebration, they saw that it meant more work, reading up on the new client and getting acclimated and new quality expectations. Since we were customer focused, we promised to customize each new client's systems and processes to meet their specific corporate reporting goals.

Mike's comment helped me understand why some of the staff's celebrations may have been a bit low key for my taste. The bar we set for our staff, when it came to customer-service expectations, was admittedly high because one of the greatest lessons I learned about growth was that just because you win a client, doesn't mean you get to keep the client (à la IBM). Growth means you need to add staff to stay in close communication with each and every client, continuing to assess their current needs and asking the all-important question: "How are we doing?" If you're in business you know the drill; it's Account Management 101. As you grow you need to continuously add more and more people to be successful; not "just enough" people to deliver the services, but also enough to hand-hold the clients along the way. We always made sure we added staff when we needed, so that everyone in the office would celebrate.

Cars, Careers & Cash

One of our first twenty clients at IMPACT Group—and one of our very first big clients—was a major U.S. automotive manufacturer. In fact, we sold our services to this company the very first year we were in business. They relocated thousands of people a year all over the world. Adding the automotive company to our client roster was so helpful in marketing our services to the other car corporations, as well as two other major Fortune 100 companies.

The car company had another division we were unaware of: their union workers. At one point, Lynette, our account manager for this client, set up a lunch with a woman and me and Susan, the relocation manager for the client's union workers. We didn't talk about business but rather just got to know each other as people. Susan and I really clicked and by the end of lunch, she requested a proposal, and shortly thereafter we were providing services for this division of the auto manufacturer. I also befriended and worked closely with Mary, the Director of Labor Relations. Mary and I often shared stories about our families and all three of us became very close.

This client ended up being one of our most enjoyable accounts. Taking this to heart and having already learned the value of account management, I made it a point to make frequent trips to Michigan to spend the day at their headquarters. Once there, they were always gracious and made not only the trip worthwhile, but also the business and ultimately the relationship. They would meet us at the hotel for breakfast, then we would visit their offices to review cases and do our semi-annual reports. Then, putting work aside to get to know each other as people, there followed the inevitable lighthearted lunches, full of stories, company updates and laughter. We would often end the day with a trip to the spa—a group of executives looking delightfully silly roaming around in robes, bathing caps and pedicure flip flops. There were always appetizers, wine and even more bonding, as our group of account managers, customer service representatives and I grew closer and closer to this client. It was wonderful, feeling like a part of their extended family. And that's how our deep, long-lasting relationship with this company began and then flourished over the years—by sharing mutually fun activities, special times and special talks. We engaged fully in the process of building life-changing relationships with them, and legitimately feeling like family.

Now, you have to understand, clients don't normally just say, "Let's be family and share whatever we want to share with each other." No, just like in life, business relationships are created one event, one day and one cry for help at a time. It takes time to develop the best ones, those based on mutual respect and trust. This is built on following through with the commitments you make, the promises you keep and by respecting the individual who seeks your friendship and trust. This is one aspect of building strong client relationships. The other, of course, is going well above and beyond to deliver what you say you're going to deliver in products and services.

One day in 2006, about ten years into our working relationship, I received an urgent call from Mary saying that something was going on and they really needed our help. She asked me to fly up to Michigan as soon as possible. I flew up the next day and found out that they were going to "idle" some plants (meaning close some plants, as the union's contract would never allow them to fully close any plants).

"You've helped us make soft landings for years for all our relocating families. Well, we're eventually laying off 40,000 people and we know you and your company have values that match ours, and we want every single one of these people to have the same soft landings."

I saw the enormity of the task immediately, so Lynette, their account manager, Susan, Mary and I locked ourselves in a room for three days to brainstorm a client-focused solution for the giant auto manufacturer that aligned with their needs, values, expectations and outcomes. Here's what we came up with.

Soft landings mean taking the time first to explain everything you're going to do, rather than charging in and making a sensitive situation a traumatic one. So, we made a DVD and gave one to each one of these 40,000 people, explaining what outplacement services were, how retirement coaching worked and what a relocation package was (for those lucky enough to be offered a relocation). The employees could bring the DVD home and watch it with their spouses and families.

Then, we selected eleven cities in Michigan where we would hold information fairs (a job fair, relocation and outplacement resource event), with the addition of many of our outplacement and relocation coaches who could help people deal with the psychological issues of being laid off, especially after decades with the company. Within the alarmingly brief time period of six weeks, we arranged two fairs in each city (creating options for people who couldn't make it to the first one), each with a minimum of twenty-two different stations set up—everything from financial planning, resume writers and counseling services to community colleges, universities, training companies, corporations and businesses in the local communities with actual job openings, and any other resource we could think of to help these 40,000 employees and their families have the soft landing that was paramount to the management at the company.

Here's the other part of what was already a daunting challenge: While pulling together this plethora of details for these events, we were basically flying blind in terms of the most important detail: the dates. The client wasn't able to tell us exactly when we would be able to schedule the fairs, because they didn't want the situation to leak out to the company before the actual layoffs had occurred. This meant that even as we arranged specific event details such as renting space for the job fairs, contacting vendors and getting them to agree to participate, having contracts signed, creating materials to distribute to UAW workers and spouses, booking hotels for our people and training them for the actual fair, we couldn't actually reveal who we were doing this for, or why. When the phone rang and we were finally told, "Okay, here are the eleven cities and here are the dates," it felt like, "On your mark, get set, go!"

This was a truly amazing feat to have pulled off. There are companies that spend a year putting together something of this magnitude. We got it done by hiring two experienced project managers and then pulling all our coaches and research department and putting them on this one project. In total, the project plan was 139 single-spaced pages.

One of the things I learned was how to hire the right people at the right time for the job at hand. We identified the right people in each of the eleven cities to coordinate with in advance. Not daring to leave anything to chance, Mike and I, along with a research assistant, even flew up to each city a couple of days in advance, rented a U-Haul and personally delivered all the materials to the event.

As Mike said, "I don't trust that these huge boxes of vital information will be delivered in time. And if they're not, this whole thing is a bust."

As entrepreneurs, Mike and I routinely did things like this because it was critical to get them right. There was no hierarchy or executive ego, nor should there be in business. Instead, there was Mike and the research assistant, Doug, unloading the U-Haul, lugging boxes inside the event space, overseeing union members setting up all the tables at each event in all eleven cities, hanging banners, and meticulously arranging the display materials on each table. This was a herculean task—and there wasn't a chance that we would leave it up to chance.

At the event, my team and I personally visited each booth, introduced ourselves and thanked each vendor for being there. Then, we shared IMPACT Group's mission, vision and values (down to the level of simple things like never sitting down while on duty and personally welcoming each guest to your booth) with them since they would be representing us to the company's employees and families attending the fair. Each fair in each city went off exceptionally well. Our client placed their trust in us so much that, when local television stations showed up to cover the various fairs, I was selected to act as the media spokesperson for the behemoth automobile manufacturer. I memorized the approved script from their marketing department, introducing IMPACT Group as number one when it came to creating soft landings in layoff and relocation situations. And I always praised the car company throughout each and every interview for handling what could be an extremely traumatic situation. For their part, our client was grateful to have me deal with it.

It amazes me to this day that we did all this in just six weeks. This was a game changer for our organization because we were the only provider selected, due to of the quality of our services and the cloak of confidentiality we had to work under the entire time. Our client also knew that we could customize a program down to every last detail for them.

Afterwards, we followed up with phone calls. We promised that someone from our team would talk to each employee or spouse within forty-eight hours of the event. One entire dedicated HR team hired 300 additional coaches to make this happen. We worked with these employees and their families for a year, until they felt satisfied.

All this time, Peggy (who had been ready to pack her things and head off for greener pastures) was there with her talent and experience. Peggy's team singlehandedly trained all those new people for this project.

As it turns out, this massive layoff was the writing on the wall. The longtime auto manufacturer was running out of money. Thirteen months later, one of America's largest automobile manufacturers was plunging toward certain bankruptcy.

Meanwhile, at the close of this project, we received a nearly unheard-of 97% satisfaction rating from the employees and their families we worked with. So, it was stunning to us the day we got a call from Mary, saying she had received our invoice and was shocked. Understand that we paid for all the expenses of these events, plus we flew sixty people between St. Louis and Michigan regularly over a six-week period, while funding their food and lodging expenses. The cumulative result was complete outplacement coaching, retirement coaching and relocation assistance for 40,000 people for a full year. It was an enormous task at an enormous cost. Our invoice was significant, as you can imagine, for a year's worth of coaching for 40,000 people plus the job fairs.

Then Mary and Susan called to tell us that they would be making a call the next week to discuss the bill.

Seeing the writing on the wall, I called in our lawyer, Bill Corrigan, a fabulous attorney at Armstrong Teasdale and a friend, and had him waiting in the wings in the next room when that phone call occurred. In the boardroom, I gathered the entire team around the table for the call. My friends at our client company got to the point quickly.

"Laura, we've received your invoice and we can't pay it. We're not going to pay this. It's time to start negotiating. That's the reality of the situation. Tell me what you'll accept," she said through the speakerphone as jaws dropped all around me at the table.

I assumed this is what a heart attack must feel like, as I mentally calculated all the costs associated with their bill that we had already paid out. The work had been done and paid for and now the client was refusing to pay for it. This type of financial hit is the kind of thing that sinks a company. I went into sheer panic and then anger. This woman and I and her director of relocation were friends, so now they thought I was naturally going to just roll over and go along with this.

I was finally able to wrench words from my mouth. "Mary, I am shocked. I can't even breathe. I can't start negotiating because you signed a contract with us two years ago. When I asked you if we were going to be operating under the same contract, you said yes."

With that, I told her I couldn't even think straight and that I would get back to her, and then I politely hung up the phone. Almost instantly, all the phones lit up around the table.

"None of you pick up those phones until I talk to our lawyer and know what course of action we're going to take," I told them, and then got up and went to the next room, where by this time Mike had materialized.

The lawyer gave it to us straight. If we dared wage war against this mega corporation, we were looking at up to six to ten years in court and all the legal costs that went with it. He pointed out that the company had tons of lawyers so we stood little chance of winning with our much smaller legal team.

"I want to settle. I just can't go through something like this and neither should you," Mike said in a strained voice.

"Absolutely not!" I cried out in fierce determination, "We did the work. We created a fabulous program for them. They agreed. We're fighting this!"

Well, before Mike and I could escalate this any further my secretary, who hadn't a clue as to what was happening behind these closed doors, came running in.

"Mary just called me and she's on the line. I told her to call this line and that you would pick up," she said.

I took a deep breath before picking up the phone, with the full intention of saying, "Mary I still haven't decided what I'm going to do."

But instead, she surprised me.

"Laura, don't worry. We're not going to have to negotiate. Your check has already been cut."

I assumed this must be what the reverse of a heart attack feels like. The elephant lifted itself up from on top of me. Relief and gratitude came rushing out.

"Thank you, Mary, thank you so much. We've worked hard for this and we will continue to work hard for the next year for these people," I gushed into the phone.

"Don't thank me, thank the accounting department because they got your invoice and already paid it," Mary said.

I was speechless once again, because it usually took this client months to pay our bills.

The dramatic ending to this story was the hefty check that showed up in the mail *the same day as these discussions.* Mike opened it and paraded it around the office, as it was the largest single check that IMPACT Group had ever received. For so many reasons, we had been blessed.

—∞— Lessons Learned —∞—

1. Use experts when acquiring companies.
Do not attempt to buy a company without outside help and guidance as to what the appropriate step-by-step procedures are. If you've done it once or twice before, or someone in your organization has done it many times, that's a different matter. But if you are going to buy a company for the first time, it is best to hire someone who is used to closing deals and who has the knowledge and the background to get you the best deal possible. We would never have been able to do our deal without the expert help of Kevin Short and his Capital Partners' team.

2. Always keep your door open.
We all have to terminate employees. Some employees will chose to terminate themselves. Always, always, be gracious. Do not burn bridges. You never know where they will land and how they might reach out to you to do

business with their new employer. Even if they leave with a chip on their shoulder, keep the door open. If I hadn't, Kathy Flora would never have made that call and handed me a $12 million company. Always take the high road.

3. Celebrate your victories.

When you close a new client or re-sign an old one, celebrate. Create a tradition. In the beginning you may not be able to afford champagne or treats, but go around the office, thank everyone for a job well done. Create a tradition. We danced around the office with champagne. You can make it fun. Take it in. Enjoy the moment and always include everyone.

I remember when *Inc. Magazine* (inc.com) ranked us the 327th fastest-growing company in America in 2009, Lauren sent everyone a $327 American Express gift card with a note thanking them for making it possible. Everyone loved it.

4. Build relationships with your vendors.

When people call on you to "sell" you something, they are there to be part of the service. Treat them well. Respect their goals and their efforts. You will not buy from everyone, but they will speak about you to many others, so give them something positive to say by giving them a positive experience.

Had I not done that, Pete, the guy who helped me save the Spherion contract deal, might never have been willing to help persuade his boss to do the deal. You see, when he first called on me we talked for a bit. I found out he was relatively new at his job, so I gave him some names of companies and helped him network. He told me later that he never forgot how much I wanted to help him succeed.

Networking is always important, but helping your network achieve their goals is even more important.

5. Build client relationships into friendships.

I always go into a new client meeting expecting to like them and when possible, develop a nice, warm relationship if not a friendship. Don't assume friendship in business means they have your back. The reality is: business is business. When there are bumps in the road during business, if you have a positive personal relationship, it will help a little bit in being given time to "fix" the problem. But, the bottom line is, the client has to report to someone and their boss might not be as patient or forgiving.

I also tell my new clients: "While we have a 97% satisfaction rate over the years, there are going to be issues. Please know that we will always do our best to create win-win solutions. Thank you for your business." Why do I do this? Because when an issue does come up, I can always say, "Yes, sometimes things like this happen, but like I told you, we will take care of it to everyone's satisfaction." This reminds them that, "Yes, Laura said there will be times like this." They know that I am honest and trustworthy.

6. Don't continue talking when you can't breathe.

When I hung up on Mary, I did so because I was in shock; I couldn't breathe and I wasn't sure if I would say something for which I'd be sorry. Don't try to talk, don't try to sound brilliant. Stop. Ask for time, or ask if you can discuss it later. Don't try to solve the issue if you are angry, dumbfounded or confused. Just say, "I need to think about this. I will get back to you." This way, both of you will have time to think, research and come up with resolutions. By politely hanging up on Mary, I prevented myself from saying things I might have regretted.

Section II

Conclusion: On Fear of the Unknown...

"Fear sees, even when eyes are closed."
—**Wayne Gerard Trotman**, Author

For entrepreneurs and intrapreneurs, fear comes after the excitement of the idea. Their passion and vision for what they want to create drives them in the very beginning. They want to tell everyone they know about their idea and how it will change the world. Their excitement is what propels them to sometimes, blindly, take a seed of an idea and nurture it and lovingly present it to people way before they have thought through the "why" and the "how." They have the "what" down, but many stop there. As a result, when people question them or challenge their vision or their product, they can get angry, frustrated or worse, fearful that their idea or product is destined to fail.

In order to keep fear at bay and not paralyze you from moving forward, it is best to step back and ask yourself, "What is my goal here? What am I trying to accomplish? What is the end result I am looking for? Am I offering a solution to an agreed-upon problem? Have I researched the need, or am I trying to create a need?" The last two questions in particular require very different strategies. The best way to combat the fear of the unknown is with the "known," with information.

If you are feeling fear in moving forward, maybe you need to really take the time to see if there is a true market for your product. Do competitive research. Who else has a product like this? What is different about yours? Focus on whether there is a need, how it is currently being met and how your solution is better. Define your market by who would buy your product and how you will take it to market. What is your unique selling proposition?

Talk to people who have done this before, who have successfully achieved a sizable success, as well as those who have failed. Knowing the road in front of you will calm you and help you put a plan together. Seek guidance from entrepreneurial resources like the Small Business Administration (SBA). SCORE is made up of retired businesspeople who volunteer to help people just like you through the often intimidating maze of the startup process (see Appendix). The wisdom of others who have already been down this path can take the edge off your fear.

Finding a mentor with experience is also a great help in moving you through the next steps of growing a company, even beyond the startup stage. Many entrepreneurial companies become stuck in the growth stage because they have not yet taken the time to overhaul their original concept. They have not taken it to the next level of potential, and suddenly new competitors enter the picture with fire in their bellies and become the newest, best thing on the market. Regardless of whether you are an entrepreneur or an intrapreneur, you must always be ready to think things through over and over to make sure you are constantly making process improvements and staying ahead of the market curve. Nothing is worse than waking up and finding your customers choosing the next best thing. As a businessperson, you have the obligation to always be thinking, "How can I make our product better, more streamlined and more responsive to customers' needs?"

However, even with all the prep work in the world, fear is a personal demon that you may find yourself fighting regularly, especially when confronted with the unknown. The most important questions to ask yourself in these situations are: *What am I afraid of? How will it impact me? My family? My future?*

When Mike and I came to many potentially fearful moments in starting and growing the business, we asked ourselves the same question: *What would we do if it didn't work?* Our answer was always the same: *As long as we had each other, then we were smart enough and resourceful enough to start over, even moving back to our $85-a-month, walk-up apartment.* But, to be clear, we did not expect to fail; we did not fear failure. We made failure impossible by doing our research, doing focus groups, constantly getting feedback, and constantly making our product and processes better. In other words, we planned, executed, got feedback and then drew up plans and sold like crazy.

I will repeat here one of my favorite phrases when coaching business people. "F does NOT = Failure; F = Feedback." Using feedback for positive change of direction or improvement will help eliminate fear. Constantly taking stock of what is working and what is not working really helps calm the devil within, who visits in the middle of the night and taunts you about all that you are not doing. Here are a few suggestions to send the devil on his way.

First, if you are awakened in the middle of the night, rather than getting irritated at it, thank your unconscious for making you aware of something you might not have known or done. Keep a way of taking notes by your bed and write down the thought that woke you up. Don't try to solve it then, but you might want to write down the first step you want to take the next morning to do so. Repeat this process for each thought that is haunting you; write down the thought and the first step you will take in the morning toward resolving it.

I embrace waking up as a way for my unconscious to send me information, remind me of what I have not done, offer ideas I have not thought about before, or acknowledge an idea and validate it. Embrace your unconscious, and thank it for being your partner. Do not feel you have to solve the problem in the moment.

Just write down the "who, what, how and why" of the situation, knowing you will fill in the details by taking action in the morning.

If your demon is scaring you beyond sleep, ask it these questions: *What is the "positive intention" of it scaring you? Is it telling you that you don't have a plan? You don't have the money? You doubt your ability to sell the idea? Is it alerting you to something that you really do need to think about, plan for or rethink?* If that's the case then set a date with yourself to revisit the issue in the light of day. Your unconscious has done its job. Thank it, pay attention to it, create a plan around it and then take action and move forward.

Fear is a friend to embrace as a warning sign of what to do next to become the success you envision.

For example, you have your product, but you hate making presentations to investors or in front of prospects. Take a speaking course, learn breathing techniques and practice in front of a mirror until you are letter perfect. Notice all of these solutions involve doing something. Take action so fear does not control you.

I am an accomplished speaker and most times I am blessed with standing ovations, but I still prepare my speech thoroughly and well in advance, delivering it to anyone who will listen and always asking for honest feedback so I can improve. This way, when I am standing in front of the audience, I know I have done my homework and can confidently go out there and have fun.

Whether you are starting your own company, growing your company or working for someone else, if you want to take charge of your career by facing fear, these strategies will work. They will keep moving you forward and help you hold up a stop sign that says: "No Fear Allowed!" for yourself and for that unconscious demon within.

PART THREE

FEARLESS!

Chapter 10

GREAT PEOPLE = GREAT COMPANY

Reflecting on impending failures of almost losing our home, losing big clients, breast cancer and all the other trials and tribulations we faced over the years while growing IMPACT Group, sometimes I had to ask: How on earth did we survive?

Even with our infinite persevering faith, the challenges we faced got to be a bit much at times. Our other saving grace though, in all these situations, is the human kind of grace: our clients, colleagues in the business world and (most importantly) our employees. Looking at the growth of IMPACT Group, it would be absolutely impossible and grossly unfair to separate our purpose, passion and profits from our people.

The success of a company has so much to do with growing it with the right people—a progression of people who keep getting better and better in proportion to the speed of your growth. The right people, aligned with company values, work ethic, skillset and culture, will ultimately propel momentum and growth.

For this reason, you absolutely must be invested in your people. You also have to hire people who make you want to invest in them. Above all, you must ensure that you have people who know how to do the job correctly. I am so pleased to share some of our finest human interest stories from IMPACT Group's hall of fame. As you meet these remarkable people who helped our company thrive, I want you to think about your own company's future hall of fame. Do you have people like this, who have the purpose, passion and skills to grow with the company?

Firsts at Bat

When we were first starting out and hiring an office manager, we got a lot more than we bargained for when Lucille Cupples, a delightfully feisty four-foot eleven-inch, sixty-two-year-old woman walked into our office. As I was interviewing her, she kept looking around, her eyes darting into every corner of the office, taking in every single detail of her surroundings. Lucille had recently retired with a nice pension after a long career working as an office manager for a large oil company in town. But, it turned out, she wasn't exactly the retiring type.

"For the past six months I have been going absolutely crazy staying at home. I'm used to managing a big, busy office. I don't know what to do with myself now," she confessed to me.

"When you say manage … an office, what exactly do you mean?" I asked, quickly realizing that I was dealing with much more than an office manager here.

"Well, everything from helping with the hiring, to assisting with accounting," she said, smiling with pride.

I encouraged her to continue.

"I got the invoices out, created processes for the entire accounting department … I just contributed what I knew to help the company," she said.

And then she said some things that I didn't know.

"You need a secretary who works for you instead of against you, so your agenda is their agenda … and you must pay special attention to every detail in your finances. Above all: communicate, communicate, communicate, and then put in writing any agreements, any employee discussions. Document, document, document every time, no exceptions."

This feisty recent retiree was educating me about everything that is critical when you're setting up a new office or just starting out in business. I felt a wave of gratitude wash over me that Lucille had walked into my office and my life. The Small Business Administration (SBA) had assisted me in writing my business plan with Ginnie Campbell's help, but Lucille's up-front information on the "who, how and why" of setting up a business were invaluable.

She was such an incredible, loyal helper and company soldier. One time, when we were short $5,000 for payroll, Lucille came into my office and closed the door.

"Laura, I would hate for you to go out of business because you were short payroll one time—money that will come in next week. I'll lend you the money to see that this doesn't happen," she told me.

She knew our hearts and acted out of generosity from hers. In return, I respected her, valued her and did whatever I could to lift her up. You stick with people like Lucille, who contribute and help you become the best you can be.

Even after she finally retired (for good) at age sixty-seven, telling me "Laura, you've grown bigger now, you don't need me anymore," we stayed good friends over the years. We broke bread together; Lucille, like so many others in the IMPACT Group family, was so much more than an employee to us. She was one of my first hires and a trusted ally.

Back in the early days of *Momentum*, long before IMPACT Group, Mike, Lauren and I barely had money to fund our peanut butter and jelly diet, let alone hire staff. We couldn't afford much, but let me tell you when that big five thousand-piece *Momentum* kit order came in from McDonnell Douglas (or so we thought at the time), I knew we needed an extra set of hands—and not just any hands, either. Enter the amazing Joyce Edelbrook and her total commitment to getting us organized and doing what was needed to get the job done. Joyce took all my ideas essentially out of a box of papers, and funneled them into clear, well-written course materials. She interviewed me, taped my comments with what I wanted to have on the *Momentum* kit tapes, and then wrote all the training tapes. Without Joyce, there is no way I would have been able to complete those packets for McDonnell Douglas, which became our first-of-its-kind *Momentum* Program for the Relocating Spouse and Family.

She would eventually be the first one to visit and then close one of our largest clients, a major U.S. automobile manufacturer. To no one's surprise, Joyce grew quickly in her career, spreading her talented wings further than the reach of IMPACT Group. She soon evolved into a fabulous public relations specialist with big ideas pumping through her veins every minute of the day. At that point in our growth, however, we needed people who could focus more on the details. In order to support her career growth I took the next step as a leader and introduced her to Ed Cohen, a wonderful marketing executive who helped arrange for me to give speeches at relocation conferences. Ed was truly responsible for giving us global exposure over the years and, to this day, he has Lauren present at many of his conferences. Ed hired Joyce on the spot and she did a lot of work for him for many years to come. The moral of this story is: when your people's talents and ambitions outgrow the needs of your company, rather than showing them the door, show them the way to their next job opportunity. This is the difference between an employer and a leader.

Our very first career relocation coach, Joanne Waldman, was a loving, caring woman who was absolutely masterful at her job. She was in her early thirties when she came to us, just getting married, and within six years of starting with us, having a baby. She helped us from day one of the Johnson & Johnson account, calling the spouses, identifying their needs and meeting them. She helped develop the many forms and paper processes we used for many years. And then, not surprisingly …

"Laura, I love what I do here but I need to be at home with my baby. I want to start my own coaching company. I hope you'll understand."

How could I not?

"I will do whatever I can to help you succeed," I told her, speaking from my heart.

Supporting Joanne in launching her coaching company was my privilege and pleasure.

Front-line Employees Must be the Best

Since that first coach hire, we have been blessed with hiring more than five hundred coaches in the past twenty-six years. We now have them in thirty-three countries and they are all certified coaches. Collectively, they speak more than twenty languages, and receive regular coaching from our training department on everything imaginable, from how to most effectively use the latest social media platforms, to all forms of technology.

While most of our coaches have a master's degree or PhD in counseling or a related field, Mary McDonald's role as a single mother of twelve made her the go-to person for helping relocate single moms. Many of our largest clients relocate their employees every three years as they move up the corporate ladder. One of our relocating clients from Johnson & Johnson insisted, "I won't move unless Mary moves me." She handled all six moves for that one family in her twenty-year career with us. Mary was able to grow her skills over the years and continued to excel.

As we do with many of our employees, over the years we shared the stories of Mary's life. IMPACT Group is founded on stories: our own, the families we relocate and certainly the stories of our employees. It would be impossible not to become entrenched in those stories. When Mary went through the tragic death of one of her sons in an automobile crash, we went through it with her. After the funeral one of her adult children told us, "We don't know what our mom would do without the friends and love of IMPACT Group." In an age when people move from company to company, Mary's empathic style, her loyalty and passion for helping others was a perfect fit for both of us.

Mary walked in on her sixty-fifth birthday with tears in her eyes: "Do I have to retire?"

I asked her, "Are you ill?"

She quietly said, "No, I just thought I'd have to retire at sixty-five."

I asked her if she wanted to retire and she shouted out "No!"

I then told her, "As long as you love what you do and you can do it well, then you'll have to come to me and tell me you want to retire."

That day came when she turned seventy-two.

Help Your People Become All They Can Be

About four years into our company, a young woman named Debbie Wampler, about twenty years old, interviewed to be our receptionist/operator. She was high-spirited and a go-getter. Learning quickly was her strength and asking, "What else can I do?" became her mantra. I really liked her. Mike saw the same thing: a positive, dynamic young woman who could really grow with our company. Mike set about mentoring her. It was then we found out that she came from a very poor family and she was on her own.

Mike asked her, "Have you ever thought about going to college?"

She said, "I would like to one day."

So we set about making sure she enrolled. Mike guided her through the financial aid maze, gave her $1,000 to get her started with books, tuition and other needs, and about eight years later, Debbie graduated with a degree in marketing. Halfway through her studies, we put her in charge of marketing. Debbie was sharp, she understood computers and she had a great intuition about people. More than once she would take me aside and say, "I think you need to be aware of so and so. They don't appear to have our passion." I wished we had moved more quickly on some of her observations, as she was usually right on.

Debbie now had the confidence to take on major marketing tasks and did a stellar job on a small budget. By this time we had reached IMPACT Group's tenth anniversary. She came in one day with tears in her eyes and said she had been offered the top marketing job for Mary Engelbreit Enterprises (maryengelbreit. com). Mary Engelbreit was an internationally known St. Louis artist who licensed her cups, shirts and paintings to shops around the world, and our Debbie landed that top marketing job. Mike and I could not have been any prouder of her than if she was our own.

Today, Debbie is married with children and we see her occasionally at the coffee shop, always greeting us with a hug and a kiss. I am proud that we invest in our people, and proud that when they have the opportunity to move on to bigger challenges, we congratulate them and thank them for a job well done. They always thank us for believing in them.

The woman who wrote our communications plan for our Spherion acquisition saw me at the airport not too long ago. She came up, gave me a hug and said, "Laura, I can never thank you enough for allowing me to work at IMPACT Group. Your philosophy of respecting flexible time for families, and understanding my needs, made my six years with you while my children grew invaluable. You allowed me to have memories I could have never had with the company I work for now."

She is currently a Director of Marketing for a Fortune 500 company that requires her to travel the country. When she left, we both agreed we gained a great deal from each other. And, of course, we celebrated her success. You launch companies and you must be willing to launch your employees when their skills expand beyond you.

There are people who will join you early on in the growth of your company who will become part of the soul of your company. That person for us was Sherry Heffington. She was a standout and another powerful, emotional example of how we make it our jobs to share in the stories of our employees' lives and, in some cases, play key roles in those stories.

When I (finally) realized that I needed an account manager to help keep all those big clients I was landing, Sherry was among my first hires. In fact, she helped me understand the role and value of an account manager, attacking her job whole-heartedly.

Five to six years into her career with IMPACT Group, Sherry wasn't feeling well. She went to her doctor and learned that she had lung cancer. This was devastating news and a total shock, especially since she was a nonsmoker. Even worse, her doctor told her that there was nothing they could do for this type of cancer, short of chemotherapy and radiation to shrink, but not eliminate, the tumor. The future looked bleak. She was given six months to live.

Sherry was managing five or six people for us at that time. When she came to work every day she was understandably depressed. As the leader, I was forced to make a judgment call, balancing my concern for Sherry with the well-being of my company. I called her into my office.

"Sherry," I said, "I love you but you just can't come to work depressed. We need you, but first you need help and we're going to do everything to help you. I want you to get some counseling so you can function better since you have made it clear you want to continue working. We will pay for the counseling."

So I sent her to my friend John, a counselor, and encouraged her to pour her heart out to him. And then … a miracle.

John referred her to a specialist in alternative medicine, who identified that Sherry's cancer was actually from mercury poisoning, a common cause of "nonsmoking lung cancer." She took a week off to have all the mercury fillings in her teeth removed and replaced with safe, nontoxic ones. This stopped the mercury leakage. After that, she changed her diet, started juicing and took additional measures to restore and preserve her health. She was a role model for taking control of one's life.

She went on to become one of our most successful managers. We made the decision to let her work as often as she wanted and when, based on how she was feeling. She told me, "Laura, had you not demanded I perform under difficult circumstances and given me that counseling, I wouldn't have lived through the year."

Sherry lived for another ten years. She came to work every day fired up and ready to go, until the last three months, when she came in whenever she felt well enough to work or she chose to work from home. At her funeral, her husband Mike opened his eulogy with words that caught Mike and me and Lauren off guard and touched us greatly.

"Sherry loved her job. And we want to thank Mike, Laura and Lauren Herring for giving her the past ten years of her life. She lived to work at IMPACT Group. And I want to thank them for giving me more time with my wife."

The good thing about being an entrepreneur is that you can make exceptions for exceptional people.

Know When to Let go

One of the hardest things about growth that I experienced early on is that some individuals wanted to claim an individual victory for their efforts. It was a difficult day to say the least, when the first woman I brought on as a manager and coached and nurtured for years, began acting differently.

She was about eight years younger than me and truly she looked up to me. I had handed her the Anheuser-Busch account when we were doing EAP referral work, counseling their employees and families. I taught her how to dress, how to manage the client and how to hire new people. We were close. She admired this one suit I had and always said so whenever I wore it. So, the day she closed her first big account, I went out, bought her the exact same suit, wrapped it up with a big red bow, drove to her house and hung it on her front door with a love note, saying congratulations. She was thrilled.

Everything changed right before her performance appraisal. She'd been talking to someone who suggested that she was perhaps not getting her due. I was oblivious to this, walking into the appraisal meeting, feeling so excited about being able to offer her 15% of the company to thank her for all the hard work and loyalty she had shown. During the four years she had worked for me, she never once hinted at wanting a percentage of the company, so I thought my offer would go over very well with her. In other circumstances it might have, however, whoever had coached her made a huge error in judgment. This person had suggested that she ask for 50% of the company. I was dumbfounded. Here I was feeling magnanimous in offering her 15% after being with me for a few short years and she wanted half of my company. Here's how I responded.

"Look, you have been very helpful in making this transition from a counseling company to a national relocation company, but you took none of the risks. You didn't double-mortgage your home, you've gotten a paycheck every week when I have not, you don't have to make payroll every week, you don't pay rent, and you were given clients from day one."

"But managing your current EAP clients has allowed you to branch out, Laura, and start the IMPACT Group Spouse and Family Transition Division," she insisted.

"Yes, but that's what I pay you to do. That's your job," I responded.

I added that whoever was coaching her was doing her a great disservice, but she stuck to her guns anyway. I don't know what made me say what followed, but it just came flying out of me and I found the guts to follow through with it.

"I am so sorry you feel that way. I am offering you 15% of the company and I was excited to do that. I didn't have to do that. But I realize now that you will never be happy with only 15%. You will always feel like I cheated you. I would hate having you feel that way, so I am left with no other alternative but to let you go. I hate doing it, as I love working with you and I have been thrilled with what we have accomplished together. But you have given me no option. You will always feel taken advantage of, so I am sorry; I have to terminate you," I said in what felt like one big breath.

She left the room in shock.

Then, I went back to my office and cried. I loved this woman, but my gut told me I was right. I had to do it.

I gained many valuable lessons from the experience. I learned to praise people in appropriate amounts and never make them feel that they are the sole reason for the company's success; that it's a team effort rather than an individual effort, and they are certainly not operating at the same level as the true risk-takers at the top—the owners and founders of the business. As a business owner, your name is on the bank note. Your home is on the line. Your sleepless nights are yours alone. Do not let anyone try to blackmail you or guilt you into giving them a raise or part ownership of the company. You must use your best judgment at all times. Trust your intuition.

I've wondered at times what this woman felt when (or if) she heard that we grew into a nearly $50 million company. If she had accepted what I saw as a generous offer, she would have received 15% of our profits for the past twenty-five years. It would have been millions of dollars.

Showing Up ... Exceptionally

What I also have experienced, and you will too as you grow, is that certain managers continued to blossom and lend their expertise to the entire company wherever they were needed. Leslie (Les) League and Linda Ryan were two of those people. Les was our first Operations/IT Director, and he followed the rule of: be the best, cut costs by shaping better processes, and offer insight to all departments. He was truly a lifesaver more than once when we needed to demonstrate our technology capabilities early on. His common-sense approach to business was a huge support to Mike and me in eventually running the operations of the company. He always put the needs of the company ahead of his or his team's needs. He was also gracious when we identified that the job got too big for him, and he stepped aside to allow more experienced leaders to take the lead.

Linda Ryan is still with us and still moving up, currently overseeing an entire relocation department. She is unflappable. It is never about her. She keeps confidences and her laugh puts a smile on my face. I cannot tell you how often I've walked into her office over the years, closed the door and said, "You are not going to believe what just happened." We would then laugh our heads off. She was my confidant. I should call her "Teflon Linda," as nothing negative sticks with her. She laughs it off, fixes it and moves on. Her motto could be: "Save the drama for your mama!"

> *"I've always compared Laura to a train: You can't really stop her. And even if the tracks were not going the right way, she just keeps going. She's just amazing.*
>
> *"She'd go sell something and she'd come back and say, 'Well, this is what we're going to do for this client.' And we're all looking at each other like, 'We don't even do that!'*
>
> *"This happened for many of our biggest clients and projects; we ended up doing things that we didn't do in our core business. But luckily she had people around her that would say, 'Okay, let's put it together and do this and that and whatever.' It didn't always make sense financially, but we did a lot of things just because it was Laura's vision."*
>
> **—Linda Ryan**, IMPACT Group

There were (and continue to be) other standout individuals who helped create the story of IMPACT Group. There are many people over the years who have been loyal, kind and dedicated. These eleven people have all been with us over 15 years: Tim Martin, Sue Wegrzyn, Paul Mueller, Tanya Fite, Anita Cole, Sheila Scott, Barbara Daniel, Virginia Gentry, Joely Kettler, Linda Ryan, and Jason Spears. Many of them have been with us for nearly two decades. All show up and do exceptional jobs every day.

And for those who outgrew IMPACT Group and moved on, I did what I could to support their goals. You see, in a well-developed company, well-developed employees are not a threat. When they outgrow you and move on, it's usually because they want to serve clients on an individual basis. As you've seen, building a full-fledged company is a different enterprise entirely. Therefore, there is no reason to resent or be fearful of employees in this situation. Instead, be thankful that they contributed great ideas that hopefully helped your company grow. Be glad that perhaps you could teach them a few things in return, and wish them well as they go out and build their own careers.

What I believe is that you should hire people who share your passion for being the best and making a positive difference. They need to love their family, spouse and whoever else is important in their lives. That gives them an emotional reason to come to work each day and be proud to be part of something bigger, someplace where they personally can make a difference each and every day. The important part of that is making them aware that they *do* make a difference.

When I was CEO, I would write each person what I call a "love note" twice a year: on their work anniversary date and on their birthday. I'd personalize them so that they knew I knew what they did, and the specific difference they were making in their department. We were growing to over one hundred people, and one day I was getting behind in my love notes when I wondered out loud to my secretary if it was worth it.

She said to me, "Walk around the building and look at their cubicles; everyone has your love notes posted for all to see!"

I did take a walk and *pow!* There they were, proudly displayed. That made a huge impression on me. They really cared that I cared about them. So, as you grow, don't grow too far from those who make your company great—those individuals who show up each day to make a positive difference in your success.

Statistically speaking, we all spend the majority of our lives working—employees and employers alike. There seems to be a prevalent, self-destructive idea that work is supposed to be a negative experience; that the invisible gray line between bosses and workers is more often than not an impermeable steel wall, where "us versus them" replaces compassion, alignment of values and goals, and purpose and passion. As entrepreneurs we have the power—and, really, the responsibility—to work on tearing down that wall. We can do this, one employee at a time and one workplace at a time. I hope that the stories shared in this chapter serve as an example of what can happen when the right people come together with the right company, and the right values and human interests become company interests.

—w— LESSONS LEARNED —w—

1. Hire passionate people.
Interview people in a way that allows them to demonstrate their passion for something in their lives. Then ask them to share specific examples of how they transferred that passion into their last job. Your job is to listen, ask questions and probe deeply to see if their passion matches yours.

2. Hire people who are not just like you.
I had to learn this lesson myself. Mike finally said to me, "You have enough ideas for fifty people. Now we need people who are detailed-oriented and can implement!" A light bulb went on. As entrepreneurs, our biggest mistake in hiring is believing we can clone ourselves and create a company that reflects who we are. But each job requires a skill set that, more than likely, you don't have. Write down each job, create the job description and then outline the skills necessary to get that job done. Most importantly, ask applicants for clear behavioral examples of how they accomplished their goals using those skills. Ask for specific stories that demonstrate they understand the process or tasks you are asking them to do, like: "Tell me about a time when a client called all upset that their order was sent out wrong and how you handled it. What was the result?" Come up with five to eight questions for each job that will force the person to dig down and demonstrate they not only have the skills necessary, but in the telling of the story you will be able to hear if they have the passion for the job.

3. Treat your staff to celebrations of them and celebrate wins!
It is not unusual to walk into our company and find everyone wearing crazy hats, crazy sweaters or both. We play together. We celebrate each other and we celebrate when we get a new client. Party-like announcements go out, cleverly

written by our marketing department, to reveal new clients, which services they bought, and bestow credit upon the sales team. There might be cookies in the kitchen—or, in Mike's case, he was the "good humor man," pushing a large cart around the office filled with tubs of various ice creams and lots of toppings and whipped cream. The women always asked Mike to dish theirs out to them, as they knew he would always give them more than they would have given themselves.

Once this culture is established, hand the celebrations over to a committee that takes it to a whole other level. Thanksgiving dinners, Halloween costume parties and contests along with trick-or-treat luncheons, holiday lunches and more. If there is a season or a holiday, our company employee committee will find something to celebrate. And, most importantly, make it about them. Thank them for their hard work and toast them.

One year at our Christmas party I surprised them. I did a take-off on Oprah's favorite things. I had four carts wheeled in, and had wrapped (with my assistant's help) four gifts for everyone: my favorite Ghirardelli caramel squares, Body Shop's orange hand cream, personalized stationery with their home addresses on it (for their own love notes), and a picture frame. I love having personal pictures surround me. They loved it! They whooped and hollered. It was fun for all of us.

It is always important to acknowledge that the new clients might mean more work until you can hire some more people, but thank them in advance. Remember, the company might have been your idea, but without them, there would be no company.

4. Be flexible.

Children get sick, parents die, spouses pack up and leave and employees have parent-teacher meetings, football games to attend and cookies to bake for homeroom. Make flex time a part of your company, if at all possible. It will be a valuable attraction and benefit of your company. As a mother, I knew the importance of showing up to the right midday school functions. Lauren, to this day, remembers my involvement before I skipped back to work. Trust me, flex time will buy you lots of loyalty, and if your company allows flexibility by circumstances, so much the better. No one resented Sherry because we let her come in only when she felt like it. They knew the same would be there for them, God forbid. It allows your people to show grace.

5. Walk around and talk to your people.

Talk to them about their work and about their family, and then make a note of it back in your office. Send a note if there is a baby, a graduation, a wedding, a new car, etc. When we grew I would ask our managers to share news updates from their employees and their families. I remember when Tim, one of the IT men, came up to me and said, "Stacy and I just bought our first home. We are so excited." After congratulating him, I ran back to my office and thought, "Oh my, I am responsible for selling enough business so Tim can pay his new mortgage!" It was eye-opening to me how many people depended on our company to be successful, so they could live the life they wanted. I always keep that in mind with every business decision. Stay connected and your people will come through for you.

6. You need different people as you grow.

Be aware when it is time to change the lineup. As departments grow, you need people who have been there and done that, and aren't afraid of complexity or growth. I can't say this loudly enough. Just because someone was a star when you were starting out doesn't mean that his or her skillsets are what you need now. Be honest during performance appraisals. Tell them where their growth areas need to be and how they can grow. Provide them the training or tools that will enable them to get to the next level. Send them to outside training, or bring training and coaching programs in to do the job. Research shows that the most important thing employees want in a job is not salary, but training to advance to the next level. Do it, and you can have your people grow with you. If they still can't do their job to the new level demanded of them, provide them outplacement and assist them in finding a new job. Treat them well and you will be remembered well. Every ex-employee is a potential ambassador for your company and a possible referral agent of new clients or new employees. Treat people well.

My biggest mistakes were with my secretaries. I needed high-powered, well-organized secretaries who could juggle not just my personal life but my clients' needs as well. I learned that I should have had two secretaries once we grew to over one hundred clients: one who could do my scheduling and travel and work with my clients; and one to do my paperwork and computer work. Ellen Sherberg, publisher of the *St. Louis Business Journal*, told me that and she was right.

7. Do not be held hostage.

No one in an organization is so critical that they could hold you over the barrel and demand either more money or a part of the organization that you are unwilling to provide. Therefore, it's important that you recognize and value your people with ongoing positive feedback, but avoid implied promises. Thank them for their contribution, but don't overdo it so that at some point they feel they are responsible entirely for your success.

Chapter 11

CREATING CLIENTS FOR LIFE

This is where you will start hearing from some new voices at IMPACT Group. And not just any new voices: the voices of my family. As you have learned by now, we are a family-owned business. My husband, Mike, and our daughter Lauren have worked alongside me in various roles throughout the years and, above all, they have absolutely had my back no matter what we faced as an organization and a family. The three of us will talk more about the dynamics, challenges and advantages of growing a family-based company in the next chapter.

In this chapter, you will hear insights from me on how to create, build and maintain strong client relationships. As well, you'll hear from Lauren Herring, the current Chairwoman and CEO of our company. As a mother, and I'm sure other parents will understand this, I will describe Lauren as indisputably the most amazing, beautiful and generous human being who has ever walked the face of the Earth. But as the founder of IMPACT Group, I can also attest that Lauren is an ambitious, energetic, intelligent and skillful leader who has already set a fresh new tone throughout the company as she confidently leads IMPACT into the future. Her bio attests to her capabilities: a magna cum laude graduate of the University of Notre Dame with an undergraduate marketing degree, coupled with an MBA from the Olin School of Business at Washington University in St. Louis. Education aside, and before she took over as CEO, she had already built IMPACT Group's international capabilities and led the Spherion acquisition. So, despite her youth, I felt confident in IMPACT Group's future.

When Lauren and I sat down to discuss this chapter—this idea of creating clients for life—the first thing we agreed on was that, in many ways, this very phrase is an oxymoron and, in Lauren's words, kind of a "Pollyanna" approach. There is realistically no such thing as a client for life. The truth is it would be foolish and (from the standpoint of the bottom line) financially imprudent for any CEO or leader to believe that their clients are there with them for life. After twenty-five years, I'm painfully aware that clients come, and sometimes despite our best account management and highest level of services, clients go. As we learned from the IBM situation, the minute you think of them as "for life," you are risking taking that client for granted somehow; you are putting yourself in a very vulnerable position. If you start getting complacent, or if you start to feel too comfortable, that's the point at which you probably start risking your relationship with that client.

But in some cases, and always with a lot invested to make it happen, we've seen that lost clients can find their way back. This is ultimately why Lauren and I decided to talk about this subject—because of how it reflects the principles behind developing strong client relationships—relationships strong enough to sometimes give you a second chance.

"It's an illusion to say we haven't lost clients, but I choose to look for opportunities to regain them," Lauren says.

Starting With a Solid Foundation

I agree with Lauren, and I would recommend that all CEOs adapt her optimistic "how do we get them back?" mentality after losing clients. It all begins with creating that solid foundation for a lifelong client relationship from day one.

"You always have to be working to provide value and demonstrate how you're going to be a true strategic partner to every client all the time. When your client sees you as a strategic partner, they see how that relationship will enable them to grow their opportunities with you down the road. It's no longer a client/vendor relationship," Lauren says.

This is so true. After providing years of outplacement services for some clients, they have ended up as our best partners to try out new products and solutions for us. So, because they have that trust and relationship, and because we've taken the relationship up to that level, we have a clear vantage point as to how to add value to other areas of the relationship. That way, when you do encounter vulnerability in the relationship, it's the day-to-day work—the investment in that client you've made over the years—that can come back and work in your favor.

This kind of vulnerability can come in many forms and work for you or against you in multiple ways, and it exists in all stages and phases of a client relationship. For instance, dialing back to day one when you bring on a new client, you're always vulnerable. First, there's the client's opinion of the quality of work you actually do compared with their expectations of what they want you to do. Second, you're vulnerable to how responsive your implementation process is, or the account manager is, to the client's needs (if that person is a good listener, a good communicator, and what they're specifically doing to make that client happy). Third, there's the vulnerability that can come if and when the client's original contact is replaced (whether via termination, retirement, etc.); there can be issues around that initial loyalty. Then, you have the vulnerability of the client's changing needs, simply because the economy changes. As much as they might love you, they might no longer have the resources to keep working with you. This has happened to us and countless other companies numerous times, especially in recent years when economic pressures have driven decisions. The last vulnerability, which we have really felt the impact of over the past twenty-five years, is when companies merge. When this happens, your new clients may already have a provider of services like yours. If that's the case, there's a decision maker who comes in and makes the ultimate choice of which vendors are kept and which are let go.

That's where having the relationship at the highest level possible within the organization makes a big difference. It's easy, and I can speak to this from personal experience, to be so attentive to your day-to-day contacts at a client company that you may not necessarily have the same tight relationships with senior leaders in the company. It is these individuals who may be the ultimate decision makers in a situation where there's a merger or similar, so it's critical to have those relationships there when you need them.

The lesson here is to make sure, as you form your client relationships, that you build horizontally across the organization while strengthening connections with executive contacts at the top of the organization whenever or wherever possible. At IMPACT, this also means forging bonds with different buyers within the same organization based on our different services. You've heard me talk mostly about our relocation solutions throughout the book so far since that is the foundation of the organization, but outplacement as well as talent development also makes up a significant part of our offerings. This requires the forging of quite a few lateral connections to ensure that we're building the strongest foundation possible for long-lasting relationships that can weather any storm.

Selling the Mission

So many people in business, especially entrepreneurs, can easily fall into the habit of hard selling versus using soft touches and quality relationship-building to seal the deal. There is a difference between being positive and refreshing, and being greedy and pushy. When you make it a point to lead from a place of compassion, mission, values and making a positive difference in the lives you touch, people will see that and it will make them want to buy from you. They will feel committed to you personally as well as to your mission. This doesn't mean there is never a time to push, but you need to check yourself in these situations and ensure that it's coming from the right place—a positive place of helping others. Overall, if you have a mission that resonates with people, even if your sales style is unpolished or a little awkward, they will connect with your heart and link arms with you as a strategic partner.

You can be aggressive as long as it relates to how it can help them. If it's aggressive just for the sake of being aggressive, it turns people off. But if you can find a way to connect with people and demonstrate value to them, then the relationship is there to be built. It comes back to the mission and your passion for making a difference.

Every entrepreneur has heard the phrase, "What's in it for me?" That's all the customer wants to know. So, if you bring the conversation back to you, from a place of greed, it's not going to work. It's about meeting the needs of the customer and the customer's customer.

Account Management

At the heart of client relationships is an understanding of what each client wants and needs from you as a service provider. It means knowing who all the clients are in the sales process (i.e. how many people will have decision-making input into the sale), how many people touch the sale, how many decision makers there are, and how you can maintain relationships with all the clients throughout the sales process and even afterward.

This requires digging in and asking about everything from preferred methods of communication and frequency of "touches" to the best contact people and (in general) how much attention the client wants and needs. Then, you find a way to meet those needs. This applies to all clients, whether you're selling to them directly, or operating via channels. The key is to maintain positive relationships with everyone involved in the customer relationship.

Different companies call this different things: account management, client support or customer service. But it's important to be clear on how your clients and prospects will be getting those soft touches. Whether it's everyday business or selling new business, there's only so much the CEO can do. Entrepreneurs should always plan to have that backup support to ensure the clients are getting what they need.

At first, I handled all this type of account management by myself, personally touching clients three or four times a year. Now I see that wasn't nearly enough. I learned as a CEO the importance of hiring great account managers, and training them on how and when to service your clients, and what quality looks like.

Solid account management allows you to manage expectations within each client relationship, so when situations do arise, you can attack them proactively. In this sense, you are much less likely to experience actual crises—just problems and road bumps that are being proactively managed. I call this making the covert overt.

The most effective overall account management is a continuous series of soft touches over time, throughout the relationship, even in the prospect stages. You look for excuses to reach out more, to say, "Hey, how are you doing?" You search for where you can add value, you share resources and ideas that perhaps you just read about in a magazine, and you follow news of the client and congratulate them on their accomplishments. It's about demonstrating and understanding what is going on in their business, reinforcing your role as a strategic partner, and consistently utilizing those touch points. You might not always be their immediate priority, but when the opportunity is right for that connection to take place, you are top of mind for them. I'm pleased to say we've created great account management systems at IMPACT Group, and Lauren is continuing to refine those systems today.

Client Appreciation

When you do it right, your client relationships will evolve from accounts to be managed, to real people to be appreciated for how they ignited your impact. Honoring our clients is by far one of my favorite things we do at IMPACT Group. I get fired up every single time we find a way to do it, and it touches my heart like very few other things can. Here are some ways that we say "thank you" to the clients who have been with us through the years, and helped make us great.

In 1998, for our company's tenth anniversary, we flew to New York and took all our East Coast and New York City clients to dinner at the top of the Met Life building. Looking around the table at dinner that night was a truly special experience. There were our clients from Pepsi Bottling Co., Johnson & Johnson, Pfizer, LexisNexis, Lucent Technologies, third-party folks, and the Vice President of Human Resources from Merck. The most special dinner guest of all, however, was my father. My mom had died a few months earlier, and more than anything

I wanted to show my father how successful the company had become and how all those people sitting around the table had become part of our IMPACT Group family. Beyond that, my father worked at Merck for 48 years so I thought that would be a great way to honor him.

I announced to the table, "You are all here because you've made such a difference in my life personally and in the lives of our employees. In total, together we have impacted the lives of over two hundred fifty thousand families (now well over a million!) that have been touched by your organizations. You have helped us create soft landings for so many people."

Then, true to our core value of storytelling, I went around the table and told a touching story about each person.

The Pepsi story started way back when I was wearing my trusty *Momentum* visor to ERC conferences, collecting as many corporate cards as I could carry. During the conference, I ended up on a bus with a gal named Olivia Holt from Pepsi. After the conference, I visited her office, contracts in hand (I *always* brought contracts with me to every meeting back then).

"I'd like to show you what we talked about on the bus back in New Orleans," I told her.

She agreed, and I presented everything we had to offer Pepsi. Olivia signed the contracts right there on the spot.

"We have three people relocating right now so we need to get started right away," Olivia said.

"That's fine. Fax their information to my customer service department and we'll get started for you," I responded, thinking that by the time I flew back to St. Louis this information might be waiting for me.

Olivia moved much faster than that. By time I made it downstairs to the lobby, I called my secretary from the pay phone (no cell phones back then) with the heads-up that Olivia would be faxing the information.

"Laura," my secretary said, "I already received the three applications a few minutes ago."

"In that moment," I told our dinner guests at the Met Life Building, "I remember getting goose bumps because I knew we had a wonderful national product."

"Olivia," I said, turning to my guest, "you and I have connected on a lot of things from that first meeting when I saw that picture on your desk of your beautiful daughter Allie and we chatted about our families, and then later on when we all started a tradition of spending time together on a regular basis. I want to thank you for being a part of my life and a part of IMPACT Group's wonderful tradition for all these years. You have helped us make a difference."

I continued to share stories, the Gary Gorran/Johnson & Johnson story, and then how the woman from Lucent started out with Bell Labs and packed us up and brought us with her when she went to Lucent, and still another company after that. When people move on in their careers and bring us along, that's part of being a client for life. After dinner, I loaded everyone into a limo and we went to see *The Lion King* on Broadway to celebrate them and thank them for a great ten years.

The reason I put together this special evening and told all these stories was to let each of these clients know that they were valued for different reasons. I wanted them to repeat the stories to others. Even if they didn't remember all the details, we had now empowered them to be storytellers for IMPACT Group. Even if the sole part of that evening they remembered was, "Wow, they helped over two hundred fifty thousand families!" it made it all worth it. I continue to be grateful to each one of these clients for helping us fulfill our mission of making a positive difference in their employees' lives.

Highest Honors

When individuals from our top client companies retire, we like to honor them in different ways. You learned all about Gary Gorran from Johnson & Johnson earlier in the book, and how critical he was in ensuring our success, especially after the rocky start with McDonnell Douglas and the van lines. To honor Gary upon his retirement, we established the Gary Gorran All Star Award, in honor of our friend, mentor and committed client who always supported our mission to make a positive difference in the lives we touch. Every year, we ask our employees to nominate one of their own—an individual who stands out amongst his or her peers in loyalty, commitment and a tireless push of oneself to be all he or she can be. The employee should also be a role model in living the IMPACT Group mission, vision and values.

Speaking of Johnson & Johnson, recall that when we left off with this particular story, Gary had bought one thousand of our kits. The problem was the way it was set up; we stored and kept track of their packages, but it was up to Johnson & Johnson to spread the word to their twenty-seven business divisions to tell their people about the product, actually sell it and then fax shipping requests to us. Well, after two years, we hadn't sent out more than two hundred kits, but they were relocating a thousand people. I became frustrated because they were stalled and our products—kits that were designed to help all those relocating employees and their families—were not getting into the very hands that needed them most. I knew exactly who to call.

I had built a relationship with Ruth Davis, manager of a division of Johnson & Johnson, early on. Ruth is very soft-spoken, kind, insightful and known by many for her listening skills. I went to Ruth's office and unleashed my frustrations on the poor sweet woman.

"Ruth, I can't seem to motivate your Relocation Managers to use our products! I'm so frustrated because I work so hard. I try calling them, meeting with them; this one is difficult, that one will never see me ...."

And all of a sudden, I did something I haven't done since. Right there on the spot, I started sobbing. The whole experience was just so mentally draining for me that I'd tumbled down an emotional rabbit hole. I continued on through my tears as Ruth gently handed me tissues across the desk with a reassuring smile.

"Ruth, I don't know if I can keep doing this. It takes so much of my time trying to get your people to cooperate with the vision Gary, Joe and Mike had for using our family services."

She looked at me, and then said in her soft-spoken voice, "Laura, I know it's been very hard on you, but trust me, just give me about two or three months and I will help you take care of it."

Still dabbing at my nose, I told her *okay*, and put my trust in her.

One month later, Johnson & Johnson announced that their relocation division was going to consolidate their twenty-seven divisions into one central relocation center, and that Ruth Davis would be the head of the center. From that day forward, Ruth made sure we got one hundred percent of the people moving with them. She started getting people to use our kits and, although it still took another year or two to get them all out of the basement and shipped to people who needed them, Ruth made sure the job got done. To this day, we are more than just a strategic partner; we are a part of their culture. They won't move an employee without us. Many of their transferees have moved twelve times with us and request their same relocation counselor, by name, each time—a true testimony to "clients for life" throughout our organization. Everyone who touches your clients is responsible for nurturing those relationships and thus has a role in keeping those clients for life.

Now, like any other special relationship, my bond with Ruth works in both directions. One day, years later, I was giving a speech out in San Francisco when I received word that Ruth's husband, who had been suffering from emphysema, had died. I got all the information from my secretary and immediately took a nonstop red eye to New Jersey, rented a car, and drove three hours Southwest of Newark to be with Ruth. I arrived just in time for the last viewing and embraced and cried with Ruth. She later told me that I was one of a few out of all the vendors who made that type of herculean effort. So much more than being a client for life: Without a thought to her being a client, I left San Francisco to be with my friend who just lost her husband, an act that sealed our friendship for life.

Recently, when Ruth learned that my breast cancer had returned, she immediately started leaving me voicemail messages. In the last one, she let me know that she planned on coming out to our house and helping Mike and me.

"You just have to call me and tell me when to be there and I will be there to do the cooking and whatever you need to get through this," she continued.

These are the kinds of things you don't read about in sales and business books, the kinds of situations that reveal a person's values. The sales books tell you to look at the walls and make observations about the client's pictures, see what they're interested in, and ask about their kids. But that's not how you create clients for life. You genuinely have to show up and be present and care about what's important to them. Nine times out of ten, it's about making them successful at their job. Another time, it just may be about their life outside of the job.

By the way, Ruth is an avid volunteer. She always has been. When Hurricane Sandy came, she was down at the Jersey shore helping every weekend for a full year to rebuild those communities. Her love and dedication to people is one of the reasons why, when Ruth retired several years ago, we named our Employee of the Year Volunteer Award "The Ruth Davis Volunteer Award." Their names are printed on a plaque that bears her name, and she always wants a picture of them so she can send her congratulations. She feels honored, and we feel blessed. It is an alignment of values that truly makes clients for life.

> *"Laura always listened. She made regular visits out to us (Johnson & Johnson), even during hefty snowstorms where I had to drive her back and forth from her hotel. We'd sit there and talk about how the program could be improved. She listened, then took the information back and hit the ground running with it. That was the key; she knew that she would get back (to IMPACT Group), work every avenue and use every resource she had to develop a program the corporations wanted. It wouldn't be sitting and talking about the same problems during every visit—she would actually do something about it. You need to be able to have an open relationship like this with service partners, with open lines of communication. That's what we had with Laura and IMPACT Group."*
>
> —**Ruth Davis**, Johnson & Johnson (retired)

What Goes Around Comes Around

Recall earlier in this chapter how we talked about the vulnerabilities that can occur when companies merge, especially some of the largest companies in the world. Here are three examples of how, under her leadership as the CEO of IMPACT Group, Lauren has managed to capitalize on some of those mergers, turning potential vulnerability into opportunity.

When I brought Olivia Holt and Pepsi on board with IMPACT Group years ago, they were Pepsi Bottling Group, which was a separate entity from PepsiCo (the global conglomerate). We had a very strong relationship with the former, but in 2010, PepsiCo bought back Pepsi Bottling Group. At the time, we did not have a relationship with PepsiCo. For years, I had been trying to get PepsiCo as a client and then Lauren, very wisely, used the merger as the perfect opportunity to begin working with the larger organization as one of multiple providers. It took some time and finesse on Lauren's part, as well as some great relationship building by others in the organization, but I'm proud to say that as of this writing, we are now a sole provider for PepsiCo, both domestic and global.

"This just goes to show how you can take advantage of opportunities to grow. You might get an opportunity to meet with one business unit or one particular population, which is a great time to look at how you can build on that relationship, demonstrate value, and go from there to move it forward to something even bigger," Lauren adds.

I will let Lauren share another tale of ups and downs:

"We had a Fortune 500 client in the telecommunications industry that recently went through a lot of consolidation. We managed the outplacement for one of their divisions, and one of our competitors was working with another division. The company decided to merge HR for the two sides of the house, and the other division (the more politically powerful division) decided to move forward with their vendor for the entire company. We didn't have a relationship with the other decision maker, and in the end, we lost the business, which was a big hit since that was a significant account for us. It wasn't that we weren't trying the whole time to meet other key decision makers or that we were falling short on the business we had, but rather we just didn't push hard enough or pull the right levers to get the right connections in place.

"I look back on that and say, 'How could we not have better relationships for one of our biggest accounts?' We knew we were doing a great job managing the relationships we did have as well as the service delivery, but we should have continued pushing ourselves for more. I will say this: Once we got the news that we were going to lose the business, I took it upon myself personally to figure out how I could leverage some of my networking and other professional contacts to get back in front of executives at the absolute highest levels. I was able to parlay some of those relationships into appointments with high-level leaders who connected me with the VP of talent management and her direct reports, who brought us full circle back to providing leadership training for the managers of their high potentials. We're not replacing the full value of the original business yet, but I am thrilled that this long-term partner is working with us on a critical talent development need that has tremendous potential to help their business, and for us to grow with them."

"These are such wonderful examples of how you're not always going to be able to get everything you want all the time, but you can always be looking at opportunities to grow and leverage opportunities in the future. It may not be about literally keeping clients for life, but you do keep them in your crosshairs for life."

—Lauren Herring

I applaud Lauren for what she has done with PepsiCo and this Fortune 500 telecommunications client; I tried for twenty years to make some of the changes she has made, just by being persistent. She'll say it's all in the timing. Sometimes I got frustrated after five years of trying and I'd put my sights on something else. Lauren has really kept her eye on the target and been absolutely focused on landing some of these major prospects and getting back other clients we've had over the years. It's about keeping these clients in your sights as well as your peripheral vision, and making sure they don't forget about you.

In Conclusion

I will say unequivocally that once you have a client, do everything in your power to make them a client for life. Respect who they are as people and as an organization, which sometimes changes leadership or ownership, and focuses more on the bottom line than on people. Nonetheless, include them in all your communication updates, newsletters and personal contacts, letting them know how much you value them and what you are doing to improve systems, processes and quality.

We can't always have clients as best friends. One of my current best friends (who was CAO of a huge global company) one day said to me,

"Laura, will you have someone else call on me from IMPACT Group? I'd rather be your friend than your client." That doesn't always happen. Clients just don't say, "I want to be your friend," but you need to treat them with the same care and concern as you do your friends. Treating them with warmth and genuineness that invites a mutual respect and a sense of appreciation builds the relationship. (We are still dear friends today and our husbands are best friends.)

I don't take my friends for granted and I don't take my clients for granted. The bottom line is: If you operate from your sense of purpose, if you do so with passion and if your approach is honest, integrity-filled and heartfelt, people will feel it, embrace it and value it. Thus they feel your passion, embrace your positive intentions and purpose, and value you for bringing your product to them. Not all of them will link arms and sing Kumbaya, but they will respect you for who you are and how you conduct business.

One woman, who did business with my competitor, told me to stop calling her. So I did. Five years later we met at an industry function and she said, "Laura, I really respect you. I told you not to call me and you haven't for five years. Give me a call; I'd like to get caught up." Right before this woman retired, she called Lauren in and gave her all her global business, as our services had grown globally and our competitor's did not. So, respecting boundaries is critical to creating clients for life.

An interesting anecdote is that I teach all my account managers how to respect and serve their accounts so they will have them for life. Unfortunately, when I let go an account manager for lack of professional decorum (that the client never saw or experienced), the same client was upset with me and pulled the account. Why? Because he really liked his account manager and felt I had been unfair. He went with our competitor. I never did tell him the reason I let the account manager go. We eventually got that client back and I have never told him why we released his former account manager. Some things need to have boundaries, and I did not feel it appropriate (or legal) to disclose the grounds for termination. You need to always maintain your integrity even when others lose theirs.

⸺ LESSONS LEARNED ⸺

1. Clients are never really clients for life.
There are bidding processes and procurement protocols; treat them as if they will be clients for life, do everything you can to respect their boundaries and invite then into yours, and there is always a possibility of keeping them forever. Be patient. Be grateful.

2. Don't ever assume clients are yours, even with friends.
Their bosses have relationships, mergers and acquisitions happen, and people leave organizations. So make relationships with all those involved with the purchasing decision of your products. You must always give these relationships what they need to be successful in their role, in order for them to value you and your product. Provide value and demonstrate how you are going to be a true strategic partner who will help them achieve their strategic goals.

3. You are only as good as your entire company!
Just because you have a relationship with the buyer or client, don't assume it will trump bad service. Make sure your entire company knows the goals of each client, their purpose and their passion. They must deliver the same purpose and passion in each role within the company. Train for it, model it and hold them accountable for it. Clients feel it.

4. Manage expectations of your clients.
Tell them what to expect if there are going to be some bumps in the road. From the start, tell them to expect some startup or implementation hiccups. Explain what they typically are, and what you like to do to prevent them. For example, our services are initiated through third-party relocation management companies. If our experience is that these third parties need training in how to do that, we offer to do it up front. The client is then alerted as how well the third party is managing the process. Clients love for us to manage their employees' expectations. They appreciate knowing what to expect so they are not caught off guard.

5. Exercise patience and gratitude.

We were also a long-term vendor for a major oil company. As an established vendor, you always operate from the goal of creating clients for life, so you learn to quickly adjust to any changes made within your clients' organizations; it's par for the course. This also frequently means competing with other vendors providing the same services.

Showing great perseverance, Lauren stayed in touch with all of this oil company's many managers over the years, building relationship after relationship and finally, through strong account management, IMPACT became the sole provider of spouse-and-family transition services for them. Did I mention that patience and gratitude are important? Never give up and never whine. The moral of this story (similar to Pepsi) is that there is no "special sauce" involved. It's all about being persistent, spotting the opportunity and then pushing it. Show up, and be caring and helpful. That is how you create clients for life.

Chapter 12

LOVE & LEGACY

So many successful companies are powered by a close-knit family of co-workers, each with their own unique skill set, coming together to help grow the business and make a difference in the lives of others. In the case of IMPACT Group, that metaphorical work family revolved around a real family: ours—the Herrings.

As a family, my husband Mike, our daughter Lauren and I have come together, each playing various roles in the company through the years, and doing what was needed to feed this entity more powerful than any one of us individually.

We've had fun doing it, too. Mike has labeled us with different personalities and animal personas: He labeled me a thoroughbred, based on his theory to "just let her run the race and she will win." He sees himself as a workhorse: "just hitch me up and I'll do whatever you want me to." Lauren was more difficult to identify, even though she told us when she was three that she wanted to be a pony when she grew up. In the end, we see her as more of an Arabian horse, the one who has incredible stamina over long distances and can outrun the competition. It seems fitting since she has run in several triathlons. Knowing what strengths we each have is critical to the success of the business and critical to determining the best roles for each of us to take on.

That said, being a family-run business has its own dynamic and its own unique set of opportunities and challenges. When your company co-workers are also your colleagues in life, the concept of work-life balance is suddenly redefined. But just like anything else in business and in life, you find a way to make it work.

One of the most important decisions Mike and I made together early on in the business was that I would always have the final say in any major decision, after taking all opinions into account. You can't have everyone serving many masters. The other decision I made—this one on my own—was there can only be one head of the household. I felt strongly that, while we were a team, he would have final say over our home. Not that we didn't collaborate, but his opinion would be preeminent. So when I walked in the door at night, I literally closed my eyes, shook off my work day and whatever may have happened, and said to myself, "I am now a wife and mother."

Does my view on this sound like it goes against the laws of feminism as we know them? I don't believe it does, especially knowing that each of us has to do what works for our own unique life. I could not be CEO at the office and CEO at home. It would not work for any of us, especially Mike, who has strong feelings about maintaining a home and being a strong family unit. He had to be boss somewhere and, although I do not believe he was conscious of my internal decision, he was aware of making the home and financial decisions because he was better at those than I am, period. Find your own rhythm, whatever works for you, but realize there can only be one CEO in any organization, work or home.

We are just one of many family-run businesses out there, past and present. There are many much larger than us, like our client Johnson & Johnson once was. America is also blessed with many smaller family-run businesses that add flavor to our streets and towns; you can probably think of a few where you live.

Each one, in its own special way, leaves its own mark on the business landscape while creating a legacy that lives on in future family members.

What is fun for me is to look back on the many roles Mike, Lauren and I have played in this wonderful company called IMPACT Group. This is our behind-the-scenes story, with all its candid moments, family secrets, and many times, even comedies.

The Good Humor Man

Every other Friday in the office, all of our employees at headquarters in St. Louis enjoyed a very special treat. A man who came to be known as the "good humor man" would wheel a cart around with gallons of ice cream and every imaginable topping, from chocolate syrup and whipped cream to sprinkles and cherries, and fresh fruit for our health-conscious people. We liked to think that this man was serving more than ice cream: He was serving happiness for the bargain price of about $10 in supplies from Sam's Club. That man also happened to be one of the company owners: Mike Herring. Everyone loved Mike, not just on those Fridays, but every day. He was their go-to guy.

Just like hiring the right person is so important, so is marrying the right person. And boy did I nail it when I married Mike. Back to the company's earliest days, he had a knack for knowing what needed to be done and then going the extra mile to do it.

There was the time when he spent ten hours at Kinko's, stretching until 2:00 a.m., to meticulously copy those original one hundred and twenty-page *Momentum* booklets, making sure that details like the binding and glossy covers were done right, and that the pages were in the right order to show it at a trade show, because our new order did not show up in time. To this day, even after all the challenges we've faced together in the company, he says that this was one of the hardest things he ever did for IMPACT Group.

Mike knew that this company was my passion and supported it in any way possible to make us (the company and our family) successful. There was no "my wife's business." Perhaps it was the lesson he learned back in the seminary: "Die unto self so that others may live." Here's how Mike describes it:

"I always felt it was my responsibility and job to support Laura in the office in any way, shape or form, as well as at home. We always knew, and reminded each other, that we're on the same team. In business this is non-negotiable, because in many cases you are putting family resources at risk, committing to hours well beyond nine-to-five, and being 'on call' during vacations and what would normally be off time for other people. The spouse of a business owner has to be a good representative and partner—a person who knows we're on the same team, we just have different roles. Even if you don't own the company together, you have to have a spouse that sees your company as an extension of you. They need to respect it and support it, and love it as you do."

In a business marriage, it's not a question of if or how one spouse will put their ego aside for the good of the business—you just do. Hierarchy within the organization and decision-making power is discussed and agreed upon before it becomes an issue. It's critical to make decision-making a non-issue.

For example, Mike's innate humility and willingness to put his own needs aside to service my dreams and the company's needs was just as valuable, if not more, than the $7,000 from his retirement fund that he initially invested in IMPACT Group. Some men in this scenario might be called "the man behind the woman." I call him the man behind the dream.

I like to say that, while I had the sales and business acumen, Mike had the human acumen. His philosophy was to be present as much as possible around the office so people would see that management was there, listening to their concerns and valuing their contributions. And, by the way, if you're picturing a man in a suit and smile strolling through the office like a king in his castle, I have a reality check for you; that is not how Mike showed he cared. Instead, he was the guy crawling under a desk that was falling apart, drill gun in hand, to fix the problem. He was the one making sure that an employee's desk was at the right height so they weren't at risk of developing carpal tunnel syndrome in their hands and wrists from repetitive motions such as typing. He was the guy on his hands and knees in the bathrooms unclogging toilets, cleaning up the kitchen and doing whatever else needed to be done so everyone could do their own jobs.

We both knew that all our people valued the fact that one of the owners was willing to get their hands dirty to do what needed to be done.

Even when Mike rolled his sleeves down and became more of an operations manager, he was still handling all the internal company issues that made IMPACT Group tick, such as programming technology, hiring and motivating people while I was on the outside, and growing the company through travel, conventions, sales meetings and client visits. So on a day when I was at the top of the Met Life building in New York City, working to close contracts, it was conceivable that Mike was back in the office trying to cut us the best deals possible on insurance or copy machines. He was keeping the ship running straight so that we could deliver on the things that were being sold. Like I said: In business, especially a family business, there is no ego. You do what is needed to grow the company.

He was also extremely committed to learning whatever it was that he didn't know, especially if it meant saving the company money. One time in our very early days at the company, I remember finding him holed up with a computer book every night for a month. It turned out he was learning about a computer system that he could operate and update himself, so we wouldn't have to pay a computer technician $50 to $100 per visit. Whether it was finding ways to cut costs, or keeping up with the latest technology, he was always learning what was needed to support the company's growth.

In Good Times and Bad

You probably recall from earlier in the book some of the more dramatic stories that played out during the early years of IMPACT Group: losing the McDonnell Douglas deal, then the van lines, later IBM, and the list goes on. As you have read, there's no such thing as a "drama-free" business, and in a family business that means your loved ones are on board the roller coaster with you, whether they like it or not.

To say our IMPACT ride was a bumpy one is an understatement. The highs and lows were something I truly wasn't prepared for when I started the business. I naively thought that when you sign a customer, you service them perfectly and you keep them for life. Silly me. So the ups and downs were, at first, surprising. Then I said, "Oh, this is how business works!"

Where I am most fortunate is that Mike held my hand during the ups and downs that made the roller coaster ride of success for IMPACT Group an exciting one, rather than a terrifying one. He not only held my hand, but he had my back.

You've heard those stories from my point of view: the sheer panic, my heart and stomach dropping to my feet, the fear that each shot at success would be my last, and always, always thinking about how my decisions would affect Mike and our family. Fortunately for all of us, Mike's perspective on these life-and-death situations was decidedly more level headed. Here's how he views the 25-year roller coaster ride of IMPACT Group:

From the Desk of Mike Herring

In corporate America and in our industry, there are people who we refer to as "high pots," or high-potential people. This is that rare group of individuals, possibly only two, three or four percent of the population, that just shines. When corporations find these people, they do whatever it takes to develop and keep them (in fact, they hire firms like ours to coach them and help them become all they are possible of becoming). These companies know that it is the high pots who will take flight in everything they do, and move the organization as a result. When I found my own high pot, I married her.

Here's an example that really shows what a high pot Laura has always been. I was in a meeting one time with her and she was selling as usual, but the guy wouldn't budge. But Laura being Laura, she's absolutely charming and refused to take no for an answer. She casually, softly said to this man, "I know you're saying no now, but if you didn't say *no*, what would you say?" The guy just sat there, kind of baffled at this powerhouse of a woman in front of him. He finally answered, "Well, I would say *yes*." And Laura said, "Now that sounds better. Let's go from there." High pots.

If Laura was the goose laying the golden eggs, than I was the goose keeper. I recognized from the get-go that she was brighter and more talented than me, so I acted accordingly, making the choice to support her in every way possible.

So when it came to the issue of Laura's path to success, road bumps and obstacles included, I had a slightly different take on the "bad stuff" than she did. You see, my father, when he retired, had a twelve hundred-square-foot house in Memphis, Tennessee, in a pretty crummy neighborhood. He was happy as could be there because he had enough. I've always said there are two ways to be wealthy: one is to make more money; the other is to want less. My father took the path of wanting less, and so he had never taken a chance in his life. He had a nice retirement from his company and was content having everything he felt he needed. So my position was always, "If worse comes to worse and Laura and I end up in a twelve hundred-square-foot house, happy with each other and doing what we want to do, so be it." Therefore, when we took these risks, like all the ones Laura has talked about in this book and more, I didn't really see them as risks. They were things we were going to have to do to get the company off the ground, and they would require spending money. I knew that from day one. I never saw any of it as a "sure thing"—far from it. But at the end of the day, no matter how things panned out, I knew we were going to be together and we'd have a great relationship with each other. We knew we had enough skills and abilities to make money and get by, so whether we were going to be tremendously successful or make a mistake and lose everything we had, I never saw it as, "Oh my God, oh my God, what's going to happen?" I didn't ever feel that I was behind the eight ball or that we were doing these incredibly dangerous things that were putting our family at risk. It was just, "take a chance and go for it".

So, earlier in this book, you heard these stories where Laura was feeling that the sky was falling and saying, "How am I going to tell Mike?" I think of it differently. It's like the teenager who has a car wreck and panics about having to tell his parents. "Oh boy, I'm going to get home and my dad's going to kill me." And then the kid gets home and dad's first question is, "First of all, are you okay?" "Yeah dad, I'm okay." "Good." Once we establish that everyone's okay and there's no bodily harm, the pressure is lifted from the situation. Sure, they'd rather come home with a straight-A report card than a wrecked car, but that's just part of life and it's also part of business, especially in a family business where outcomes reflect more than a paycheck. If business were easy, everybody and every business would be plugging along successfully, without any issues. At the end of the day, no matter how big the crisis, I would always ask Laura the same question: "If we lose this business and have to close the doors, will we still be together?" And of course, she'd always say, "Yes," and I'd respond, "Okay, then we're good."

Any problems we had early on in our marriage (and who hasn't had them?), we resolved early and then made a commitment to be together always. So we kept marching on, hand in hand, together.

There is also the fact that, in Laura's case, she was talking about a level in business that few people ever experience—let alone have the opportunity to panic about. Just the fact that she was dealing with a company like McDonnell Douglas was pretty darn impressive to me. The deal falling through at the last minute was almost an afterthought. I was just so proud of her for taking it that far in the first place.

I remember one time when we got IBM as a client, and Laura's mother was just incredulous. She asked us, "How did you get IBM as a client?" It was one of the largest corporations in the world, so most people wonder where you even start to make that happen. The answer Laura gave to her mom was, "One telephone call at a time."

So in the midst of the challenging times, you just have to remember that success is around the corner, and every building has numerous corners. You just keep turning, keep walking, keep going after it and, sooner or later, good things happen.

We could say we're lucky, but luck often happens to people who work a lot harder than the next person. I've said before that everyone—every single person out there—has a million-dollar idea. Only millionaires actually follow through with them. It really does take work. Someone once said to us, "Gosh, I wish I had my own company so I could take off whenever I felt like it." As if we took off all the time—what a thought! The thing that people don't see about having your own business is all the behind-the-scenes work that goes into it. We rarely took time off in the beginning. We had to be there almost every second for the first fifteen years. Even when we were away on vacation, visiting family, or whatever, we were always working. With connectivity nowadays, it's even more so. There were calls back and forth to the office, emergencies to be dealt with, urgent faxes and other things that come with the job. Lauren can attest to this, having grown up hearing us constantly "talk shop" at the dinner table, in the car, in the living room watching movies and everywhere else. Once you start your own company, it is a twenty-four-hour-a-day deal. There's the importance that Laura has talked about throughout this book, of making sure that everything she was doing comes from a passion and purpose to make a difference in the lives of others. Without those powerful driving forces, I would imagine that the amount of work required in relation to the outcome might not be worth the struggle. Other people have driving passions, but they are not always about making a difference. The key is to be passionate and follow through. We were fortunate to share the same values and to want to make a positive difference in this world. That is the success of our relationship, and that is the success of IMPACT Group.

—**Mike Herring**

Now do you see why I am crazy about him? He gives me all the credit. Not so, Mike Herring!

The Company Mom and Dad

As owners of the company and providers of paychecks, Mike and I were more than a little aware that our employees looked to us as a barometer of how well the company was doing. At home early on, we had one dependent (Lauren), but as soon as we walked through the doors at IMPACT Group, that number grew to over one hundred, and eventually three hundred. And boy, were they all aware of everything that went on between Mike and me.

We made it a pact that we would never argue or disagree in front of the staff. From our early days with a staff of three, we knew that if we argued in front of our employees, productivity would take a nosedive as word would quickly be whispered throughout the entire organization—from the water coolers to the kitchen, to the bathrooms to the parking lot.

"Mike and Laura are arguing? Do you think they're going to get a divorce? If they get a divorce it may mean they have to close the business. Oh my God, I'm going to lose my job. Maybe I should start looking for a new job!"

This is the kind of thing that gets carried on in a family-run organization, simply because everyone is dependent upon us to pay their home loans, their car notes and everything else. We realized early on, through trial and error sometimes, that we had to put on a brave face as Laura and Mike, company owners (versus Laura and Mike, the married couple), even when we didn't feel like it. Therefore, we never argued in front of the staff or Lauren.

What we did and how we acted was reflected back to us through our employees like a giant, freshly cleaned mirror. If we gave one hundred percent, they would say to themselves, "Well, Mike and Laura are giving one hundred percent, so I should be giving more, too." This also applies to the flipside. Just like when parents at home are fighting, the energy rubs off on the kids who immediately become rambunctious and start acting out. The same is true at the office. If we're complaining, it promotes complaining at the office. If we're down on each other, our employees are given permission to do the same. It's crucial to remember that you're always being watched.

When we treated each other with respect and avoided name-calling or yelling, there would be a trickle-down effect; the attitude became that we're all in this together and on the same team. This reminds me of a funny "employees are always watching and guessing" story.

One time I was rushing out the door, and the wind caught it and it slammed shut. *Bam!* People in the office immediately got very concerned and the whispers started buzzing: "What's she mad at? Oh my God, she just slammed the door! She never slams the door. Did I do something wrong? Is someone going to get fired? What's going to happen to us?" Mike had to calm them down and say, "Look, it's windy out, the wind slammed the door! She is late and rushing. End of story." They are always watching you. It's nice to have someone have your back—if not a husband, then a manager or assistant. You need someone to interpret and manage the small things so they don't get to be big distractions.

This is a great lesson: If you want productivity within the organization, you want people to treat each other with respect, you want people working on your business versus obsessing about what's happening with the bosses, and you have to realize that you're constantly communicating your feelings and emotions policy through all your words and actions—at all times.

Born into It

Meanwhile, our daughter Lauren Herring has had her own unique journey through the pages of the IMPACT Group story—starting as a curious observer of our family-run business from her seat at the kitchen table, all the way to the executive suite where she is now CEO.

Lauren was ten years old when we started the company. From the standpoint of the family tree, Lauren is an only child. From the standpoint of the family company, however, Lauren likes to say, "I wasn't an only child. I had a little sister and her name was IMPACT."

In retrospect, this is true. As you might expect, almost every aspect of IMPACT Group managed to work its way into Lauren's life. Even with the initial *Momentum* product, our daughter was one of our first employees, sitting with me at the kitchen table, helping mom collate, hole-punch, bind and ship relocation kits. Then, as we grew, Lauren was the first to feel the effects. For instance, she'd come home from school, backpack loaded with homework, only to find that she no longer had a desk to work on. "Let me guess," she'd say, "you hired a new employee and needed a desk."

This was just one of many insightful observations Lauren made through the years. She also quickly got an idea of who did what in the company, telling one of her teachers as a little kid that she wanted to be Vice President of IMPACT Group someday. "Why VP?" her teacher asked. "Well, my mom is the President and she brings work home, and my dad is a VP and he doesn't bring work home." It would be unrealistic to think that a child growing up in a family business wouldn't notice most everything.

Even in the middle of it all, however, I was careful never to forget for a minute that in addition to being President, I was also mom. There were times when I would go home from the office at 2:30 p.m. just so I could meet Lauren's school bus, have a snack with her and talk about her day. But around 4:00 p.m., I'd go back to work again when Mike got home. As it turns out, Lauren had a slightly different point of view about our mother-daughter quality time.

"When I would come home, honestly I just wanted to watch cartoons but Mom wanted to talk about my day instead," she says.

So much for good parenting intentions. In all seriousness, though, Lauren was the furthest thing from a demanding child. Even at a young age she seemed to have a very grown-up understanding of the dynamic we developed between home and work, and our own unique mother-daughter balance. In retrospect, that perspective grows even wiser.

"I think I got plenty of time with my mom, despite her busy schedule. When I was in high school, for instance, my mom made the conscious decision to travel less and be home more. So yes, in a sense, she probably could have grown the company so much more, but that wasn't her choice. I know today, possibly more than ever, there are a lot of conversations about balancing motherhood and work. I get that question a lot too, especially as the child of a female entrepreneur. All I can speak to is my own experience, in which I felt I was still a priority for her, despite her bringing work home or her travel schedule. As an ambitious woman myself, I appreciate the role model she provided for me," Lauren says.

Now, just like I gave Mike the floor earlier, I'll let Lauren tell the story of how she made the eventual choice to join the family business.

Rising to the Occasion

When I first came to work at IMPACT Group, in August 2001, it was supposed to be temporary. Mom had just been diagnosed with breast cancer and I wanted to be close to her to help, so I decided to put my personal career plans on hold and stay home to be with family and help out at the company. This was a very simple decision. Working in the company felt completely natural to me, especially after all those years watching it grow. I realized immediately that I had certain information about the company that the other employees didn't have; I also had a deep understanding of who we were and what we did—the purpose and passion pieces my mom talks about. Nevertheless, the plan was to help out with a number of projects with our relocation management partners on a temporary basis while mom received her treatments. But by October, I decided to stay.

Prior to that, I had a definite "grass is greener" syndrome when it came to my future. I had grown up in St. Louis while being aware of IMPACT Group, but not having any personal aspirations around it. I wanted to make my own mark in my own way, and I envisioned living the hipster life in some exciting city like San Francisco or Dallas. When I made the decision to accept a permanent position with IMAPACT Group, I realized that all those other cities were only a plane ride away, so I wasn't really sacrificing as much as I initially thought.

By 2007, after I'd settled in, mom and dad started having conversations about what would happen to the company long-term. I was about twenty-eight at the time, and not feeling extremely confident about taking on the CEO role; even putting the words "CEO" and "Lauren" in the same sentence just felt very unnatural to me. For one thing, I have always looked very young (and I was young), and I struggled with other people's perceptions of me. How would people take me seriously as the CEO of this big company? Mom went gray prematurely and, on some level, I was hoping that I would follow suit, just for that extra bit of gravitas. It was only after I started getting those gray hairs that I realized I was vainer than I thought. And, in the process, I learned that gravitas has nothing to do with gray hairs. It's something that comes from within. It has to do with how you carry yourself and how you think of yourself. I may have grown up in the company, but I knew I still had to prove myself, which I felt I did, and I ultimately decided that I wanted to own this opportunity.

—Lauren Herring

Mike and I can vouch for the fact that Lauren never had anything handed to her. We brought her in as an entry-level employee at an entry-level salary, and she worked extremely hard to learn the ropes and rise through the ranks on her own merit, not her bloodline. She seemed more and more to be a product of Mike's humility and willingness to set his ego aside to do what needed to be done, along with my drive to sell, sell, sell.

Starting as an account manager and learning the ropes from IMPACT greats like Sherry Heffington, Lauren then took on an operational leadership role as a manager in our research department, followed by marketing manager and eventually Director of International Development. That led to the company's first big push to expanding into international business. Once Lauren led the charge, breaking down global walls with lots of international growth opportunities, the sky was truly the limit. She made the choice to do something I (essentially a self-made entrepreneur) had never accomplished: Lauren got her MBA. She made this decision as a way of broadening her horizons as well as expanding her opportunities outside the walls of IMPACT Group to grow and develop her skills. From a personal standpoint, I understand that there was also a little bit of a validation issue.

"I knew that with the MBA I would have the opportunity to learn from resources outside the company. This was important to me since I wanted to learn and grow from experts, which can sometimes be hard to find in a small-company environment. It was also a kind of external stamp of approval that I felt was helpful given my age," Lauren says.

And in the middle of it all, while finishing up her MBA and rising through the ranks, Lauren also played a major leadership role in the Spherion acquisition that you read about earlier in the book. This was no small feat for an up-and-coming CEO to take on the integration, with all its complexities, that doubled the size of the organization.

Legacy

Obviously, when company leadership changes hands, changes will be made. And when the handoff of the CEO position is from mother to daughter, the plotline has its own unique nuances.

There are new people. After the plane scare, we empowered Lauren to put her own team in place. Max Barnett, Martin Meador, Brook Grokowski and Ed Chaffin are now working alongside Lauren toward her long-term goal of $100 million.

There are also new systems and policies. In Lauren's case, one of these was rolling out "all hands" phone calls policy, where she opens up the books to the staff, revealing key financial information. While this is not something I personally would have done, this is one of those moments where I realize that Lauren is now the CEO of IMPACT Group. She has the right to make these decisions, and from her standpoint, this decision is about empowering her people to really dig in and analyze the company's bottom line; more specifically, her employees can see how their individual actions ultimately affect the bottom line. I understand that, and I understand that by handing her the reins I also handed over a lot of leeway to run the company as she sees fit.

Now, here's Lauren beautifully summing up what it meant for her, first to work for, and then take over, the family business:

"I think a lot of second generation leaders in business have to deal with the question, *How am I going to make my mark on the company?* And a lot of people probably don't go into the family business because they want to find their own way; they don't want to just follow in mom or dad's footsteps. I had some of those same, emotional conversations with myself while I was still in college. It wasn't even a thought process. It was more of an assumption: I didn't want to go into the business. I wanted to do my own thing. I wanted to make my own way. I didn't want to be seen as just coming in and taking over the business. Then, during an internship between my junior and senior years, I was talking to a friend about our future plans and she asked me, "So, your family has a family business, right?" I said, "Yes." She said, "So why don't you want to work there?" I told her I wanted to do my own thing, and this friend just looked at me and said, "Wow, if I had a family business to go into, I think I'd just be all over that." I still remember that conversation because it made me think a little bit more seriously about the opportunity, whereas I had always just kind of shut the door before. Why did I really not want to join IMPACT Group?

Then I started having even more conversations with myself, with thoughts like, *Well, if I were to come to IMPACT Group, who says that I won't be able to put my own stamp on it?* I think I had this impression for a long time that if I came here, I would be purely walking in my mom's footsteps; that I would always be in her shadow and ultimately not be able to make my own way. Then a light bulb came on: If companies keep on doing things the way they have always been done, they go out of business. You have to change in order to stay viable. And so, I came to the realization that if I came to IMPACT Group, there's no reason why I wouldn't be able to make it my own. Once I realized that, I came to peace with the opportunity.

—Lauren Herring

IMPACT Group was ultimately built on a foundation of my own purpose and passion for making a difference. Then, through the circle of life, Mike was my humble workhorse, steadfast by my side in a role of service, doing whatever he could to help build my dream into our dream. Then, as the circle continued to revolve, a new person, with her own voice, her own ideas, and her own ambitions started doing things in the company that I'd never imagined possible. And somewhere along the way, that person, our daughter Lauren, found her own unique purpose and passion.

The core values and heart of the company remain the same—to make a difference in the lives of others. Now that you've heard my stories and our stories as a family, it's time to write stories of your own. It's time to architect the foundation of your purpose and passion and put strategies in place to turn them into profits.

And remember: NO FEAR ALLOWED!

—⚬— Lessons Learned —⚬—

1. In any business, but especially a family business, a "tone" of the company is set.

We tried to create the tone that we are all in this together. We are a team. Decide what kind of tone you want to create in your business. Realize that this tone eventually becomes known as the corporate culture. Your company mission, values and policies have to reflect that culture. Be purposeful when creating a corporate culture, as it will infiltrate the very core of your business, all the way down to how you treat your customers.

2. Just because you are a family-owned business does not mean hiring family is your only option.

Not all of your family may want to be in your business. It was easy for us to want Lauren to be a part of our business because she was bright, a hard worker and never took anything for granted. At first, we hoped she would work somewhere else for five to ten years to gain management and leadership experience in a different organization. If children in the family are not capable of learning/

handling the day-to-day tasks required of running or being a part of your family business, let them know early and directly that they do not have what it takes to be a part of the company. Realize, also, that your children may have dreams of their own that don't include being a part of your company. Allow them wings and celebrate their individual choices.

3. As a husband and wife in business, Mike and I learned early on that we needed to make a commitment to each other.

Earlier in our marriage, like in any marriage, we had our ups and downs and periods of dissatisfaction with each other, as all married couples experience. The key to a successful marriage is to get help when you need it. We highly recommend finding a trusted counselor or someone you trust to speak with about your relationship. Fix the problems and move on. Forgive each other for the disappointments and ask how you can keep it from happening again. Then move on. Become a passionate team at home and in business and you will find comfort in realizing you fought for what you ultimately wanted—each other.

4. Always remember: Your employees are watching you.

Act in a way that will garner respect, admiration and gratefulness that they work for you.

CONCLUSION

The feeling of fear is real. How you respond to it is the most important choice you make in business. It can move you forward or stop you dead in your tracks. Which path do you usually take? How is that choice serving you?

Typically, how you respond to it is determined by what you learned early on about yourself or others, and what you believe about the world. Is it friendly or not? Is it safe or not? Will people support you or not? These are belief systems that we internalize very early on in life and which turn into self-talk. You know that voice inside of you, the one that shouts in your ear, either *Go for it!* or *You don't want to go there.* My self-talk tends to say *What can I do?* not *What can't I do?*

Asking myself *What can I do?* automatically feeds my mind with possibilities instead of fear. Somewhere along the way, these three words were planted in my head: "No Fear Allowed!" Keep moving and keep doing. We are taught belief systems early in life, but later on, our point of view becomes our decision. Choosing the mindset of doing versus fearing launches us into a whole new world of possibilities, with an abundance of new and exciting questions to be answered like: *How will I do it? Who will be involved? What will it look like?*

Fear-based Beliefs

I'm not sure what early event triggered this belief in possibilities that has stuck with me, but it has been with me since I was about ten years old. Perhaps the first time I flew to New York by myself to visit my Aunt Marge, who was the first woman Vice President of McCrory's. That eye-opening journey to New York must have been a forever-empowering moment for me—one that somehow conveyed to my unconscious, *Young lady you are going places, you know how to get there, and you know how to create moments that will inspire you forever!*

However, empowered thinking like this doesn't automatically become a shield, keeping out all the arrows. Believe me, lying on the floor of my office crying after that client canceled, wondering out loud "What have I done?" was not a high point. But not for one moment did I regret my decision to take a leap, leave my stable teaching career, and go into private practice for myself. I did not allow fear to seep in—just the opposite. It inspired me to get up and start dialing for dollars, reaching out to even more schools, community centers, churches and other counselors, offering them free speeches, workshops and consultations. That moment of fear moved me into action. So what is similar about these two events? One, when I was ten and the other at twenty-six? I tuned into the belief that I can and must make things happen. And, in challenging times, ask myself what I can do to get a different outcome.

As a psychologist, I saw many clients, families and couples believe that they were helpless, or worse yet, victims of their pain, fear or inertia. A lot of your fears are from the labels you accepted throughout your life. A belief is simply a PFA, a label directed at you that may not be true, but you have chosen to believe as true. Simply put, PFA means "plucked from air." Think about it: As you grow up, people constantly label you. Dad says, "You're lazy," your older sister says, "You're stupid," and then a teacher says, "You're not trying hard enough." Teachers, parents, aunts, uncles, brothers and sisters and even strangers all have and eagerly offer up opinions about us—some positive, some benign and others downright negative. These are labels plucked from what real, trusted people told us. Perhaps they were true or descriptive of you then. But are they truly, accurately defining who you are today? You can either choose to agree, disagree or become confused by these labels, particularly those that you feel don't fit who you feel you really are, or you can allow them to define you. For example, if you were told at six years old that you were clumsy or not pretty or bad at math or disorganized or stupid, those labels started to define you. Every day you have an option to change those beliefs by choosing to act differently and think of yourself differently.

Ask yourself, *Would I allow a six-year-old to manage my checkbook?* Hopefully you said *Absolutely not!* But why, then, would you allow your six-year-old self to run your emotional bank account?

When we are young, most of us do not have a solid enough life experience to firmly disagree or agree with those labels, so we start looking for moments in time in our young life that either confirm or disprove those constant PFA labels heaped upon us. It is important that we ask ourselves who *we* want to be and then take steps throughout our life to become that person—that image of our desired true self. The most important point is to own who you want to become, and then take daily actions that are congruent with becoming that person.

For example, when I moved to Memphis and felt somewhat left out, I decided to be smart instead of popular. It took the hurt away. Even though I was a B student before then, I took college prep classes, studied hard, worked hard, made National Honor Society, won a partial college scholarship and made the *Who's Who* in colleges and universities list (whoswhoamongstudents.com). You are who you decide to become. It is a decision you can make any day of your life. At any time, you can choose to believe: "No Fear Allowed!" Realize that fear is a natural part of life, but it should never be allowed to define you or stop you from becoming the person you want to be.

I have a friend who owns a small business and she said to me, "I'd like to be a CEO of a real company someday."

She thought of herself as a small-business owner—more of a service provider than anything.

Immediately I said, "Call yourself a CEO now; begin acting like a CEO in this moment. Delegate when possible, hire earlier rather than later, set a strategic plan, work the plan, create a relationship with the bank, build your brand now, and grow into it.

She began doing this that very day. Today, there are no networking meetings this lady doesn't attend. Her introductions are now, "I am CEO and Founder of my company," rather than introducing herself as the owner of a little marketing company. You must first know who you want to be and "act as if" you already are that person. That is when you say: "No Fear Allowed!" I know what I want, who I want to be, I know what I need to be, what I need to learn, and what I need to do. Now I just have to dig in and do it!

"No Fear Allowed!" is a belief system that you must have in order to keep moving through life to become the best you possible. The truth is we do not really know fear until someone reacts to us doing something, or someone else is doing something that is labeled dangerous. Fear, often times, is a learned behavior, like "don't cross the road without looking both ways." This is great information, but until you see someone else almost hit by a car you do not actually experience the fear of what might be.

Our bodies have a natural fight or flight response to protect us during times of actual danger. Having this internal trigger that says *You are in danger!* is a valuable indicator for us to react: run, hike, climb a tree, just keep moving and think on our toes.

In business, an angry customer, a lost deal, a blown sale, or a situation can trigger fight or flight response. And when that fight or flight response kicks in, it can absolutely feel life-threatening because our body doesn't know the difference. It doesn't know if we're in the woods being chased by a bear or in the conference room trying desperately to save a client relationship. It takes a strong person to keep moving in the face of fear in business. Fear needs to be quickly turned into a trigger of *What do I need to do here to survive?*

Move into Action

"No Fear Allowed!" means not giving into fear and allowing yourself to stop moving forward. It means thinking through the choices you have in taking action. Let's say sales are down and you can't pay the rent, make payroll or electricity. You first determine how long it will take to stop the downward cycle.

Weeks? Months? Years? What actions can you take now to stop the fear and move to action?

There are many options:

1. Call the landlord, renegotiate the rent and ask for some time to regroup. Meet to discuss options with your landlord rather than suffering in silence, paralyzed by your fear of the unknown.
2. Call current customers and try to sell additional orders; create the sale rather than waiting for it to happen.
3. Work with the utility company to reduce payments.
4. Cut staff hours and don't take your full salary.
5. Borrow money from family or friends with interest.

Whatever you do, don't let fear move you into a state of doing nothing. You must move into action. You must analyze what is working and what isn't. Reach out to people who can help you think through solutions; maybe it's the SBA, your networking group, other business owners, a coach or a mentor. The most important thing is to think it through, create a plan and then act on it.

Don't let fear stop you in your tracks, no matter what life throws at you. Know what your purpose is, what your passion is, and go for it. Do everything you need to do in order to be successful. Embrace your purpose, follow your passion, and your profits will come to you.

Own who you want to become and take daily actions toward that goal. Know what is important to you and keep moving toward your goal. Let "No Fear Allowed!" become your mantra, and you will be successful.

ACKNOWLEDGMENTS

For me, writing this book was an act of love for all those people who helped make IMPACT Group a success. This includes our employees, our corporate clients, those who received our services and everyone who supported us along the way.

It goes without saying that my family of origin—my mom and dad, Rita and Carl House, my brother Doug House, and my sisters Karen McLane, Cheryl Moore and Lisa Malatino—gave me the inspiration to develop a relocation program for families. Our own personal journey is what impacted my heart at age thirteen, and the effect it had on all of us still motivates me to reach out and make a positive difference in our clients' lives.

My parents always taught us, by example, to be the best that we can be and to participate in our community and make a difference. Dad coaching me in sports and my mom's willingness to drive me to all the events in my life allowed me to be me, and made the difference in who I am. The power of a parent to influence your life is so important. They inspired me with both their positive attributes and their flaws to become who I am today, and shaped the kind of parent and leader I wanted to be. For them, I will always be eternally grateful.

One of the first people to hear my dream of helping relocating spouses was my brother-in-law, Chuck Moore. He and I were both idea people. Chuck and

I would often stay up late, coming up with ideas that would keep us excited about our respective companies. I would talk about building a kit with plan books and tapes for the relocating spouse and their families. We would help each other think through specifics of emerging dreams and goals, and create titles for yet unwritten materials, always planning the future. Thanks, Chuck, for encouraging me to be creative and go for it.

Another brother-in-law, Joe Herring, was the businessman in my husband's family. It was at our annual Herring family reunion—fifty-six Herrings strong—at Fall Creek Falls State Park in Tennessee, where I showed Joe my first draft of this idea that was to become IMPACT Group's MOMENTUM Program for the Relocating Spouse and Family. I said, "Joe do you think this could be successful?" He looked through it and said, "Do you?" I said, "Yes, I know there is a definite need." He said, "Then do it!" It is funny how those few moments in time helped to build my confidence that our *Momentum* program for relocating spouses was the right solution at the time. I want to thank them both. It just goes to show how little it takes to motivate people to follow their dreams. It also shows how important it is to surround yourself with positive people. Fortunately, long before Joe died, I told him how his encouragement was so important to me and our success.

A very special thank you goes out to my sister Karen, her husband, John, and their kids Brian, Andy, Matt and Meagan, for inviting me into their home in Muscatine, Iowa, to photographically document their painful twenty-second move. This emotional slideshow became my most important marketing tool when speaking to corporations. Your family's vulnerability touched the hearts of many who, in turn, bought our programs in hopes of addressing these painful, dual-career relocation goodbyes for their employees and colleagues.

My sister Lisa Malatino was an HR Staffing Specialist. Frequently, she became my go-to person to sound out my people issues. Thanks Lisa.

I also want to thank the first employees who believed in our vision and in me. Maureen Kammerer was a McDonnell Douglas spouse who worked day and night to help me finish our prototypes, and whose experience as a relocating spouse was invaluable as we wrote our programs and created a model. Joyce

Edelbrock, who was my first editor and created our first marketing materials, was amazing as she pulled from air design ideas and unique marketing strategies (like copying the ERC's membership book, cutting it up by company, and arranging according to ZIP code). Her thorough efforts enabled me to make the most corporate calls per day per city, by calling on those in the same or nearby ZIP codes. It was Joyce who first closed our big automaker client who, as you read, became our largest client ever.

There were so many good-hearted employees who joined us early on. Joanne Waldman, Debbie Wampler, Lucille Cupples ... and the list goes on of those who were with us very early, each always contributing their very best. I appreciate you all, as well as the hundreds of employees who came throughout the years and built our company as a team with shared values. I thank you for believing in our mission and our vision, "Making a Difference in the Lives We Touch."

Special thanks goes to Linda Ryan, Sherry Heffington, Mae Moore, Virginia Gentry, Barb Daniels, Tanya Fite, Paul Mueller, Tim Martin, Les League, Karen Hasheider, Melanie Winograd, Dan Coffey, Kristi Nygaard, Wendy Frados, Mary McDonald, Margaret Barnhardt, Kathy Johnson, Sheila, Scott, and Linda Costello (my personal assistant). We could not have done it without you.

One of the most important people in this book is Gary Gorran, our first client from Johnson & Johnson. Gary's unwavering faith in our services and me personally has been the cornerstone that became IMPACT Group. Thank you, Gary and Gail (Gary's wife), for your continued friendship and love.

Ruth Davis' unfaltering belief in my mission and vision, and her love and support as the Manager of Relocation at Johnson & Johnson, secured our future and paved the way for other "pharma" companies to follow suit. Ruth, I will always be indebted to you both personally and professionally.

This journey has introduced us to some of my dearest friends and clients. Joe and Pat Morabito, Marge and Gary Fisher, Ed Cohen, Marita Strictland, Jennie Spring and Cheryl Hammonds all provided the support and friendship that is so necessary to strengthen your belief in yourself.

Joe, thank you for believing in IMPACT Group and passing our name along to all your clients. You helped build our early foundation of success. Your continued friendship has allowed our families to grow up together and has given me a dear friend for life: your wife, Pat.

Marge, thank you for offering your home, friendship, support and a bed to sleep in whenever I traveled to the East Coast. Our conversations over wine and dinner during these twenty years have forged a truly special friendship, deeply rooted in mutual passions and respect, not to mention late-night psychotherapy sessions where we changed the world.

Ed, thank you for highlighting me at all your conferences and offering me the spotlight to shine on the needs of relocating families. Also, a big thank you for continuing to support Lauren in your international programs.

Marita, thank you for your continued support of IMPACT Group through thick and thin.

Jennie and Cheryl, I cannot thank you enough for your belief in me, and in IMPACT Group's ability to serve you and your fellow workers through some of the roughest times of their lives. Your trust in the more than three hundred IMPACT Group employees who served more than forty thousand of your colleagues will never be forgotten. Because of you, we have set up a foundation that serves Variety, the Children's charity that provides services and equipment to serve the needs of disabled children; Siteman Cancer Center in St. Louis and its breast cancer research; college education scholarships; and numerous social and business educational programs for women and children.

There are many other good relocation friends and partners who believed in our quality services throughout the years, and who made sure we were in the RFPs and on the speaker's platform—to you I am also grateful. Relocation management companies such as RRI, Sirva, Brookfield Relocation, Altair, Weichert Relocation, MI Group, Pinnacle, Primacy, Cartus and Graebel. We truly appreciate the trust you continue to place in us.

Elke and Paul Koch, dear friends of thirty-five years who saw me unravel due to fatigue created by the stress of growing a global company and dealing with cancer at the same time, thank you for swooping me up and taking me to The Sanctuary in Arizona for a four-day, much-needed spa vacation. I will never forget that feeling of being loved and cared for by people who had nothing to gain, but just loved me. Your continued support and kindnesses are treasured.

And to Kathy Flora, who has come back into my life several times, who has weathered both business and breast cancer setbacks, but who always emerges positive and supportive. Kathy, you reaching out to me and encouraging me to go for the telephone support outplacement program will never be forgotten. Recommending us to Spherion to purchase their Human Resources consulting division, which added $12 million to our revenue and more than one hundred corporations to our client list, will always remain a highlight of my career with IMPACT and my friendship with you.

And then there were friends I met along the way who will continue to be a part of my life. Starting as a client with Peabody Energy and now a friend for life, Sharon Fiehler and husband, Dale, continue to play a major role in our lives sharing families and homes.

Kathy Cramer, author and psychologist, and her husband, John Davis, are the two most positive influences in our lives and have become supporters of my writing and my purpose and passion.

Lisa and Greg Boyce, book club co-founder and neighbors, add grace notes to our lives and continue to be a very special part of our support system.

Karen Hoffman, who nominated me to the RCGA, helped propel my visibility to the leadership in St. Louis and whose positive, loving energy has culminated in her non-profit, Gateway to Dreams, is the epitome of total loving, positive support and giving.

Gen. John and Mickey Handy, for your belief in my vision for military spouses, and for your loving friendship over the years, I thank you.

To Linda Rothleder, thank you for coaching me as to the ins and outs of the military family center powers that be.

To Mike Washbourn for giving me a second shot at Pfizer.

To Carolyn Parrot and Pam Growsiki for their leadership during the Spherion acquisition, and for taking such good care of the Spherion employees who have become our trusted and valued IMPACT Group colleagues.

And my good friend, Karen Kotner, who played a dramatic role in our major auto manufacturer's downsizing by bringing Linda Wessel into our organization and putting together the most comprehensive project management plan, the likes of which I had never seen.

Allen Hauge, Chair of Vistage 175, and all my Vistage friends who walked the journey with me and supported me every step of the way. Allen, thank you for chasing me down and convincing me to become part of the Vistage family.

To Joanne Griffin, who nominated me for The Committee of 200's Protégé Program, which inspired me to strive to grow to be a $20 million company so I could join this prestigious organization. To this day, I am blessed to call members of this wonderful organization—Kathryn Swintek, Larraine Segil, Mindy Meads, Roberta Sydney and Laurie Ann Goldman—dear friends whom I treasure and who nurture and support me. And of course, Lauren in building IMPACT and in nurturing me on my personal health journey.

I also owe a debt of gratitude to Nancy Baumann, The Book Professor, CEO of Book Karma and a good friend, for encouraging me to complete my book and tell my story. She helped me envision the opening scene and we went from there.

To Kris Swanson, CEO of The Zap Lab, for patiently recording this book and for his passion for NO FEAR ALLOWED.

Also, I could not have stayed in Reno without the love and support of my "Walkie Talkie" friends, Dede, Lindy, Jan, Pat, Jeanne, Elisa, both Margarets, KiKi, Janet and Donna. Okay and wannabe, Lynne, who is a hilarious walkie talkie by email and a dear friend. Without all your love and support and listening and laughter, I would have lost interest long ago.

I want to also thank my book club, Literary Ladies, for allowing me to flit in and out of our book club over the years, reflecting the special love and bond we share. Thank you Lisa, Jolynn, Lynne, Vicki, Sue, Karen, Christine, Maureen, Elke, Nancy, Julie, and Jeanne.

And to all my friends Laurie Ann Goldman for writing the forward, Maxine Clark, Nina McElmore, Beth Stroble, and Arlette Murphy. And to all my friends who have contributed quotes in support of this book. I am grateful and honored to call you friends.

Thank you, Linda McLean, for your prayers and for introducing me to my editor, Christine Whitmarsh, CEO and Founder of Christine, Ink. This book would not have been possible without her. Having dropped off three hundred and twenty-five pages, she masterfully put them together into an outstanding flow, which allowed me to tell my story. Her organizational skills and her ability to pull brilliance from chaos was a gift I will always treasure. This book took five years to write and only a few months to get organized and polished by this competent woman's hands. Seeing the impact my book had on Christine while she was helping me tell my story convinced me it was worth all the hard work. Thank you Christine and team, especially Stefanie King, for setting up all the interviews and keeping us on track. Christine, you are amazing and you and your team's reputation as the "Biographers to the Movers, Shakers and Stars" is well deserved. Thank you from the bottom of my heart also for introducing me to Adryenn Ashley, who designed my cover and managed an unbelievable publicity roll out, incorporating social media and all the things that go with it. Thanks to my Team Fearless!

And, of course, my two biggest thanks go to Lauren and Mike. Lauren, thank you for coming home when I had cancer the first time and for helping me navigate IMPACT Group through all its twists and turns. Your love and support have been invaluable to me, to be able to call and just sound out thoughts, feelings, visions and strategies. Your stepping up and taking on our international development was such a brave thing to do and yet you saw it only as an opportunity. Taking on the integration of Spherion immediately after getting your MBA was *fearless*. I stood in awe as you integrated IT, Finances and everything in between. Your love and support as a daughter has been such a blessing in my life. You can't imagine the pride and joy I feel watching you grow IMPACT Group and embracing your global Mobility and Talent Management vision. I so appreciate you and your openness to learn and grow and, especially when you were younger, never voicing jealousy of the time I spent at IMPACT Group. You once said that you "learned to think of IMPACT Group as your sister and you had to share me with her." You have treated your sister well and I see the love. However, the best gift you have given me is your friendship and love.

And finally, to my husband Mike, I want to say thank you for allowing me to dream big and to take risks. You have walked alongside me every step of the way. You protected me from the day-to-day snafus that happen in every business. You always had my back. Your steadfastness allowed me to continue to act fearlessly throughout our journey. Your love, quiet strength and non-judgmental attitude kept me afloat and kept me calm through the many storms. Thank you for believing in me and taking the growth of IMPACT from the very beginning as part of our journey. We worked as a team and we are luckily enjoying the blessings of our journey together. Thank you for being you.

And thank you God for being with me through thick and thin, for showing me the way more than once, and forgiving me when I challenged your sense of humor by throwing obstacles in my way. I couldn't have done it without you.

Thank you readers for reading this and for paying forward anything you learn from "No Fear Allowed!"

God bless you all,

Laura Herring

Appendix A

RESOURCES

eWomen Network

eWomenNetwork, Inc. is recognized as the Premier Women's Business Network in North America. They focus on women entrepreneurs, business owners and corporate professionals. Their mission is "to help women and their businesses achieve, succeed, and prosper." They focus on helping their members acquire more clients and customers, market and promote who they are and what they offer, and access important resources, ideas and opportunities.

eWomenNetwork was founded in 2000 by Sandra and Kym Yancey. Since then, the network has grown into the largest women's business event company in the world, with 118 U.S. and Canadian chapters producing more than two thousand events every year. Thousands of speaking opportunities are available through the network, and the skilled professionals who head each chapter ensure that this organization showcases the "best and brightest thought leaders and experts."

"Give first, share always" is the philosophy of eWomenNetwork, and this idea is what drives the network to produce so many opportunities for women to connect and collaborate with each other. Every year, they produce the International Conference & Business Expo, the largest in North America. The conference is four eventful days of workshops, lectures, coaching sessions and other programs for visionary women entrepreneurs to gain not only important information for their business, but also to make lasting connections with other women who may have similar stories.

After attending her third conference, Margot Morgan of Business Coach Executive Coaching Group, Inc., said, "I came home, not only fired up and inspired, but because of the powerful teaching, with new actions to move my business forward ... some already in place." Tricia Reynolds of Reynolds Business Solutions, Inc., said, "The conference ignited in me the passion that I had lost over the years of running my own business. It rekindled my desire for abundance and to give back. It started me on a path of rediscovery of my passions and purpose in this life. My business is changing and so am I."

Once a member of this network, you will be able to make an online profile and search for thousands of women in many different business categories through the member search engine. The network also provides members with access to online forums and discussion boards. You will also choose two exclusive one-on-one coaching sessions from a team of Premier Success Coaches. Members also enjoy other benefits such as events, workshops and conferences. Everything the eWomenNetwork does is designed to help members advance their careers and gain more business.

If you are interested in becoming a part of the eWomenNetwork to expand your business, make new connections through their online search engine, or participate in the many events that they host every month, you can find this information and join the network directly through their website (ewomennetwork.com).

Committee of 200

In 1982, a group of the most powerful women in business got together to raise money for The National Association for Women Business Owners. Realizing the difference they could make, the founders created a larger plan that evolved into what we now know as the Committee of 200.

The Committee of 200 is made up of the world's most successful women entrepreneurs and corporate leaders. Its mission is "to foster, celebrate, and advance women's leadership in business," and it promotes success among its members and with future female leaders.

C200 serves as both a professional and personal support system for its members. Members gain access to networking events and member-to-member support that allows them to meet with other women who have built businesses and gained experience as leaders. C200's annual conference gives members a chance to learn valuable lessons from world-renowned leaders as well as their C200 peers. The goal of these conferences is to demonstrate to members the possibilities of how to stay innovative not only in their personal life, but also in the not-for-profit world.

Membership to the Committee of 200 is by invitation only, and one must meet specific criteria to be considered. A Corporate Candidate must be responsible for the full profit and loss of either the parent company or division generating annual revenues of at least $250 million, with a title such as CEO, COO, General Manager or Operating President. An Entrepreneur Candidate must be a company founder and/or a majority or controlling owner, responsible for the profit and loss of the company, and reporting at least $20 million in annual revenues. The committee also considers many other factors when considering potential members, such as board involvement, track record of success and personal and professional integrity.

If you are interested in learning more about the Committee of 200 or looking into the criteria for membership, please visit the C200 website (c200.org).

National Association of Women Business Owners (NAWBO)

The National Association of Women Business Owners was started in 1975 when a group of businesswomen gathered to share information in an attempt to strengthen their entrepreneurial interests. Now, NAWBO has expanded across the United States, with chapters in every state, as well as an affiliation with the World Association of Women Entrepreneurs, which gives NAWBO a global reach that extends to 60 countries.

NAWBO represents the interests of more than 10 million women-owned businesses across all industries in the United States. It focuses on creating change in the business culture to help strengthen these companies, as well as encouraging these business owners to build strategic alliances. NAWBO also works to transform public policy on behalf of the women it represents.

Katrina Markoff, Founder and CEO of Vosges Haut Chocolat and Wild Ophelia, claims, "NAWBO is a great organization for women entrepreneurs that provides an outlet for women business owners across the country to share their creativity and [to] inspire and support each other in their pursuits." NAWBO offers regional, national and international events such as the Women's Business Conference to give women entrepreneurs the opportunity to connect with each other and expand their networks. It also offers Chapter Leadership Boot Camps, which provide training and resources for current and future NAWBO leaders. This program is designed to empower each participant to "BUILD a sustainable chapter infrastructure, STRENGTHEN your leadership skills, and IMPACT the legacy of the women's business community at large."

Members of NAWBO receive many benefits, such as partnerships, exclusive online resources and communications, and leadership development. If you are interested in learning more about member benefits or would like to apply for membership, please visit the NAWBO website (nawbo.org).

Women's Business Enterprise National Council

The Women's Business Enterprise National Council is "the largest third-party certifier of businesses owned, controlled and operated by women in the United States." The WBENC's mission is to help advance the success of its Corporate Members and of certified women's business enterprises (WBEs). The organization's Corporate Members are major corporations that pay membership fees and have an active Supplier Diversity program. They are also required to actively conduct business with WBENC-certified WBEs, which includes any women-owned business entities that have been granted WBENC certification and have paid all relevant fees. These WBEs are not classified as members of WBENC, but as Beneficiaries. WBENC certification and recertification is administered by fourteen Regional Partner Organizations located throughout the U.S.

WBENC's tagline, "Creating Opportunities ... Recognizing Excellence," proves the dedication of the organization to helping its members gain opportunities for success. With this focus in mind, WBENC provides programs, events and tools to connect Corporate Buyers with the certified WBEs that can help meet their business needs.

WBENC also provides helpful resources to their Corporate Members, such as training, trends and tools to help grow their Supplier Diversity programs and professional development. WBEs are also offered training and tools to help better operate their businesses and grow to meet corporate needs.

If you are interested in learning more about WBENC, becoming a Corporate Member or becoming a WBENC-certified WBE, you can find more information on their website (wbenc.org).

Women 2.0

Women 2.0's mission is to increase the number of female founders of technology startups. Women 2.0 supports entrepreneurs with a network, resources and knowledge to take your startup from an idea to launch (women2.org).

Astia

Astia propels women's full participation as entrepreneurs and leaders in high-growth businesses, fueling innovation and driving economic growth (astia.org).

Count Me In

Count Me In's focus is on promoting economic independence and the growth of women-owned businesses (makememeamillion.org).

Hatch Network

This organization gives women a business school of their own—a place to learn to start and grow a business of any size (hatchnetwork.com).

Women Impacting Public Policy (WIPP)

WIPP advocates for and on behalf of women and minorities in business in legislative processes, creating economic opportunities and building bridges and alliances to other small-business organizations (wipp.org).

Girls in Tech

Girls in Tech's mission is to focus on the engagement, education and empowerment of like-minded, professional, intelligent and influential women in technology (girlsintech.net).

Savor the Success

This organization pulls together resources to offer affordable PR tools for women entrepreneurs both online and offline (savorthesuccess.com).

Ladies Who Launch

This is a cleverly named organization with a mission to make entrepreneurship accessible to every woman (ladieswholaunch.com).

Women Initiatives

Women Initiatives builds the entrepreneurial capacity of women to overcome economic and social barriers and achieve self-sufficiency (womensinitiative.org).

Forum for Women Entrepreneurs & Executives (FWE&E)

FWE&E connects exceptional women leaders—entrepreneurs and intrapreneurs—with people and ideas that enhance their impact on the world (fwe.org).

Women Presidents' Organization

Women Presidents' Organization (WPO) is a non-profit membership organization for presidents of multimillion dollar companies. Founded by Marcia Firestone, members of the WPO take part in professionally facilitated peer advisory groups in order to bring "the genius of the group" and accelerate the growth of their businesses (womenpresidentsorg.com).

Young Presidents' Organization

The Young Presidents' Organization unites successful young chief executives around a shared mission: "Better Leaders through Education and Idea Exchange." The organization is made up of approximately twenty-one thousand business leaders in more than 125 countries, with around four hundred local chapters. YPO continues to focus on the basic principles that were important to the company when it was founded in 1950: "the value of a peer network and trusted mentors, the importance of ongoing education, and the need for a 'safe haven' where issues can be aired in an environment of confidentiality." As founder Ray Hickok stated, "YPO is first, last, and always a uniquely personal experience."

To become a member of YPO, you must be under forty-five years old and have the title of CEO, President, Chairman, Managing Director or Partner, Publisher, or an equivalent title. YPO strives to bring young chief executives a powerful network not only for business purposes, but also to build lifelong friendships. Despite the many different locations and chapters, every member of YPO is capable of connecting with members across the globe through YPO's web and mobile technologies. Through these technologies, members are able to access videos, a confidential member-to-member exchange and an exclusive social networking platform. Members are provided with the YPO Global Pulse tool, which uses YPO company performance metrics combined with regional and global trends to predict the economic outlook. YPO is the only organization in the world with this powerful of an economic forecasting tool.

YPO's largest annual event, Global Edge, brings more than three thousand members together with world leaders to address key issues in business, politics, philanthropy and humanities. By bringing these talented young business leaders together with speakers from around the world, YPO hopes to help these leaders shape the world of tomorrow. Dave Maney, YPO member since 1998, said, "YPO's Global Leadership Summit is the convening of remarkable entrepreneurs who bridge the gap between Wall Street and Main Street. This is far from an ordinary gathering; YPO's Summit is truly where you can glimpse the future of the global economy."

The Young Presidents' Organization believes that "learning is lifelong." Their goal is to give members access to resources that they would be unable to find anywhere else. Through Global Conference Calls, peer exchange and events all around the world, the organization hopes that the young chief executives involved will be able to make connections with people around the world and use the lessons they learn to help them run great companies.

If you are interested in joining the Young Presidents' Organization, you can find more information regarding membership and requirements on the YPO website (ypo.org).

BUSINESS ORGANIZATIONS AND BEYOND

World Presidents' Organization

The World Presidents' Organization is the next chapter of the Young Presidents' Organization. It was founded in 1970 "to sustain and enrich the education and idea exchange that began for its members when they joined YPO." WPO is for members ages fifty and older who have either graduated from YPO or been members of YPO for at least three years and left in good standing. Among the many members of WPO are diplomats, senior elected officials, appointed government officials and more.

Similar to the goals of YPO, WPO promotes peer exchange not only between its members, but with the members of YPO as well, mentoring and encouraging the next generation of business leaders. Along with the benefits of YPO membership, WPO members receive exclusive benefits such as discounts on international dues, the option of no annual dues through a lifetime membership, and Aon WorldAware, which gives members and their families safe travel solutions as well as emergency medical assistance.

If you meet the qualifications to become a member of WPO and are interested in joining, you can find a membership application form on their website (wpo.org).

Vistage International

Vistage International is an organization for CEOs, business owners and executives of small- to mid-sized businesses. It began in 1957 when Robert Nourse met with fellow CEOs and found that sharing lessons and experiences could help each other improve performance in their businesses. Vistage now has more than eighteen thousand members in fifteen countries. Their goal is to bring more success to the companies of those involved by bringing together executives from across a broad array of businesses.

Vistage believes that peer advisory allows for new perspectives in members and is one of the most important tools for them to achieve results in their businesses. Vistage Chairs facilitate group meetings of up to fifteen people to be sure that every member gets the most out of every session. In addition to these group meetings, members receive one-on-one coaching sessions with their Chair to determine their business needs and the best opportunities for the future.

Aside from these small group meetings and one-on-one sessions, Vistage offers exclusive events that allow members, Chairs and guests to learn valuable lessons that they can apply to their own businesses. Organized at local, regional and international levels, these events can provide insight into the experiences of their business peers. Members also gain access to vast online resources and connectivity with other members.

When Jay Steinfeld's mom-and-pop drapery business transformed into Blinds.com, he said, "I had no idea what being a real boss, or especially a CEO, even meant." The website was doing well, but Steinfeld had high hopes. "It's one thing to have a business that's doing okay, but if I wanted to really launch this and make a dent in the blinds business, I needed to learn more." He decided to join Vistage, where he learned how to be a CEO and how to focus more on the business as a whole than just on the "nuts and bolts" of it. Steinfeld says that he cannot imagine his success without the help of Vistage.

If you are interested in taking your business to the next level, you can access more information about Vistage on their website. Then, fill out their online profile form and a representative from their Membership Development Team will contact you (vistage.com).

SCORE

SCORE Association is a nonprofit organization supported by the U.S. Small Business Administration that provides free business mentoring services to entrepreneurs in the United States. Once known as the Service Corps of Retired Executives, SCORE offers mentoring services to assist small businesses. Since SCORE began in 1964, they have been "dedicated to helping small businesses get off the ground, grow, and achieve their goals through education and mentorship."

Along with their mentoring services, SCORE offers many easily accessible resources through their website, such as articles, online workshops and blog posts. Free advice is available by browsing profiles and emailing a mentor that best meets your needs. SCORE also offers business workshops and seminars throughout the country for a fee.

With these resources, potential entrepreneurs have been able to get the help they needed to launch their dream company. When Marni Vyn decided to leave the national company she had been working at to start her own resume-writing company, she turned to SCORE. With the help of her mentor, Chosen Resumes, LLC has increased its annual sales for three years in a row. Marni says, "In addition to the practical business assistance, [my mentor] has helped me to overcome intangible obstacles. His support and guidance has provided me with the confidence I need to grow as a business owner …. He has a supportive style that pushes me to stretch and go beyond what I think I can achieve."

With more than three hundred and twenty chapters, SCORE has volunteers near you ready to help you start a new business or expand an existing one. Schedule a meeting with a mentor, get free advice via email or search for upcoming workshops on SCORE's website (score.org).

The U.S. Small Business Association (SBA)

The U.S. Small Business Administration was created as "an independent agency of the federal government to aid, counsel, assist and protect the interests of small-business concerns, to preserve free competitive enterprise and to maintain and strengthen the overall economy of our nation." The SBA believes that small business is a crucial part of building America's future and strengthening the economy.

SBA provides small businesses with many different kinds of financial assistance, from small needs in microlending to substantial debt and equity investment capital. SBA also offers free counseling and low-cost training for small businesses in over eighteen hundred locations throughout the United States and U.S. territories.

In addition to these services, SBA advocates for small business in the government. The Chief Counsel of this specific office is appointed by the President of the United States and conducts research on American small businesses so that the Office can testify on behalf of small business.

In May 2014, Maria Contreras-Sweet was sworn in as SBA Administrator. In a blog post a month later, Contreras-Sweet writes, "As I reflect on an eventful first month, the word that stays in my head is 'inspirational.' As our field team knows so well, our work does more than help America's small businesses succeed and our economy grow. So often, what we're really doing is empowering our entrepreneurs to give back and lift up entire communities."

SBA has sponsored several programs and laws that directly affect small-business owners. Among these are the Small Business Jobs Act of 2010, Startup America, and the SBA Emerging Leaders Initiative. If you want to learn more about these programs, find out about small-business events or share your ideas on how SBA can better serve small business, visit the SBA website (sba.gov).

Webster University

Webster University is an American university with a global perspective, founded in academic excellence in 1915 in Webster Groves, MO. Webster University is the only Tier 1, private, nonprofit university with campus locations around the world including metropolitan, military, online and corporate plus traditional American campuses on four continents: North America, Europe, Africa and Asia.

Their study abroad programs are ranked in the top two percent by U.S. News and World Report's " America's Best Colleges 2013". With 22,200 students at locations around the world, it is proud of its diversity, average class size of ten and Faculty-to-student ratio of 1:9.

For more information go to (webster.edu).

U.S. Chamber of Commerce

The U.S. Chamber of Commerce was created in 1912 by President Taft, who hoped to counterbalance the labor movement happening at that time. Since then it has become a strong influence in government, and is now the world's largest business organization. It represents more than 3 million businesses and advocates for pro-business policies to create jobs and grow the economy.

More than 96% of U.S. Chamber members are small businesses with one hundred employees or fewer. The U.S. Chamber strives to be the "leading voice for small businesses in Washington, D.C." Members and supporters of the Chamber "have access to key policy information, news, marketing tools, networking opportunities and events." Every year, the U.S. Chamber brings together those involved in small businesses through America's Small Business Summit. This event connects these owners, managers and entrepreneurs and allows them to network and share tools and strategies to compete in today's market. The Chamber's Council on Small Business allows small businesses to be involved in determining the U.S. Chamber's business strategy. This group also "assists small-business members in creating effective grass roots actions and strategies on legislative, regulatory and international initiatives." The U.S. Chamber also offers Small Business Nation, an online community encouraging the exchange of information, ideas and issues between members.

With their main goal to strengthen the U.S. economy in mind, the Chamber of Commerce focuses on ten key challenges: tax and entitlement reform, energy, health care, international trade and investment, a competitive workforce, capital markets, reliable and secure infrastructure, legal reform, innovation, and regulatory reform. The Chamber works to develop and implement policy on these major issues.

The Chamber has several different programs focused on addressing these key challenges, such as the Campaign for Free Enterprise, the Center for Women in Business, the Workforce Freedom Initiative, and many more. These programs allow the members to get involved in the issues important to them and to more clearly see the Chamber's policy goals and what they are doing to achieve them.

If you have an interest in having your voice heard in Washington regarding your small business or any of the issues that the Chamber of Commerce addresses, you can read more on their website and find links to all of the programs that the U.S. Chamber of Commerce offers (uschamber.com).

Christine, Ink.—Writing with Impact

Every mover and shaker in corporate America has a story to tell. Christine, Ink. has quickly gained the reputation as the "biographers to the movers, shakers and stars" to ensure that those stories get told right and each author has an impact on their world (Christine-ink.com).

Military.com

Military.com was founded in 1999 to provide a way for Americans involved in the military to stay connected. The site refers to itself as "the largest military membership organization, connecting over 10 million to benefits, news, resources, discounts and each other." It offers resources for active duty, National Guard, reservists, spouses, dependents, veterans, military retirees, DoD personnel, those considering joining, and military enthusiasts and supporters.

This site is extremely helpful for military families. It offers discussion boards where members can post about hot topics, women in the military, veteran's issues and much more. The site offers support for military spouses, helpful tips for those interested in joining the military, and news stories specific to all services.

Military.com has so much to offer not only for those currently enlisted in the military, but for anyone seeking a better awareness. If you have an interest in the military, this website is a great place to connect with people and gain valuable knowledge about all the aspects of its services (military.com).

Siteman Cancer Center

The Alvin J. Siteman Cancer Center at Barnes-Jewish Hospital and Washington University School of Medicine is an international leader in cancer treatment, research, prevention, education and community outreach. Each year, with more than three hundred and fifty research scientists and physicians, Siteman is able to provide care for eighty-five hundred newly diagnosed cancer patients, giving them access to many treatment advances enhanced by more than two hundred and forty clinical studies. Siteman Cancer Center's mission is "to prevent cancer in the community and transform cancer patient care through scientific discovery." Along with their nationally recognized treatment and research programs, Siteman uses an outreach program to focus on prevention, screening and education. Through their website alone, Siteman Cancer Center gives access to prevention and screening podcasts posted by researchers and physicians, tips on how to stay healthy and prevent cancer, and screening guidelines. The prevention team at Siteman Cancer Center also provides a website called *Cancer News in Context*, which breaks down popular cancer-related news stories and summarizes them to readers in an attempt to "make the headlines make sense."

Siteman Cancer Center is the only cancer center in Missouri and one of only forty-one institutions in the United States to hold the Comprehensive Cancer Center designation from the National Cancer Institute. Siteman received this prestigious status in 2005 after a rigorous review of its basic and clinical research programs as well as its cancer prevention programs and its control and population-based research.

Along with their esteemed designation from the National Cancer Institute, Siteman became one of twenty-five institutions that make up the National Comprehensive Cancer Network in 2006. The NCCN is "a nonprofit alliance of leading centers dedicated to improving the quality and effectiveness of cancer care." This membership allows Siteman to share in the group's development of resources such as treatments and clinical trials.

Siteman Cancer Center aims to make the treatment process as smooth as possible, with one centralized location for all outpatient services: the Center for Advanced Medicine on their main campus in St. Louis. This allows for patients to schedule all necessary appointments and exams at the same location, often on the same day. However, Siteman also offers satellite locations for patients who want to receive their care closer to home. Aside from just the physical recovery of their many patients, Siteman also focuses on patient and family recovery through support groups and counseling services, which they offer at their three St. Louis locations.

Ken Steinback found comfort in the Siteman Cancer Center when he was diagnosed with non-Hodgkin's lymphoma. "In my opinion, that is one of the great advantages of a university hospital and being in a place like Washington University," he said. "You get the opinion of a lot of experts, not just one." After the doctors helped Steinback into remission, he donated $100,000 to establish the Kenneth B. Steinback Endowed Fund for Cancer Research, saying that he has "always been a believer in giving back to the community."

If you are interested in making a difference in the research and treatment of cancer at the Siteman Cancer Center, you can access online giving forms as well as a list of volunteer opportunities on their website (siteman.wustl.edu). If you are donating in response to Laura Herring's book, NO FEAR ALLOWED, please mention so on your donation form. Laura is donating all profits from the sale of her book and speaking engagements to the Siteman Cancer Center.

Printed in the USA
CPSIA information can be obtained
at www.ICGtesting.com
JSHW022320140824
68134JS00019B/1211